1996

THE FEMININE S

THE FEMININE
SUBLIME

GENDER AND EXCESS
IN WOMEN'S FICTION

BARBARA CLAIRE FREEMAN

University of California Press
Berkeley · Los Angeles · London

University of California Press
Berkeley and Los Angeles, California

University of California Press, Ltd.
London, England

© 1995 by
The Regents of the University of California

Library of Congress Cataloging-in-Publication Data

Freeman, Barbara Claire.
  The feminine sublime : gender and excess in women's
fiction / Barbara Claire Freeman.
      p.   cm.
  Includes bibliographical references (p.   ) and index.
  ISBN 0-520-08863-8
  1. American fiction—Women authors—History and
criticism.   2. English fiction—Women authors—History and
criticism.   3. Women and literature—United States—
History.   4. Women and literature—Great Britain—History.
5. Femininity (Psychology) in literature.   6. Sublime, The, in
literature.   7. Authorship—Sex differences.   8. Feminism and
literature.   9. Sex role in literature.   10. Aesthetics, Modern.
I. Title.
PS374.W6F67 1995
813.009'9287—dc20   94-27508
                                                          CIP

Printed in the United States of America

9 8 7 6 5 4 3 2 1

For my mother,
Marjorie Cahn Freeman Block,
and in memory of my father,
Bernard Freeman

Contents

Acknowledgments

One of the pleasures of completing this book is being able to express my gratitude to the people who enabled it. I would like to thank those friends and colleagues whose encouragement, insight, counsel, and wisdom made this book possible. To Judith Butler, Cathy Caruth, Diana Fuss, Marjorie Garber, Barbara Johnson, Robert Kiely, Diane Wood Middlebrook, Walter Benn Michaels, Thomas Richards, Hayden White, and Patricia Yaeger I owe the sort of debt that cannot be calculated. Each has been an invaluable source of support throughout the writing of this book and it could not have been undertaken, let alone completed, without their assistance and care.

I thank as well my seminars at Harvard University for stimulating conversations in the fall of 1991 and spring of 1992 when this project began to take shape. The English Department at Harvard University supported my research through generous grants from the Clark and Robinson/Rollin Funds, and provided a semester of leave that greatly facilitated the completion of the manuscript. I am extremely grateful to Marshall Brown and Diane Elam for their astute comments and suggestions. I am also grateful to Doris Kretschmer, Edward Dimendberg, and Edith Gladstone of the University of California Press. It has been a great pleasure to work with them.

I must finally express something well beyond gratitude to my companion Gary Shapiro, without whom this book would have been unthinkable. If there indeed are limits to his wit, compassion, and intelligence, I have not discovered them.

Early versions of Chapter Three appeared in *SubStance* and *The Yale Journal of Criticism*. I am grateful to their editors for permission to reprint them here.

Introduction

The Feminine Sublime

If we had a keen vision and a feeling for all ordinary human life, it would be like hearing the grass grow and the squirrel's heart beat, and we should die of that roar which lies on the other side of silence.

(George Eliot, *Middlemarch*)

The Borderlands are physically present wherever two or more cultures edge each other, where people of different races occupy the same territory, where under, lower, middle and upper classes touch, where the space between two individuals shrinks with intimacy. . . . A border is a dividing line, a narrow strip along a steep edge. A borderland is a vague and undetermined place created by the emotional residue of an unnatural boundary. It is in a constant state of transition. The prohibited and forbidden are its inhabitants.

(Gloria Anzaldúa, *Borderlands/La Frontera*)

She listened, but it was all very still; cricket was over; the children were in their baths; there was only the sound of the sea. She stopped knitting; she held the long reddish-brown stocking dangling in her hands a moment. She saw the light again. With some irony in her interrogation, for when one woke at all, one's relations changed, she looked at the steady light, the pitiless, the remorseless, which was so much her, yet so little her, which had her at its beck and call (she woke in the night and saw it bent across their bed, stroking the floor), but for all that she thought, watching it with fascination, hypnotised, as if it were stroking with its silver fingers some sealed vessel in her brain whose bursting would flood her with delight, she had known happiness, exquisite happiness, intense happiness, and it silvered the rough waves a little more brightly, as daylight faded and the blue went out of the sea and it rolled in waves of pure lemon which curved and swelled and broke upon the beach and the ecstasy burst in her eyes and waves of pure delight traced over the floor of her mind and she felt, It is enough! It is enough!

(Virginia Woolf, *To The Lighthouse*)

Woman is not to be related to any simple designatable being, subject, or entity. Nor is the whole group (called) women. One woman + one

I

woman + one woman will never add up to some generic entity:
woman. (The/a) woman refers to what cannot be defined, enumerated,
formulated or formalized. Woman is a common noun for which no
identity can be defined. (The/a) woman does not obey the principle of
self-identity, however the variable x for self is defined. She is identified
with every x variable, not in any specific way. Presupposed is an excess
of all identification to/of self. But this excess is no-thing: it is vacancy
of form, gap in form, the return to another edge where she re-touches
herself with the help of—nothing. Lips of the same form—but of a
form that is never simply defined—ripple outwards as they touch and
send one another on a course that is never fixed into a single
configuration.

(Luce Irigaray, *Speculum of the Other Woman*)

To hear the roar that lies within silence, and write it; inhabit a border (not
a waste) land in which boundaries overlap and differences of race, class,
sexuality, and geography collide; see waves of light breaking upon the
beach as a movement in which otherness appears; or define "woman" not
as a shared fantasy of sexual identity, but in a way that contests any notion
of essence, feminine or otherwise: across different trajectories Eliot, Anzaldúa, Woolf, and Irigaray articulate crucial aspects of the feminine
sublime, for each makes explicit the female subject's encounter with and
response to an alterity that exceeds, limits, and defines her.[1] The central
tenet of this book is that the feminine sublime is neither a rhetorical mode
nor an aesthetic category but a domain of experience that resists categorization, in which the subject enters into relation with an otherness—
social, aesthetic, political, ethical, erotic—that is excessive and unrepresentable.[2] The feminine sublime is not a discursive strategy, technique, or
literary style the female writer invents, but rather a crisis in relation to
language and representation that a certain subject undergoes.[3] As such it
is the site both of women's affective experiences and their encounters with
the gendered mechanisms of power from the mid-eighteenth century
(when the theory of the sublime first came to prominence) to the present,
for it responds specifically to the diverse cultural configurations of wom-
en's oppression, passion, and resistance.

From Longinus' day until ours writers have viewed the sublime as a
more or less explicit mode of domination. The vast majority of theorists
conceptualize it as a struggle for mastery between opposing powers, as
the self's attempt to appropriate and contain whatever would exceed, and
thereby undermine, it. Within the tradition of romantic aesthetics that

sees the sublime as the elevation of the self over an object or experience that threatens it, the sublime becomes a strategy of appropriation. For Kant, its most authoritative and influential theorist, the sublime moment entails the elevation of reason over an order of experience that cannot be represented. Typically, the sublime involves a moment of blockage followed by one of heightened lucidity in which reason resists the blocking source by representing its very inability to represent the sublime "object"; it thereby achieves supremacy over an excess that resists its powers.[4] Thus, the central moment of the sublime marks the self's newly enhanced sense of identity; a will to power drives its style, a mode that establishes and maintains the self's domination over its objects of rapture. I certainly do not wish to domesticate the sublime by defusing its profound and important connections to the realms of power, conflict, and agency, or suggest that the feminine sublime is merely another, more intense version of the beautiful; yet rather than represent the object of rapture as a way of incorporating it, as the traditional sublime of domination does, the feminine sublime does not attempt to master its objects of rapture. It is my conviction that another account of the sublime lies hidden within and is repressed by metaphysical theories of sublimity, and that the story of this other sublime has yet to be written. The central purpose of this book is to begin to tell that story.

I try, in the pages that follow, to make explicit the crucial yet unexamined role gender plays in the articulation of the theory of the sublime and to explore some of the ways that fiction by American and British women, mainly of the twentieth century, responds to and redefines what the tradition has called "the sublime." In chapters concerned with Longinus, Burke, and Kant I show that the theory of the sublime not only describes the subject's encounters with excess but also defines the ways in which excess may or may not be conceptualized. The sublime is a theoretical discourse, with its unique history, canon, and conventions, about the subject's diverse responses to that which occurs at the very limits of symbolization. One main contention of the book is that the canonical theories that seem merely to explain the sublime also evaluate, domesticate, and ultimately exclude an otherness that, almost without exception, is gendered as feminine.[5] Through readings of the texts that form the canon of the sublime—Longinus' *Peri Hypsous* (On the sublime), Burke's *Enquiry*, Kant's third *Critique*—I argue that, at the level of theme, its principal theorists are able to represent the sublime only through recourse to metaphors of sexual difference and, equally significant, that the structure of the sublime depends upon (and results from) a preexisting construction of "the feminine." What appears to be a theory of how excess works actually functions to keep it at bay. Therefore we must address the ideology at stake in traditional theories of the sublime, as well as in some of its more recent critics.[6] I argue for a reading of the sublime as an allegory of the construction of the patriarchal (but not necessarily male) subject, a self that maintains its borders by subordinating difference and by appropriating rather than identifying with that which presents itself as other.[7] My principal concerns are to demonstrate that the discourse of the sublime has typically functioned not to explicate but to neutralize excess and, as I examine fictions that represent our encounters with it, to explore other ways of envisioning and writing the sublime.

The notion of spectatorship as the site of sublime experience is one of the principal strategies through which such a neutralization occurs. Joseph Addison's "Essay on the Pleasures of the Imagination," from *The Spectator* papers of June 21 through July 3, 1712 (Nos. 409, 411–21), emphasizes sublime experience as that of the spectator of an overwhelming event, landscape, or text, and thereby suggests a principal avenue of inquiry that Burke and Kant were to explore more thoroughly. Why, he asks, do we "take delight in being terrified or dejected by a Description, when we find so much Uneasiness in the Fear or Grief which we receive from any other Occasion?"[8] Addison explains that such pleasures depend upon a comparison between our own state of safety and the danger or terror we contemplate:

> When we look on such hideous Objects, we are not a little pleased to think we are in no Danger of them. We consider them at the same time, as Dreadful and Harmless; so that the more frightful Appearance they make, the greater is the Pleasure we receive from the sense of our own Safety. . . . In the like manner, when we read of Torments, Wounds, Deaths, and the like dismal Accidents, our Pleasure does not flow so properly from the Grief which such melancholy Descriptions give us, as from the secret Comparison which we make between our selves and the Person who suffers.[9]

One of the purposes of this study is to argue that the distinguishing features of the sublime unsettle the very notion of spectatorship upon which Addison and subsequent theorists rely. Although Addison, Burke, and

Kant regularly posit a subject who observes pain or terror without partaking of or being directly affected by it, the very hallmark of sublime experience is an identification between auditor and orator or between reader and text in which, as Longinus was the first to observe, "we come to believe that we have created what we have only heard" (7.2).[10] Such a moment, in which the subject, whether in thought or in fact, merges with that which she perceives distinguishes sublime discourse from language that, in Longinus' words, is merely "persuasive and pleasant" (1.4). We will explore the nuances and complexities of the Longinian sublime in chapter one. For the moment, it is important to emphasize that the very nature of the sublime—its ability to blur distinctions between observer and observed, reader and text, or spectator and event—undercuts the claim upon which its theorists rely to explain and defuse its peculiar force. The internal contradiction so central to the history of the sublime is that its theorists regularly claim for the spectator a state of detachment that, were it to exist, would nullify the very features of rapture, merger, and identification that characterize and define the sublime, for the sublime event is precisely one in which what happens to "the other" also happens to the subject who perceives it.

By retaining the category of "women's fiction," with its apparent endorsement of feminine, generic, and authorial identities, I do not wish to reinscribe the formulations of either femininity or the sublime that are the object of critique. The notion of a women's fiction with its own tradition and specificity functions as a necessary descriptive and sociological category and has profound importance for feminist theory and practice, but the use of preexisting or universal concepts of feminine identity, writing, or authorship would force us to equate the sublime with the presentable and thereby sustain precisely that notion of the sublime I would resist. For this reason I do not put forward a concept of the sublime that might be equated with "the feminine": to do so would be to suggest that the feminine is presentable and, hence, not sublime. The notion of a "feminine sublime" does not refer to a particular representation of either femininity or sublimity, which would domesticate sublime excess through a conceptual elaboration of its very incommensurability. Rather than a transhistorical or essential category, I employ the notion of "women's fiction" to underscore the categorical instability of a socially constructed body of writing that bears the traces of women's shared history of oppression. Theorists such as Hélène Cixous and Julia

Kristeva frequently introduce works by male writers (Céline, Genet, Joyce, Lautréamont, Mallarmé) to exemplify the semiotic practice of an *écriture féminine*; I examine novels written by women because the uniqueness and commonality of women's oppression inflect their articulation of sublimity.[11] Whether a man could write, or indeed has written, a version of the feminine sublime is not a possibility this study explores or denies. My wish is not to reconcile but to heighten the paradox that lets the feminine sublime displace the categories underlying it, and to underscore the necessity for a double practice that revises the theories it would critique.

In describing a feminine sublime I also take issue with many critical responses to twentieth-century women's fiction. For the issues foregrounded by the sublime—the construction and destruction of borders (be they aesthetic, political, or psychic), the permutations of identity formation and deformation, and the question of how such limits may or may not be represented—are extraordinarily important elements in women's fiction of this period, and these are precisely the elements critics tend to pass over without engagement or comment. Quite simply, critics often view the female protagonist either as exclusively passive, as society's victim, or as an accomplice of the economy that excludes her. Without minimizing the extent and importance of women's oppression, I argue that a too exclusive focus on women's victimization may lead us to misread the orders of discourse through which women exert agency, even as they confront its limits. Faced with Edna Pontellier's encounters with the ocean during Kate Chopin's *The Awakening*, Lily Bart's final speculation with the narcotic chloral in Edith Wharton's *House of Mirth*, Sasha Jensen's apparently eager assent to sex with a man she detests in Jean Rhys's *Good Morning, Midnight*, or Sethe Suggs's murder of her daughter in Toni Morrison's *Beloved*, critics frequently condemn the heroine's self-indulgence or blame the society that victimizes her. But if we look at such novels in terms of the sublime, we can raise complex questions about the nature and exertion of agency and understand these protagonists somewhat differently: as subjects who exert will, even at the cost of self-destruction, and thus not merely as victims who are acted upon.

My choice of novels reflects the canon of theoretical writing on the sublime represented by Longinus, Burke, and Kant, for these are not only the theorists who define the very terms in which the sublime has been thought, they are also the authors to whom contemporary critics and theorists of the sublime most frequently respond. I discuss *The Awakening*, *The House of Mirth*, *Frankenstein*, *Good Morning, Midnight*, and *Beloved* because they represent differing articulations of the feminine sublime and because, consciously or not, they minutely respond to the arguments, metaphors, and ideological underpinnings at stake in the sublime's most definitive theorists.

I do not wish to suggest that many other novels could not provide valuable insights about the sublime in women's fiction. The works we examine offer particularly insightful critiques of traditional theorizations of the sublime as they suggest alternatives to it but do not fill the rubric of the feminine sublime. By focusing upon twentieth-century women's fiction, we take up only one aspect of women's literary tradition and inheritance among the periods, perspectives, and literary genres of the feminine sublime. Since a primary aim of this book is to demonstrate the dominant ideology of misogyny that haunts canonical theories of the sublime and to suggest another mode of envisioning it, I have chosen novels whose structure, characters, and themes make explicit the blind spots within the history of the sublime's theorization. These works disclose a conjunction between apparently dissimilar domains, the theory of the sublime and the genre of the novel, and thereby allow a more complete understanding of each. Each novelist seeks language adequate to the task of representing something of the unstable and discontinuous relation between self, world, and other—the capacity to hear and make audible Eliot's roar of sound, or Woolf's waves of light.

Our focus on the genre of the novel rather than on poetry, drama, or autobiography as the primary vehicle for the investigation of the feminine sublime ought not to imply that the study of other genres would yield few insights. While the novel's very diversity and open-endedness is perhaps its most noteworthy feature, frustrating any totalizing claims about its essential or defining features, the genre has a profound affinity with the theory of the sublime and therefore represents a particularly appropriate medium for investigation of this topic.

It is no accident that the rise of the novel occurs at the same time that the sublime comes to the fore in eighteenth-century aesthetics, for both depend upon—or perhaps help to construct—a distinctly modern subject. A new conception of the individual, one who, as Thomas Weiskel observes, experiences "an incurable ambivalence about authority," and a correlative concern with the extremity and variety of personal experience, can be seen as a fundamental factor in the rise of both discursive modes.[12] The novel and the sublime both emphasize the primacy of the individual and appeal to individual experience as the ultimate arbiter of reality; share a concern with the process through which, at least since the eighteenth century, identities are formed; and reflect upon the value and diversity of individual taste. Just as important, both offer a fundamentally narrative account of that subject's nature and development.

That many readers may think of romantic poetry in connection with the sublime does not diminish its affinity with the novel. The sublime of Wordsworth, Coleridge, Keats, and Shelley finds its most typical expression in epic or narrative, rather than lyric, poetry, yet there is nothing inherent in the genre of poetry that makes it uniquely suited to or evocative of the sublime. The genre of sublime poetry was effectively closed to women. Dorothy Wordsworth, or any woman of her period, could not have written a poem such as "Tintern Abbey," with its celebration of "A presence that disturbs me with the joy / Of elevated thoughts; a sense sublime / Of something far more deeply interfused" and abiding faith in the poet's infinite ability to "revive again."[13] Wordsworth, the poet of the "egotistical sublime" that so provoked Keats, inherits as his birthright a self-assurance, entitlement, and confidence in his right to speak and be heard that no woman of his era could share. The moment of conversion Wordsworth experiences in *The Prelude* when he encounters a blind beggar in the streets of London, "My mind did at this spectacle turn round / As with the might of waters" (VII, 643–44), is a paradigm of romantic transcendence and celebrates a kind of power that was forbidden to women. It also privileges a subject who subsumes all experience into an infinitely expanding "I," as if the goal of the Wordsworthian sublime were to consume the very otherness it appears to bespeak and demonstrate mastery over an experience that had seemed overwhelming.

Keats criticizes the "wordsworthian or egotistical sublime" as "a thing per se" that "stands alone." Unlike Wordsworth, he views the sublime as residing in the extinction and not the enhancement of identity: "poetical Character," he observes, "is not itself—it has no self—it is every thing and nothing—it has no character": to be sublime is to have "no Identity . . . no self."[14] As with Keats, Coleridge's sublime also depends upon the self's awareness of its own absence. His comments upon the sublimity of a Gothic cathedral provide a striking contrast to Wordsworth's response to the craggy peaks in the Mount Snowdon passage of *The Prelude* or Shelley's rhapsodic identification with Mont Blanc:

> But Gothic art is sublime. On entering a cathedral, I am filled with devotion and with awe; I am lost to the actualities that surround me, and my whole being expands into the infinite; earth and air, nature and art, all swell up into eternity, and the only sensible expression left is, "That I am nothing!"[15]

Whereas Wordsworth's sublime culminates in what Weiskel describes as "an infinitely repeatable 'I am,'" in the sublime of Keats and Coleridge individual consciousness is subsumed by the eternal.[16] The grandeur of the Gothic church suspends Coleridge's self-awareness; all the self can know of itself is that it is "nothing."

In contrast to Wordsworth's "I am every thing" and Coleridge's "I am nothing," the feminine sublime neither celebrates self-presence and the self's capacity to master the other nor consecrates the immediacy of its absence.[17] If Coleridge's identity is diminished by the sublime while Wordsworth's expands, Irigaray contests the logic of identity that conceives of the self in exclusive terms of presence or absence. Her articulation of the feminine self as a "no-thing" for which "no identity can be defined" partakes of a very different order than Coleridge's sense of the self as "nothing."[18] Rather, she envisions a sublime in which the self neither possesses nor merges with the other but attests to a relation with it.

It is not my intention to identify the feminine sublime with the work of Irigaray, or with that of any particular theorist or theoretical practice. Nor do I imply that an innate femininity or unique style of women's writing accompanies the feminine sublime. Indeed, the very search for an essential difference that would function outside any specific context to fix, determine, guarantee, and control meaning is precisely what the sublime contests. At stake in the notion of the feminine sublime is the refusal to define the feminine as a specific set of qualities or attributes that we might call irreducible and unchanging. I employ the term "feminine" as that which contests binaries, including a rigid notion of sexual difference that would insist upon separate male and female selves. The appeal to a "feminine sublime" is not to a specifically feminine subjectivity or mode of expression, but rather to that which calls such categories into question. It is one name for what we cannot grasp in established systems of ideas or articulate within the current framework in which the term "woman" has meaning.

To investigate the feminine sublime is not to embark upon a search for an autonomous female voice, realm of experience, or language, although these categories may be valuable as a dimension of the strategic interventions of feminist practice. What is specifically feminine about the feminine sublime is not an assertion of innate sexual difference, but a radical rearticulation of the role gender plays in producing the history of discourse on the sublime and the formulation of an alternative position with respect to excess and the possibilities of its figuration. To assert the importance of the feminine in this context is not to reinscribe normative gender categories, but to offer a critique of a tradition that has functioned historically to reassert masculine privilege. In this sense, the notion of the feminine does not refer to a particular affinity group, gender, or class, but rather to a putting in question of the master discourse that perpetuates the material and psychological oppression of actual women.

I use the word "feminine" in at least two ways: on the one hand, to refer to the socially constructed category of woman that has endured universal and transhistorical oppression and thus to underscore the reality of women's suffering; on the other, to indicate a position of resistance with respect to the patriarchal order, whether it is perpetuated and sustained by biological women or by men. Here the term does not so much refer to actual women as designate a position of critique with respect to the masculinist systems of thought that contribute to women's subjugation. Although such a conception of the feminine does not suspend reference to existing women, it does suspend the notion of an ultimate feminine identity that could function as the ground of sexual difference. Rather it becomes one name for a residue that disrupts the oppositional structure male/female and thereby calls for a radical rearticulation of the symbolic order. My central question is not, what is the feminine sublime? but rather, how does it signify? It refers to what, in Anzaldúa's sense, is a site of passage and border crossing in which meanings collide and transform one another, an ongoing process of re-metaphorization in which we may perceive, in Judith Butler's wonderful phrase, "the movement of boundary itself."[19]

The sublime has been aligned with a wide variety of political practices. Although an interest in it often marks the conservative (Burke, for example, lauded the sublime but condemned the French Revolution), a

number of theorists associate the sublime with the possibility of liberty and
freedom.[20] Subsequent chapters will argue that there is no single, unchanging politics with which one can identify the sublime. Indeed, the
fact that it can so readily embrace political positions of every persuasion
attests to its metamorphic capacity and ability to exceed any particular
designation, definition, or category.[21] That the sublime has no inherent
politics, however, does not mean that its effects are not inevitably and
necessarily political. And while the present study is not political in the
sense of proposing a specific blueprint for social action, it does, I think,
imply a strong sense of the form a politics of the feminine sublime might
assume.

The dimension of the unrepresentable would be a central feature of any
sublime politics. One of the main contentions of this book is that the
sublime involves an encounter with a radical alterity that remains unassimilable to representation. Such an encounter marks the very limits of the
representable, for it entails the question of symbolizing an event that we
cannot represent not only because it was never fully present, but because
it presents the subject with an unrecuperable excess of excess. In the
formulation of Jean-François Lyotard, for example, the sublime is not the
presentation of the unpresentable, but the presentation of the fact that the
unpresentable exists.[22] To invoke the nondemonstrable—not as a familiar
feature of aesthetics but rather in the context of the incommensurable—is
to situate the sublime as a site of resistance to aestheticism and also to
underscore its political and ethical dimensions. In this sense, the notion
of alterity eludes particular ethnicity, sexuality, class, race, or geopolitical
positioning but implies both a general concept of the unrepresentable as
that which exceeds the symbolic order of language and culture, and the
particular otherness of actual others, who remain nameless insofar as they
are outside its borders.

Unlike the masculinist sublime that seeks to master, appropriate, or
colonize the other, I propose that the politics of the feminine sublime
involves taking up a position of respect in response to an incalculable
otherness.[23] A politics of the feminine sublime would ally receptivity and
constant attention to that which makes meaning infinitely open and
ungovernable. As Bill Readings suggests:

> A sublime politics would not attempt to subject politics to the radical
> indeterminacy of the sublime as a questioning of rules and criteria . . . it
> is to refuse society as the locus of modeling and authority, to argue for

heteronomous community in which there can be no absolutely authoritative instance and no consensus that might legitimate such an authority.[24]

Such a practice would authorize concrete strategies and tactics of resistance
without the need either to identify itself permanently with any one
particular political position or to depend upon a fantasy of collective
identity as the basis for consensus. Its most enduring commitment would
be instead to sustain a condition of radical uncertainty as the very condition
of its possibility. It would not, for example, attempt to represent the total
and unspeakable horror of American slavery but offer, as does Morrison's
Beloved, a mode of historical witnessing that, through the ghostly figure
of Beloved, signifies both the traumatic institution of slavery and the
immensity of that which cannot be said. This textual and political practice
opens language to the necessary task of giving voices to those who have
been silenced and finds words for the silence within speech that language
cannot say—and thus makes resonant what Kate Chopin hears as "the
everlasting voice of the sea."[25]

I

The Awakening

Waking Up at the End of the Line

The sublime does not so properly persuade us, as it ravishes and trans-
ports us, and produces in us a certain Admiration, mingled with Astonishment and with Surprize, which is quite another thing than the barely
pleasing, or the barely persuading: that it gives a noble Vigour to a Discourse, an invincible Force, which commits a pleasing Rape upon the
very Soul of the Reader.

(John Dennis, *The Grounds of Criticism in Poetry*)

You can't make a political "program" with it, but you can bear witness
to it.—And what if no one hears the testimony, etc.?

(Jean-François Lyotard, *The Differend*)

Love is lak de sea. It's uh movin' thing, but still and all, it takes its
shape from de shore it meets, and it's different with every shore.

(Zora Neale Hurston, *Their Eyes Were Watching God*)

These waters must be troubled before they can exert their virtues.

(Edmund Burke, *A Philosophical Enquiry into the Origin
of our Ideas of the Sublime and Beautiful*)

Longinus cites only one female poet in his influential *Peri Hypsous* (On
the sublime), the first-century treatise whose fame was revived by
Boileau's French translation and commentary of 1674.[1] That poet, of
course, is Sappho of Lesbos (early sixth century B.C.), and Longinus
chooses her lyric *phainetai moi* to illustrate his view that literary excellence
depends upon the writer's ability to harmonize differences and create an
organic whole.[2] Anticipating the New Critic's demand that the perfect
poem, like a "well-wrought urn" or "verbal icon," achieve the status of
an autonomous unit, Longinus praises Sappho's ability "in selecting the
outstanding details and making a unity of them" (10.1) as particularly
exemplary of sublime writing. What is striking, however, is the disparity
between Sappho's poem and Longinus' interpretation of it. Whereas the
lyric describes an experience of total fragmentation when the speaker hears
her lover's "sweet voice" (10.1), Longinus commends Sappho's skill in

creating the illusion of wholeness: according to him, she is able to join diverse parts in such a way that "they co-operate to form a unity and are linked by the bonds of harmony" (40.1).

Given this poem's crucial role in establishing Longinus' account of the sublime, it is worth examining in some detail. I cite versions of the poem as it appears in two eminent and recent translations of Longinus, the first by D. A. Russell, the second by G. M. A. Grube.[3]

To me he seems a peer of the gods, the man who sits
facing you and hears your sweet voice
And lovely laughter; it flutters my heart in my breast.
When I see you only for a moment, I cannot speak;
My tongue is broken, a subtle fire runs under my skin;
my eyes cannot see, my ears hum; Cold sweat pours off me; shivering
    grips me all over; I am paler than grass;
I seem near to dying; But all must be endured . . . (10.2)

The translation in Grube's edition renders the last two stanzas as follows:

Yea, my tongue is broken, and through and through me
'Neath the flesh, impalpable fire runs tingling;
Nothing see mine eyes, and a noise of roaring
Waves in my ears sounds;

Sweat runs down in rivers, a tremor seizes
All my limbs and paler than grass in autumn,
Caught by pains of menacing death, I falter,
Lost in the love trance (10.2)

And here, in Russell's translation, is Longinus' commentary:

Consider Sappho's treatment of the feelings involved in the madness of being in love. She uses the attendant circumstances and draws on real life at every point. And in what does she show her quality? In her skill in selecting the outstanding details and making a unity of them . . . Do you not admire the way she brings everything together—mind and body, hearing and tongue, eyes and skin? She seems to have lost them all, and to be looking for them as though they were external to her. She is cold and hot, mad and sane, frightened and near death, all by turns. (10.1–3)

Longinus' insistence that the poem's sublimity resides in its representation of unity, its ability to connect disparate elements and "bring everything together," is especially puzzling given that Sappho seems so little concerned with univocity. Longinus values the poem because he believes it achieves precisely the opposite of what in fact it does: despite his assumption that its excellence depends upon Sappho's skill in replacing the diverse with the singular, there is little, if any, textual evidence for his celebration of homogeneity. Sappho juxtaposes such apparent dualisms as life and death, hot and cold, or sanity and madness not, as Longinus would have it, in order to create harmony, but rather to unsettle the notion of organic form upon which his notion of the sublime depends. Rather than unify the disparate, Sappho foregrounds the activity of self-shattering. Instead of warding off fragmentation, she insists upon it. It is as if the goal of Longinus' commentary were to domesticate and neutralize the very excessiveness Sappho's text bespeaks.

My principal concern, however, is not with the strength or weakness of Longinus' literary criticism. I wish instead to examine the function Sappho's lyric plays in Longinus' treatise in order to suggest that his is a paradigmatic response to the irruption of a threatening and potentially uncontainable version of the sublime, one that appears to represent excess but does so only the better to keep it within bounds. The move Longinus makes in relation to Sappho is particularly instructive since, as we shall see, later theorists echo it time and time again. Longinus' commentary on Sappho plays a constitutive role in the sublime's theorization by shaping the ways in which the subject's encounter with excess, one of the sublime's most characteristic and enduring features, may and may not be conceptualized.[4] Neil Hertz's brilliant "Reading of Longinus," which is itself representative of late twentieth-century American theorists' commitment to a romantic (or Wordsworthian) sublime, continues this tradition by repeating the very same scenario.[5] Hertz not only recuperates an instance of difference in a literary text and reads it as forming a unified whole; perhaps more important, he constructs a theory of the sublime that perpetuates its tactic of exclusion.

This chapter's exploration of significant misreadings in the history of the sublime, along with the role and place of gender in producing that history, will let us look at ways in which the sublime might be written otherwise, were that dimension not repressed. Kate Chopin's novel *The Awakening* amplifies and elucidates precisely those elements of the sublime that Sappho foregrounds and Longinus obscures. *The Awakening*, which stands at the dawn of twentieth-century American women's fiction and brings forward some of its basic preoccupations and themes, also suggests a particular version of the feminine sublime, here understood not as a transhistorical or universal category, but rather as the attempt to articulate the subject's confrontation with excess in a mode that does not lead solely to its recuperation. At stake in Chopin's novel is the very "transport" (*ekstasis*) Sappho inscribes, a "going close to death" that marks the limits of the representable. Here the sublime is no longer a rhetorical mode or style of writing, but an encounter with the other in which the self, simultaneously disabled and empowered, testifies to what exceeds it. At issue is not only the attempt to represent excess, which by definition breaks totality and cannot be bound, but the desire for excess itself; not just the description of, but the wish for, sublimity.

I

As Chopin remarks, "The beginning of things, of a world especially, is necessarily vague, tangled, chaotic, and exceedingly disturbing."[6] We begin with a discussion of Longinus not only because, as the author of the first treatise on the sublime, he defines the set of problems that will coalesce under this name, but because his treatment of Sappho is paradigmatic of the kinds of disturbances that are at the very heart of the sublime's theorization. In order to grasp the significance of his response to Sappho, however, we need to understand Longinus' view of sublimity, the better to ask in what ways Sappho's lyric both exemplifies and undercuts it.

First and foremost, the sublime is a certain kind of linguistic event, a mode of discourse that breaks down the differences and involves a merger between speaker (or writer) and hearer (or reader). "Sublimity," according to Longinus, "is a kind of eminence or excellence of discourse" (1.3). It is not an essential property of language but rather makes itself known by the effect it produces, and that effect is one of ravishment; as Russell puts it, "whatever *knocks the reader out* is sublime" (xiii). Sublime language disrupts everyday consciousness: "great writing . . . takes the reader out of himself"; it "tears everything up like a whirlwind, and exhibits the orator's whole power at a single blow" (1.4).[7] The sublime utterance, which itself attempts to represent excess, also involves its production: it is accompanied by a threefold identification between speaker, message, and listener in which the latter comes "to believe he has created what he has only heard" (7.2). This identification displaces the identity of its participants and is characteristic of the moment of *hypsous*, that state of transport and exaltation that for Longinus is the mark of sublimity. One of the defining features of sublime discourse is its ability to blur customary differences between speaker and hearer, text and reader. As Suzanne Guerlac points out, "this paradoxical moment is presented by the text as being both the effect and the origin of the sublime, which engenders itself through 'impregnating' the soul of the listener."[8]

Unlike the listener's experience of discourse that seeks merely to please or to persuade, the effect of sublime language entails a certain loss of control. Longinus emphasizes that the sublime "produces ecstasy rather than persuasion in the hearer" and insists that this "combination of wonder and astonishment always proves superior to the merely persuasive and pleasant. This is because persuasion is on the whole something we can control, whereas amazement and wonder exert invincible power and force and get the better of every hearer" (1.4). The discourse of the sublime, then, is integrally bound up with the subject's responses to what possesses it, to the nature and effects of such a merger, and to the ways in which various forms of identification may be understood. At stake is the question of how to theorize ravishment.

Although Longinus never explicitly confronts this issue, his treatise suggests (or is most frequently read as if it suggested) that the moment of *hypsous* becomes a struggle for dominance between opposing forces, an almost Darwinian contest in which the strong flourish and the weak are overcome.[9] For the sublime not only produces an identification between speaker and audience but entails a modification in relations of power between the parties involved, and the diversity of ways in which such modifications may be conceptualized is at the heart of critical debates regarding the sublime.[10] Bloom's theory of the anxiety of influence has as its origin Longinus' precept, itself borrowed from Hesiod, that "strife is good for men" (13.4). The orator attempts to possess the auditor in much the same way that the poet wishes to transport the reader; the view of creativity as bound up with the quest for mastery and ownership shapes Longinus' view of literary production itself. Poets struggle amongst themselves to best one another: even Plato would not have attained greatness without the need to show his superiority to his rival Homer, for he could not have "put such a brilliant finish on his philosophical doctrines or so often risen to poetical subjects and poetical language, if he had not tried, and tried, wholeheartedly, to compete for the prize against Homer, like a young aspirant challenging an admired master" (13.4). Many contemporary American theorists of the sublime reinforce this claim.[11] Thomas Weiskel, for example, insists that "discourse in the *Peri Hypsous (on Great Writing)* is a power struggle," while according to Paul Fry, "the Longinian sublime appears in a climate of antagonism, as rivalry between authors."[12]

But if the sublime is, to borrow Fry's phrase, always "a drama of power" and "a struggle for possession," I must stress what Longinus and the majority of his critics do not: that the kind of power at stake in Sappho's lyric differs in important respects from the other examples Longinus cites as illustrative of the sublime.[13] For Sappho's ode affirms a form of possession that redefines traditional modes of domination and relations of power. By exploring the differences between Sappho's ode and Homer's—since he is the other poet Longinus chooses to exemplify "excellence in selection and organization" (10.1)—we will see that Sappho's lyric offers an alternative to Longinus's belief that the sublime entails a struggle for domination in which one party submits to another, and that his misreading of Sappho has significant consequences for the sublime's theorization.

For Longinus, who believes that "sublimity will be achieved if we consistently select the most important of those inherent features and learn to organize them as a unity by combining one with another" (10.1), the ability "to select and organize material" is one of the factors that "can make our writing sublime" (10.1). Comparing Sappho's skillful description of "the feelings involved in the madness of being in love" (10.1) with Homer's talent for portraying storms, he especially praises the latter's skill in depicting "the most terrifying aspects" (10.3). And both poems provide impressive examples of realistic description. Sappho conveys precisely what "lovers experience" (10.3); "she uses the attendant circumstances and draws on real life at every point" (10.1); the result of her art is "that we see in her not a single emotion, but a complex of emotions . . ." (10.3). Indeed, their similar gift for accurate representation prompts Longinus' comparison of the two poets. Like Sappho, Homer is a genius because he is able to choose the details that will convey the essence of an experience. Longinus cites a passage in which Homer likens Hector to a storm at sea as exemplary:

> He [Hector] fell upon them [the Greeks] as upon a swift
>   ship falls a wave,
> Huge, wind-reared by the clouds. The ship

Is curtained in foam, a hideous blast of wind
Roars in the sail. The sailors shudder in terror:
They being carried away from under death, but only just. (10.5)

Sappho and Homer share the ability to select and combine the most disparate elements of an awesome event in order to present a complete, unified portrait of it. But Longinus implies that the two poets have more in common than rhetorical or stylistic facility: he also suggests that each poet is concerned to describe a version of the same experience, as if the terror of almost dying at sea were the same as almost dying of love. This assumption, however, conflates two very different kinds of near-death experiences and ignores a crucial distinction between the kind of death, or perhaps more important, the kind of ecstasy, at stake. Sappho's and Homer's lyrics may be alike in that both depict the speaker's encounter with death, but they do not exhibit the same concern with self-preservation. While Homer writes about escaping death, Sappho describes the process of going toward it. And whereas the Homeric hero either wins or loses, lives or dies, Sappho's protagonist can only "win" by losing and "death" becomes one name for a moment of *hypsous* whose articulation eludes any literal description. Sappho, unlike Homer, is not concerned with strife or combat, nor does her poem support the notion that the sublime entails the defeat of death. Moreover, the kinds of power relations about which she writes do not involve dominance, in which one identity subjugates another, but a merger in which usually separate identities conjoin. Such a junction displaces the ordinary meaning of "possession" wherein one either owns or is owned, and instead suggests that the poet/lover can possess that by which she is also possessed.

Sappho's lyric thus articulates a version of sublimity that differs radically from the Longinian sublime of power and rivalry. In so doing, it foregrounds what Longinus and subsequent theorists ignore: the deployment of agency to intensify and underscore the wish for dispossession, and to recognize in the scene of self-dispersal a site of self-empowerment. What is particularly striking about the poem, to echo Chopin's phrase, is Sappho's affirmation of the need for "the unlimited in which to lose herself" (29). But whereas Sappho's poem refuses any binary formulation of life and death, Longinus' commentary, like Homer's lyric, reinforces their separation, and we shall see that Longinus' repression of a certain heterogeneous and irreconcilable desire has far-reaching consequences in the history of the sublime's theorization.[14]

II

It may seem a long way from Longinus' treatise to Neil Hertz's *End of the Line: Essays on Psychoanalysis and the Sublime* (1985), but Hertz's notion of the sublime, especially as evidenced by his well-known "Reading of Longinus" (first published in *Poétique* in 1973), is strikingly congruent with Longinus'; and I have chosen to focus the discussion of Sappho's lyric through a meditation upon this essay not only because it exemplifies, if not defines, an important moment in late twentieth-century American studies of the sublime, but because Hertz's and Longinus' responses to Sappho have significant affinities.

According to Hertz, the sublime moment involves a turn or "transfer of power" (7), a crucial movement in which the subject shifts "from being 'under death' to being out from under death" (6). Precisely because no such "turn" occurs in Sappho's poem, it is particularly surprising that Hertz chooses her ode to support this account of the sublime. Although there is a marked difference between the beginning and the end of the poem (the speaker, for example, begins by reporting specific sensations ["my eyes cannot see, my ears hum"] and concludes by describing general ones ["I am paler than grass; I seem near to dying"]), such a progression bears no relation to the notion of "the sublime turn" upon which Hertz insists. It is also surprising that Hertz reverses the order of Longinus' text; he quotes Homer's poem before beginning to discuss Sappho and then cites only the last stanza. Just as Hertz points out that "Sappho's ode serves Longinus' purposes" (7), so she serves his: reading her poem as if it were a microcosm of Homer's lends credence to his view that the sublime entails a chiasmatic reversal, a shift from "victimized body" to "poetic force" (7). According to Hertz, what Longinus writes of Homer—that he has "tortured the words to correspond with the emotion of the moment" and has "in effect stamped the special character of the danger on the diction: 'they are being carried away from under death'" (10.6)—is equally true of Sappho. Hertz thus ignores the crucial differences between the two poems and reads Sappho's lyric as if, like Homer's, it celebrates a "turning away from near-annihilation" (6), which, for him, is the hallmark of the sublime. In a telling comparison, Hertz compares Sappho's alleged turning away to two lines from Wordsworth's *Prelude,* lines that will also figure in Hertz's subsequent "Notion of Blockage in the Literature of the Sublime" (1978): "Sappho's turn from being 'under death' to being out from under death . . . is, characteristically, the sublime turn (compare Wordsworth's 'my mind turned round / As with the might of waters')" (6).[15] Hertz's agenda is to show that Longinus' treatise authorizes and endorses a basically Wordsworthian sublime that, precipitated by a collision with mortality, celebrates the self's triumph over anything that would undermine its autonomy or interfere with its movement toward transcendence.

It is crucial both that Hertz establish the structure of the sublime as a transfer of power and that he define this turn as one of "disintegration and figurative reconstitution" (14), a movement from chaos to unity. Insisting that "the turn itself, the transfer of power, can take place only if some element can shift its position from one side of the scheme to the other" (7), Hertz reads Sappho's text "not simply (as) a poem of passion and self-division but one which dramatizes, in a startlingly condensed fashion, the shift from Sappho-as-victimized-body to Sappho-as-poetic-force" (7). Hertz's insistence upon a clear and present difference between (defeated) "victimized body" and (triumphant) "poetic force" parallels his view that the sublime moves from a state of "disintegration" to one of "figurative reconstitution"; moreover, both distinctions endorse a view of the sublime as entailing the transcendence of an overwhelming obstacle or force. But is there any textual evidence that such a shift occurs? As we have seen, Sappho does not conceive of the speaker's experience in terms of victory or defeat, nor does the poem confirm Hertz's view that her body is "victimized." At the end of the poem the speaker proclaims herself "near to dying" (or in Grube's translation, "caught in the pain of menacing death"), yet neither phrase supports Hertz's contention that the poem illustrates "the transfer of power" or "shift from-body-to-force" that supposedly characterizes the sublime turn; neither attests to the essential turn "away from near-annihilation" that is indeed central to Homer's lyric. Sappho rather describes a kind of excess that cannot exist within Hertz's (or Longinus') conceptual framework.

If libidinal and linguistic energies are not quite the same, her poem implies, they may also be less neatly separable than Hertz might wish. In so doing the poem exhibits a sublime that, at once visceral and verbal, inscribes both "body" and "poetic force" without collapsing the difference between them. Hertz's contention that the sublime entails a transfer of power that progresses from defeat to victory (or from body to mind) thus upholds precisely the dualism Sappho's poem denies. An important question, then, is not simply what authorizes Hertz's characterization of

Sappho's body as "victimized," but why he fails to see that her text resists and critiques such a theorization of sublimity? The relevance of gender to this question cannot be underestimated, and this issue comes to the fore in Hertz's second essay on the sublime, "The Notion of Blockage in the Literature of the Sublime"(1978). Published two years after Thomas Weiskel's influential *Romantic Sublime: Studies in the Structure and Psychology of Transcendence*, Hertz's "Notion of Blockage" examines what his earlier essay had overlooked: the notion of a potentially unrecuperable excess that, in Jacques Derrida's famous phrase, cannot "be brought back home to the father" (52).

In this new essay Hertz continues to emphasize that the sublime entails a transfer of power, a movement in which the self is first "checked in some activity . . . then released into another order of discourse" (44). Here, however, his explicit focus is the problem of excess raised both by the mind's movement of blockage and release at play in Kant's mathematical sublime and by Weiskel's psychoanalytic reading of Kant. For Weiskel as for Kant, the sublime arises from a moment when the self confronts and overcomes an obstacle or "blocking agent." Because Hertz wants to consider "both the role it (the moment of blockage) played in eighteenth- and nineteenth-century accounts of the sublime and the fascination it still seems to exert on contemporary historians and theorists of literature" (41), he examines the function of "blockage" in texts on the sublime by Samuel Holt Monk and Weiskel. In each case a feminine figure (or traditional symbol of femininity such as water or chaos) becomes a metaphor for the obstacle or "blocking agent."[16]

The first indication of a relationship between femininity and the notion of blockage emerges in Hertz's discussion of Monk's magisterial study of the sublime. Monk begins "with a careful paraphrasing of Kant" (45) because the latter's paradigm of the sublime as a moment of blockage followed by a compensatory positive movement provides a defense against total immersion in the labyrinth of eighteenth-century speculation about the sublime. The sheer magnitude of writing about the sublime during this period is, in effect, a version of what it purports to describe: it would, Monk says, "be unwise to embark on the confused seas of English theories of the sublime without having some idea as to where we are going."[17] (Note the remarkable recurrence of images of the sea as metaphors for the sublime: Homer's "huge wave batters the ship, bringing the sailors close to death"; Sappho hears the sound of roaring waves as sweat runs rivers down her body; and in "The Notion of Blockage" Hertz remarks upon "the rising tide of academic publications" just before he cites Wordsworth's image of "the Fleet waters of a drowning world" [41].) We will return to the link between the sea and sublimity in connection with *The Awakening*. For the moment, it is important to remark that English theories of the sublime, here aligned with the threat of excess Monk attempts to ward off, are symbolized by femininity. Monk begins his introduction by likening speculation about the sublime to "the confused seas" and proceeds to compare it to a woman in disarray: "theories of beauty are relatively trim and respectable, but in theories of the sublime one catches the century somewhat off its guard, sees it, as it were, without powder or pomatum, whalebone and patches" (6). Perhaps English theories of sublimity, the confused seas, and a woman caught without makeup are, for both Monk and Hertz, parallel terms. Speculation about the sublime becomes the obstacle the scholar needs to overcome in order to construct its definitive study and, appropriately enough, a woman unfit to be seen presents herself as the appropriate symbol for this inhibiting, yet necessary, force.

Weiskel's study of the romantic sublime contains a similar movement of thought that represses femininity in order to construct identity. Whereas Monk relies upon Kant, Weiskel finds in Freud's Oedipus complex—the "structure beneath the vast epiphenomena of the sublime" (11)—means to chart a course upon the perilous seas. Because Kant's sublime is equivalent to the "moment in which the mind turns within and performs its identification with reason," the sublime moment "recapitulates and thereby reestablishes the Oedipus complex, whose positive resolution is the basis of culture itself" (93–94). Weiskel thus identifies Kant's notion of the moral law with the Freudian superego in which, as Hertz points out, "an identification with the father (is) taken as a model" (51). But Hertz also remarks Weiskel's suspicion that the Oedipus complex does not function as the "deep structure" (103) of the sublime, and that it wards off a terrifying heterogeneity for which the theory cannot account; indeed, Weiskel worries that he has "arrived at [the] model by pressing one theory and suppressing a multitude of facts for which it cannot account" (99). The Stolen Boat episode in *The Prelude* (1.357–400), in which the speaker suffers overwhelming remorse after Mother Nature persuades him to steal a boat in "an act of stealth / And troubled pleasure," leads Weiskel to conclude that the boy's guilt conceals "a deeper, original ambivalence" (102) that cannot be explained by the notion of "an ambivalent struggle against an essentially benevolent pedagogy" (102). "Could it be," he wonders, "that the anxiety of the sublime does not ultimately result from the pressure of the super-ego after all?" (103). It will come as no surprise that the frightening excess that, if unleashed, might block the theory's success is, for Weiskel as for Longinus, Monk, and Hertz, symbolized by the feminine.

The magnitude that cannot be "returned to the father" leads to the territory of the mother. Although Weiskel does not use the term "pre-Oedipal," his explanation for this new anxiety of the sublime calls up an invocation of the desire and terror at work in the (maternal) pre-Oedipal phase, in which the infant is still bound in symbiotic union with its mother:

> The very gratification of instinctual aims, in its quality of excess, alerts the ego to a danger. There is simultaneously a wish to be inundated or engulfed by pleasurable stimuli and a fear of being incorporated, overwhelmed, annihilated. This is hardly a rigorous formulation of the original "oral ambivalence," but it helps to account for the peculiar, ambivalent quality of the abyss image. . . . Our line of thought postulates a wish to be inundated and a simultaneous anxiety of annihilation: to survive, as it were, the ego must go on the offensive and cease to be passive. This movement from passive to active is technically a reaction formation, and the Oedipal configuration we have remarked thus appears as itself a defense against the original wish. (104–5)[18]

Becoming a self, in this scenario, requires a transfer of libidinal energy from the mother to the father, as if the mother were herself the threatening agent that, without paternal intervention, would interfere with the formation of the child's separate identity. Yet Weiskel does not remark that the shift from passive to active (or pre-Oedipal to Oedipal) is accompanied by a correlative shift in which the father replaces the mother, or that "survival" depends upon her repression. The excess that might have impeded the theory's performance again turns out to instantiate it, for Weiskel concludes that "though the sublime of magnitude does not originate in a power struggle, it almost instantaneously turns into one as the secondary Oedipal system takes over" (106). In every case, the gender of the blocking agent that seems to interfere with but in fact enables the sublime moment is feminine.

Given Hertz's attunement to the connections between issues of gender and motifs of scapegoating, it is surprising that he does not notice the reenactment within his own work on the sublime of the very strategies of repression he explores so astutely within the works of Monk and

Weiskel. His conclusion regarding Weiskel's use of the pre-Oedipal phase and the scholar's wish for the moment of blockage are particularly instructive:

> We might even see in Weiskel's invocation of the [maternal] pre-Oedipal phases, in his interpretation of them as constituting the deep (hence primary) structure of the sublime and yet as still only a tributary of the Oedipal system into which it invariably flows, a more serious and argued version of Monk's joke about the woman not fit to be seen. The goal in each case is the Oedipal moment, that is, the goal is the sublime of conflict and structure. The scholar's *wish* is for the moment of blockage, when an indefinite and disarrayed sequence is resolved (at whatever sacrifice) into a one-to-one confrontation, when numerical excess can be converted into that supererogatory identification with the blocking agent that is the guarantor of the self's own integrity as an agent. (53)

Hertz and Weiskel employ similar strategies in their wish to bring the sublime safely back home to the father. Conceiving of excess only as a frightening (and feminine) other provides the occasion for a confrontation that enables the (masculine) self to confirm, or enhance, its own existence. Excess in such a formulation cannot be defined as heterogeneity, but rather is understood exclusively as a hostile, persecutory force; as in Longinus, the sublime becomes synonymous with the self's ability to master the other.

Although it is to Hertz's credit that his essays make explicit the rhetorical strategies by which such mastery is achieved, he fails to envision a sublime that does not depend for its construction upon the repression of excess. He concludes "The Notion of Blockage" with an alternative formulation of the sublime, "not the recuperable baffled self associated with scenarios of blockage, but a more radical flux and dispersion of the subject" (58), yet does so only the better to exclude the notion of this more "radical flux" in the very act of describing it: while "the moment of blockage might have been rendered as one of utter self-loss, it was, even before its recuperation as sublime exaltation, a confirmation of the unitary status of the self" (53). The second half of the sentence disqualifies the possibility the preceding phrase had seemed to affirm; the sublime "of utter self-loss" serves merely as the exception that confirms the theory's rule. Once again excess is thematized as a "blocking agent" that guarantees the self's own "unitary status." What seems to be the articulation of a problem functions as the form of its dismissal.[19]

Whereas Hertz appears to examine a kind of magnitude that cannot be read as "a confirmation of the unitary status of the self" (53) and one that, in Weiskel's phrase, does not "dramatize the rhythm of transcendence in its extremist and purest form" (22), his treatment of excess repeats and enacts the very movement it appears only to describe: the theorist *needs* a potentially uncontainable form of excess (or "blocking agent") in order that the model, by successfully defending against it, may strengthen and thereby confirm itself. The "common function of the moment of blockage in sublime scenarios" (60) is to legitimate differences, restore continuity, and ensure that the boundary between self and other will remain unblurred. And although Hertz may be correct to insist that while "some remarkable effects can be generated by crossing the line . . . the line needs to be established in order to be vividly transgressed" (59), we need to reassess a critical tradition that can consider the sublime exclusively in terms of a model of transgression. What notion of the sublime might ensue if one could no longer determine exactly where a line ends, or what crossing it entails?

It is not surprising that the specter of difference that haunts Weiskel and Hertz is one to which Hertz's reading of Sappho was blind: that of a kind of excess (and ecstasy) that not only cannot "be brought back home to the Father" (52) but that, within the terms of the tradition, is never addressed as such. The pages that follow attempt to redress this omission by attending to what the Longinian-Hertzian model of sublimity excludes. At issue is the articulation of a sublime that not only does not conform to the pattern of "preordained failure, and the consequent feeling of bafflement, and the sense of awe and wonder" that for Monk exemplifies "the sublime experience from Addison to Kant" (58) and that so many of its recent theorists continue to uphold, but to which writers such as Sappho bear witness without attempting to contain. It is this "more radical flux and dispersion" that Sappho describes and Chopin's novel affirms, for in *The Awakening* Edna Pontellier embraces the solubility Monk, Hertz, and Weiskel so fear. Faced with what Monk could theorize only as "the confused seas of the sublime" (6), she walks right in.

III

Words at their most sublime have the force and feel of water. The ocean is *The Awakening*'s central character, the axis around which the narrative turns. From the beginning it is represented as a linguistic presence, possessing a voice that speaks to Edna's soul. What it says simultaneously resists and impels symbolization. Unlike the green and yellow parrot whose voice inaugurates the novel by mechanically repeating the same unintelligible phrase and who, Chopin tells us, speaks "a language which nobody understood" (3), the sea speaks the language of the unsayable.[20] Its voice, "seductive, never ceasing, whispering, clamoring, murmuring, inviting the soul to wander for a spell in abysses of solitude; to lose itself in mazes of inward contemplation" (15), necessarily partakes of many tongues and reaches Edna "like a loving but imperative entreaty" (14). Perhaps because the ocean possesses a multitude of voices, the command it proscribes is never reducible to any single precept or act.

The sound of the ocean haunts the novel. Like a lover's half-forgotten touch, it betokens absence; indeed, it is a carrier of absence, giving Edna—or whoever hears it—access to a certain kind of knowledge. Hearing it, for example, implies the ability to hear the sound of "wake" within "awakening" and thus to recognize that the same word can signify both life and death, for "wake" simultaneously denotes consciousness of life and a funeral rite, a collective ritual for the dead. (There is a wake within *The Awakening*, but it takes place before Edna's death, at a feast she gives as a gift to herself.) That the same word has contradictory meanings, or means contradiction, points to the irreconcilable coexistence of opposites without the possibility of resolution. Signs of life are equally signs of death, and hearing the ocean's voice impels knowledge of their proximity.

Chopin consistently refuses a dualistic formulation of the relation between life and death, sleeping and waking, or pleasure and pain, and in so doing radically alters a Homeric (or romantic) view of the sublime in which the protagonist's encounter with a potentially overwhelming obstacle leads to heightened powers and a resurgence of life. Displacing the notion that the sublime attests to a polarization of opposites is the novel's insistence upon their co-implication. The voice of the sea indicates polarities only to combine them. Although, for example, Edna perceives the sea's touch as "sensuous, enfolding the body in its soft, close embrace" (15), its waves also "sway," "lash," and "beat upon her splendid body" (27). Chopin thus implies that what lulls may just as easily lash, that what soothes also inflames, and that nursery songs can kill.

Sappho's lyric and Chopin's novel both describe what occurs in response to hearing a beloved voice. In *The Awakening*, as in *phainetai moi*, hearing the other's voice makes something happen: it is a singular event that engenders shock or crisis. The novel's beginning thus reproduces Longinus' description of the unique relation between orator and auditor at play in the sublime, in which the hearer's (or reader's) identification with the speaker (or text) allows the latter to imagine that he "has created what he has merely heard" (1.4). The rapport between Edna and the ocean's voice replicates not only that between orator and auditor in the Longinian sublime, but that between lover and the beloved in Sappho's poem: hearing its address inaugurates a desire where previously there was none. In this case the reader hears through Edna's ears, and what she hears is the ocean.

Chopin's representation of the ocean continually emphasizes its independence from the domain of vision. It is significant, for example, that Edna hears it for the first time in total darkness. Wakened after midnight by the return of her husband, Léonce, Edna sits alone on the porch and suddenly hears "the everlasting voice of the sea, that was not uplifted at that soft hour," a voice that breaks "like a mournful lullaby upon the night" (8). Absence of light allows awareness of a kind of presence one does not need eyes to discern: the sea's "mournful voice" breaks like a lullaby, a song sung by mothers to comfort their children and send them to sleep, as if its capacity to offer solace suggests a relation between the representation of absence and a distinctly aural register.

Throughout the history of the sublime the sea has often served as its most appropriate, if not exemplary, metaphor; and it is worth recalling some traditional representations of this relation the better to understand just how dramatically Chopin's construction of the oceanic sublime differs from them. In both Longinus and Burke, the sea is a major source of sublime sentiment. For Longinus the ocean's majesty is self-evident: he holds that "a natural inclination . . . leads us to admire not the little streams, however pellucid and however useful, but the Nile, the Danube, the Rhine, and above all, the Ocean" (42, Russell). For Burke the ocean is so appropriate a symbol of sublimity that he chooses it to illustrate the precept that "whatever therefore is terrible, with regard to sight, is sublime too" (53). Our differing responses to the sight of "a level plain of a vast extent on land" and to the "prospect of the ocean" show that the latter "is an object of no small terror" in a way that the plain, despite its vastness, is not: the ocean's capacity to arouse terror is the source of both its power and its sublimity (53–54). In Schopenhauer the ocean actually outranks all other forms of natural display. Transfixed and uplifted by its sight, the "undismayed beholder" watches "mountainous waves rise and fall, dash themselves furiously up against steep cliffs, and toss their spray high into the air; the storm howls, the sea boils, the lightning flashes from black clouds, and the peals of thunder drown the voice of the storm and sea." Indeed, Schopenhauer holds that such oceanic immensity yields "the most complete impression of the sublime."[21] In each case, however, the ocean's sublimity is bound up with vision: the sea is something a detached observer looks at, usually from afar. That Edna is transfixed by the ocean's sound rather than its sight is important because here Chopin revises typical constructions of the oceanic sublime. Edna transgresses Kant's injunction that "we must be able to view (it) as poets do, merely in terms of what manifests itself to the eye [*was der Augenschein zeigt*]—e.g., if we observe it while it is calm, as a clear mirror of water bounded only by the sky; or, if it is turbulent, as being like an abyss threatening to engulf everything."[22] Edna's relation to the ocean would, according to Kant, be neither poetically nor philosophically correct: merely looking at the sea holds no particular interest for her. She has a natural, if untutored, aptitude for painting and "a serious susceptibility to beauty" (15), yet only the ocean's voice and touch affect her. Chopin's oceanic sublime is not something "we must regard as the poets do, merely by what the eye reveals," but rather functions as a mode of address.[23] As in Sappho, sublime encounters are occasioned by something heard.

Edna's first encounter with the sublime is marked by an identification with what she hears. The sound of the ocean's "everlasting voice," which disrupts the everyday world she has taken for granted, speaks a language radically different from any she has previously heard and it leaves a mark: "an indescribable oppression, which seemed to generate in some unfamiliar part of her consciousness, filled her whole being with a vague anguish. It was like a shadow, like a mist passing across her soul's summer day" (8). Sound tears and Edna has been torn. Thus begins her awakening.

Learning to swim is merely its continuation. Although hearing the ocean's voice awakens her desire, Edna does not venture into it until she has been touched by another kind of sound, namely, by one of Chopin's preludes. Listening to music composed by the artist whose name replicates the author's own is a prelude to immersion in that which she has heard. Passion comes in waves that sway the soul, but sound also gives rise to waves and hearing them precedes Edna's awakening.

Toward the end of a festive midsummer soirée, Robert Lebrun arranges for Mademoiselle Reisz, a renowned but eccentric pianist, to play for the assembly. Hearing the prelude has a dramatic effect on Edna: usually music "had a way of evoking pictures in her mind" (26), but now she sees nothing; what she hears possesses and overcomes her. That Edna's most profound encounters are occasioned by what she hears suggests that hearing may entail entanglement in a way that seeing does not. For hearing, as Gerald C. Bruns reminds us, is not the spectator's mode:

> The ear is exposed and vulnerable, at risk, whereas the eye tries to
> keep itself at a distance and frequently from view (the private eye). The
> eye appropriates what it sees, but the ear is always expropriated, always
> being taken over by another ('lend me your ears'). The ear gives the
> other access to us, allows it to enter us, occupy and obsess us . . . hear-
> ing means the loss of subjectivity and self-possession . . . [and] puts us
> in the mode of being summoned, of being answerable and having to
> appear.[24]

Bruns's gloss on Heidegger's *On The Way To Language* also applies to Edna's response to Chopin: "the very first chords which Mademoiselle Reisz struck upon the piano sent out a keen tremor down Mrs. Pontellier's spinal column . . . she waited for the material pictures which she thought would gather and blaze before her imagination. She waited in vain. She saw no pictures of solitude, of hope, of longing, or of despair" (27).

How to say something that cannot be said, that confronts us with the inability to present it? The problem that has occasioned the discourse and theory of the sublime is the same as that posed by *The Awakening*: the difficulty of symbolizing an excess that resists visual or linguistic formulation but is there nonetheless. Edna's experience of what Hertz would call "blockage"—her inability to translate sense-impressions into images—calls for a radically different mode of perception, but one that does not lead to an enhanced sense of self. Adorno's conviction that music's value resides in its ability to call "for change through the cryptic language of suffering" is enacted by the prelude's effect on Edna: she trembles, chokes, is blinded by tears, and then, as if to seek deeper knowledge of the "cryptic language" she has heard, she learns to swim.[25] The figurative parallel between the prelude, whose notes arouse passion in her soul, and the ocean, whose waves like music beat upon her body, is established just before Edna, with the other guests, walks down to the ocean and swims for the first time.

Edna's first swim is neither an attempt to appropriate the ocean's power nor a submission to it. It does not represent a struggle for dominance over a force that, as in Homer, has the power to engulf her, but rather, as in Sappho, allows a relation to "the unlimited" in which she seeks "to lose herself" (29). Swimming offers a way of entering apartness; finding her "self" is, paradoxically, a matter of entering the water of the Gulf of Mexico and learning how to lose that which she has found:

> That night she was like the little tottering, stumbling, clutching child, who all of a sudden realizes its power, and walks for the first time alone, boldly and with over-confidence. She could have shouted for joy. She did shout for joy, as with a sweeping stroke or two she lifted her body to the surface of the water . . . she turned her face seaward to gather in an impression of space and solitude, which the vast expanse of water, meeting and melting with the moonlit sky, conveyed to her excited fancy. As she swam she seemed to be reaching out from the unlimited in which to lose herself. (28–29)

Learning to swim also entails awareness that the ocean can be lethal. Swimming too great a distance from the shore and at the limits of her strength, Edna experiences a "flash of terror"; "a quick vision of death" smites Edna's soul but she manages to regain the land.[26] She perceives her experience as an "encounter with death" (29) yet makes no mention of it.

Nor do most of Chopin's critics. For although, as Sandra Gilbert and Susan Gubar point out, "in the past few decades *The Awakening* has become one of the most persistently analyzed American novels,"[27] surprisingly few critics have discussed the role of the ocean and its voice, an omission made all the more startling given Chopin's insistence upon it.[28] Dale Bauer, Sandra Gilbert, Susan Gubar, and Patricia Yaeger discuss the ways in which the sea functions as a metaphor for Edna's awakening, yet none of these critics recognize that it is also a metaphor for language itself. Nor are they attuned to the ways in which Edna's newly awakened desire must also be understood as a desire for the sublime.

In "The Second Coming of Aphrodite: Kate Chopin's Fantasy of Desire," Gilbert and Gubar offer a meticulous and insightful interpretation of "oceanic imagery" in *The Awakening*. According to these persuasive critics, the sea provides an alternative to patriarchal culture: lying "beyond the limits and limitations of the cities where men make history, on one of those magical shores that mark the margin where nature and culture intersect" (102), it also provides an element "in whose baptismal embrace Edna is renewed, reborn" (103). For Gilbert and Gubar the novel not only tells the story of Edna's awakening and initiation into a "pagan paradise" in which "metaphorically speaking, Edna has become Aphrodite, or at least an ephebe of that goddess," but examines the consequences that "would have befallen any late-nineteenth-century woman who experienced such a fantastic transformation" (106). They propose that the novel be read as "a feminist myth of Aphrodite/Venus, as an alternative to the patriarchal Western myth of Jesus" (96), in which the Gulf, incarnated by the white foam of the sea from which the goddess emerges, is Aphrodite's birthplace. Just as Gilbert and Gubar find in Edna a modern Aphrodite, so they mythologize and idealize the sea and its "magical shores," for their apparent attentiveness to the ocean ignores the very register Chopin emphasizes—that of sound, not sight. Privileging vision, in this case the image of Venus rising from the waves rather than the voice of the ocean Edna hears, allows them to offer the comforting, if implausible, message that the embrace of Chopin's ocean promises only fulfillment, never terror, and that the one may be neatly separated from the other. Such an idealization upholds a vision of plenitude that a more sustained attention to the ocean's voice would function to resist. Chopin's construction of the ocean suggests not self-presence but self-dispersal; it invites the soul "to lose itself in mazes of inward contemplation" (15); and what it instills is the desire for loss.

Emphasizing only the sea's beneficent aspects, Gilbert and Gubar are able to put forward an entirely reassuring interpretation of it. Not only is Edna swimming "into a kind of alternative paradise"; the novel is itself "a new kind of work, a mythic/metaphysical romance that elaborates her female fantasy of paradisal fulfillment" (104). Their reading ignores not only the question but the consequences of asking what hearing the ocean's voice entails and enables a view of the novel's conclusion in which the ocean functions solely as a redemptive site, an "alternative paradise": "Edna's last swim may not seem to be a suicide—that is, a death—at all, or, if it is a death, it is a death associated with a resurrection, a sort of pagan female Good Friday that promises an Aphroditean Easter" (109). Gilbert and Gubar's commitment to a thematics of redemption mirrors Hertz's and Weiskel's treatment of the sublime as a sustained, if interrupted, progression toward transcendence. In each case what is envisioned is an ocean without undertow, a voice that is able to tell everything it knows, and the possibility of desire without loss.

For Dale Bauer, however, the ocean does not speak at all, an extremely surprising omission given that her Baktinian reading of the novel emphasizes such notions as "dialogue," "heteroglossia," and above all, "voice." In Bauer's view, Edna's relationship to the sea reflects her need to withdraw from a constraining and oppressive society and return "to a womb-like sea. Hers is also a retreat to the imaginary realm in which the only 'voice' with which Edna must contend is the sea's."[29] That Bauer puts the word "voice" in quotation marks is perhaps indicative of her own assumptions about language, namely that the domain of the unrepresentable and excessive, here symbolized by the sea, belongs to a "pre-linguistic, imaginary realm" (149) that has no relation to speech and language. Bauer's assurance that we can distinguish the cultural (or spoken) from the natural (or silent) elides Chopin's representation of the ocean as that which blurs the difference between the two. Whereas *The Awakening* foregrounds these issues, Bauer's reading precludes them. And whereas the sea as represented by Chopin conjoins realms usually assumed to be separate, Bauer reinstates the distinction the ocean's voice displaces. Her failure to hear is perhaps symptomatic of the view that language is, or ought to be, a site of plenitude, offering a realm in which everything can be said and nothing need go unheard. That language may possess a force that, as in Sappho, threatens to overwhelm the auditor and bring her close to death is perhaps something that current readings of *The Awakening* wish to avoid.

While Patricia Yaeger's "'A Language Which Nobody Understood': Emancipatory Strategies in *The Awakening*" is unquestionably the most sophisticated critical treatment of these issues, it nonetheless shares the assumption that language, in principle if not practice, should offer a refuge from, rather than an amplification of, the unsayable. According to Yaeger, Edna's quest is for an alternative form of communication, a speech and voice of her own. In this regard she compares the speech of the parrot to the voice of the sea: both are expressions of "the absent or displaced vocality" Edna seeks; both "emphasize Edna's need for a more passionate and intersubjective speech that will allow Edna to revise or rearticulate her relation to her own desire and to the social reality that thwarts this desire."[30] But whereas Yaeger conflates the voice of the parrot and that of the sea, I wish to emphasize their differences. While Yaeger finds in the parrot's nonsensical jabber and the sea's voice alike metaphors for "a potential lack of meaning in words themselves" (203)—meaning, that is, in the words available to Edna—I contend that the voice of the ocean attests to the incommensurable in a way that the parrot's mechanical babble does not, and that in so doing it depicts an alterity that is, strictly speaking, unsayable.

Yaeger is the only critic of *The Awakening* to find in Jean-François Lyotard's theory of "the differend" a useful way of explaining Edna's linguistic predicament and its outcome. And while I agree that "Edna's absent language is not a manifestation of women's permanent expulsion from 'masculine speech' but of what Lyotard calls '*le différend*'" (204), I disagree with her understanding of just what this concept implies. According to Lyotard:

> In the differend, something "asks" to be put into phrases, and suffers from the wrong of not being able to be put into phrases right away. This is when the human beings who thought they could use language as an instrument of communication learn through the feeling of pain which accompanies silence (and of pleasure which accompanies the invention of a new idiom), that they are summoned by language, not to augment to their profit the quantity of information through existing idioms, but to recognize that what remains to be phrased exceeds what they can presently phrase, and that they must be allowed to institute idioms which do not yet exist.[31]

Lyotard employs the notion of the differend to describe practices that remain beyond the grasp of representation. Unlike Wittgenstein's injunction, "What we cannot speak about we must consign to silence," his goal is to make the presentation of the fact that the unpresentable exists as much the concern of a critical politics as of aesthetic practices. Lyotard's differend has much in common with his concept of the sublime.[32] For the differend, which entails both "the feeling of pain which accompanies silence (and of pleasure which accompanies the invention of a new idiom)" (13), foreshadows Lyotard's insistence that the sublime entails "the pleasure of a displeasure" (165) and recalls his famous definition of sublimity in *The Postmodern Condition*: "the real sublime . . . is an intrinsic combination of pleasure and pain: the pleasure that reason should exceed all presentation, the pain that imagination or sensibility should not be equal to the concept."[33] In *The Differend* pain accompanies silence while pleasure accompanies the invention of a new idiom, but for our purposes what matters is that the differend and the sublime both emphasize something that is fundamentally inexpressible.[34] Both concepts underscore the dimension within language that, like the voice of Sappho's beloved or Chopin's ocean, testifies to the unsayable. Both signify neither absence nor presence but rather the possibility of an absolute and untranslatable otherness.

Yaeger's essay precludes consideration of the single element upon which Chopin and Lyotard insist: the force of the incommensurable. Whereas Lyotard maintains that to testify to the differend is a matter of calling attention to the disjunction between radically heterogeneous genres of discourse, for Yaeger such testimony is equivalent to recovering the silence left by the ocean's, and Edna's, not yet articulate voice, and by replacing the unsayable with speech. According to Yaeger something crucial is missing and language—a new idiom—will repair the differend by putting speech in the place of silence. I would contend that the ocean's voice intensifies the hearer's relation to that which cannot be translated into speech, making audible an absence to which she must nonetheless bear witness. In *The Awakening* hearing entails the recognition that something remains to be said, and this linguistic residue exceeds what can be put into words. The search for new "idioms," then, is not simply a matter of putting speech in the place of silence, of filling in gaps and replacing absence with presence, but of attesting to an excess that resists the attempt to translate sheer heterogeneity into a univocal message. Chopin's evocation of the ocean functions as a differend not because it replaces a flawed or missing speech-act with a more successful one, but because it stresses the impossibility of paraphrasing the singularity and particularity of its voice, and thereby allows us to hear a silence that might otherwise have remained unheard.

IV

Critics of *The Awakening* continue to be perplexed by the nature of Edna's desire. As Walter Benn Michaels argues convincingly, what is most confusing about the novel is not that Edna's desires are frustrated, but rather that so many of them are fulfilled: as he points out, the narrative "is marked by Edna's inability . . . to reshape her own ability to get what she wants."[35] And Edna's wishes do appear to be granted without apparent effort on her part. She wants to become an artist and quickly finds a market for her work; longs for freedom from her husband, children, and domestic routine and soon has personal and financial independence; desires sexual adventures and has them; indeed, the only thing Edna wants and does not get is Robert's love, but the reader suspects that had he not left her she would have left him, that frustration rather than fulfillment conditions her desire. The view of Edna as suffering somewhat narcissistically from the "problem" of getting nearly everything and everyone she wants draws support from her own assessment of her capacity to desire: "there was no one thing in the world that she desired. There was no human being whom she wanted near her except Robert; and she even realized that the day would come when he, too, and the thought of him would melt out of her existence, leaving her alone" (113). Edna's world seems simultaneously to offer her nothing she can want at the same time that it satisfies her every whim, and Michaels's assessment of the novel's conclusion, in which he holds that Edna's suicide "may best be understood neither as the repudiation of a society in which one can't have all the things one wants nor as an escape from a society in which one can't want all the things one can have but as an encounter with wanting itself" (498), would appear irrefutable. I argue, however, that understanding Edna's desire within the context of the sublime offers an alternative to this interpretation.

What does "an encounter with wanting itself" entail? On the one hand, Michaels implies that such an encounter signals the death of desire. Getting what you want means no longer being able to want it, for desire's satisfaction implies its annihilation. Seen in this light, Edna's desire can be understood only as an addiction to the unavailable, as a never-ending quest for something new to want. But Michaels also suggests another interpretation of such an encounter, "in which the failure of one's desire for things and people need not be understood as exhausting all desire's possibilities" (498). Basing his second account upon Edna's remark to Dr. Mandelet that "I don't want anything but my own way," he implies that Edna's desire "can survive both the presence and the absence of any desirable things" (498) but is nonetheless doomed to failure because it is separated from the realm of subjects and objects. Seen in this light, Edna's problem is not her inability to desire, but her "submersion in it and idealization of it, an idealization that immortalizes desire by divorcing it both from the subject (which dies) and the object (which is death) that it seems to require" (498–99). In either case, for Michaels "an encounter with wanting itself" entails an encounter with death. The specificity of

Edna's desire, however, redefines both of Michaels's accounts; Edna's "encounter with wanting itself" is unintelligible unless we explore what Michaels ignores: her wish for "the unlimited in which to lose herself." For although, as Michaels points out, "no body in Chopin can embody the infinite" (499), Edna desires precisely what she cannot embody.

What, or perhaps more important, *how* does Edna want? In *The Awakening* fulfillment entails not satisfaction but prolongation; it is neither a matter of getting what one wants (independence, money, sexual freedom, etc.) nor of removing desire from the realm of contingency. Rather, it involves a certain relation to excess, one that requires the representation or "embodiment" of that which one cannot possess. What Michaels fails to notice is that Edna's encounter with desire is simultaneously an encounter with language, here embodied by the ocean's voice, and that she wants the ocean's "everlasting voice" because it alone signifies that which is in excess of any boundary or limit. Like the bluegrass meadow that "she traversed as a child, believing that it had no beginning or end" (114), the ocean offers itself as sustaining a relation to that which she cannot represent. Given the choices available to her, the "fulfillment" of Edna's desire can only be merger, and presumably death, in the element that first awakened it. And although Edna wants to maintain a relation to what the ocean represents, her world offers nothing beyond the satisfaction of her demands. In this case, then, "desire gives birth to its own death" (496) because death within the force that awakened desire is all that remains for Edna to want. By the end of the novel there remains "no one thing in the world that she desired" (113)—a situation that comes about not because she is now incapable of wanting nor because she wants too much. The "object" of Edna's desire is neither a person nor a thing but a sustained relation to the ocean and everything it signifies.

To make what is unnameable appear in language itself—the desire at stake in the sublime is akin to Edna's desire for the ocean's voice: both defy the subject's representational capacities and can be signified only by that which, to borrow Lyotard's formulation, "puts forward the unpresentable in presentation itself," seeking "new presentations not in order to enjoy them but to impart a stronger sense of the unpresentable."[36] At issue is not a mastery of the ineffable, as in Hertz's and Weiskel's account of the romantic sublime, but rather an attestation to the unspeakable and uncontainable elements within language itself. This version of the sublime contests what Weiskel contends is the "essential claim of the romantic sublime: that man can, in feeling and speech, transcend the human" (3). Indeed, Edna wants the opposite: to find in "the unlimited" not a site of self-transcendence but rather a means of self-loss.

Edna's final swim—her going (and coming) "close to death"—must be understood both within the context of her initial encounter with the ocean and as the consequence of having awakened to desire in a social and political milieu that, as Gilbert and Gubar so rightly suggest, offers no means of articulating and sustaining her capacity for desire.[37] When, at the end of the novel, Edna tells Doctor Mandelet "perhaps it is better to wake up after all even to suffer, rather than to remain a dupe to illusions all one's life" (110), nowhere does her culture allow a means of representing her connection to the voice by which she has been called. In this context Edna's love for Robert bears no relation to his availability but rather results from his ability to manifest and facilitate her connection to the other. He is the only character attuned to Edna's need for the unlimited and until his departure for Mexico he is central to her intensifying relationship with it. Edna wants Robert because he sustains rather than satisfies her desire.

If Sappho's lyric ends by representing a merger that conflates the difference between any two sets of terms without at the same time annihilating their difference, so the end of *The Awakening* underscores the proximity and irreconcilability of opposites. Offering disparate accounts of Edna's walk into the ocean, Chopin first compares Edna to a crippled bird whose disabled wings make flying, or, in this case, living, impossible. Standing at the edge of the Gulf, Edna sees that "a bird with a broken wing was beating the air above, reeling, fluttering, circling disabled down, down to the water" (113), images that lead us to interpret Edna's last swim as a sign of her failure to survive in an oppressive world. But Chopin proceeds to suggest just the opposite. Before going into the sea, Edna removes her old bathing suit: she casts "the unpleasant, pricking garments from her, and for the first time in her life she stood naked in the open air, at the mercy of the sun, the breeze that beat upon her, and the waves that invited her" (113). Standing naked under the sky Edna feels "like some new-born creature, opening its eyes in a familiar world that it had never known," reversing the earlier connotation in which she saw that "all along the white beach, up and down, there was no living thing in sight" (113). As in Sappho's lyric, Chopin maintains the residue within language that is unhearable at the same time that she finds a new idiom for presenting its voice. But Edna's last walk into the ocean does not institute "a new idiom" in the sense that it puts speech in the place of silence (thus upholding the view that language is merely a vehicle of communication). Rather her response bears witness to the incommensurable voice she has heard. This is a "going close to death" that cannot simply be rendered by a phrase but to which phrases can testify nevertheless. Chopin's construction of the ocean's voice and the woman's response presents itself as one example of such an idiom: as a figure for the sublime, the ocean is also a figure for the unfigurable.

The novel's final paragraph, which describes Edna's last moments of consciousness, continues to foreground contradiction:

> She looked into the distance, and the old terror flamed up for an instant, then sank again. Edna heard her father's voice and her sister Margaret's. She heard the barking of an old dog that was chained to the sycamore tree. The spurs of the cavalry officer clanged as he walked across the porch. There was the hum of bees, and the musky odor of pinks filled the air. (114)

Chopin insists upon the disparate. Images of triumph—looking into the distance, vanquishing "the old terror"—coincide with symbols of authority and oppression, and then give way to sensory impressions that can be construed in neither context: the "hum of bees, and the musky odor of pinks." As Jane P. Tompkins remarks:

> Contradictory signs are everywhere. . . . The sight of an injured bird implies defeat, but Edna's shedding of her bathing suit signals rebirth. The act of swimming out so far seems both calculated and almost unconsciously performed. Edna's final vision, as she goes under, is sensual and promising, Whitmanesque, but qualified by images of a chain and spurs.[38]

But whereas Tompkins chastises Chopin for leaving the reader at sea in ambiguity, Chopin's conclusion foregrounds the very incommensurability Edna desires but cannot represent. Concluding the novel by placing images that apparently exclude one another in a relation of mutual interdependence, Chopin refuses to satisfy the wish for a single or definitive interpretation of Edna's last act, and in so doing constructs a sublime in which there is no end of the line.

2

"Sublime Speculations"

Edmund Burke, Lily Bart, and the Ethics of Risk

Hypocrisy, of course, delights in the most sublime speculations, for, never intending to go beyond speculation, it costs nothing to have it magnificent.

(Edmund Burke, *Reflections on the Revolution in France*)

Ah, how she'd always envied women with a natural wave! No difficulty for them in eloping with explorers. Of course they had to undergo the waving ordeal now and then too, but not nearly so often . . .

(Edith Wharton, "Permanent Wave")

The hatred of expenditure is the *raison d'être* of and the justification for the bourgeoisie; it is at the same time the principle of its horrifying hypocrisy.

(Georges Bataille, "The Notion of Expenditure")

No excess is good.

(Edmund Burke, *Reflections on the Revolution in France*)

As a young man writing *A Philosophical Enquiry into the Origin of Our Ideas of the Sublime and Beautiful*, the book that was to establish him as a major force in eighteenth-century British intellectual and cultural affairs, Edmund Burke favored an aesthetics of the sublime. He held it to be "the strongest emotion which the mind is capable of feeling."[1] The sublime, an experience bordering on terror but productive of delight, "derives all its sublimity from the terror with which it is generally accompanied" (60), and although Burke's notion of terror may have nothing to do with what Edith Wharton describes as the "terrible god of chance," their conjunction suggests a profound link between sublimity, chance, and speculation, categories that haunted Burke from the beginning to the end of his career.[2] But whereas Burke attempts to banish terror and everything that accompanies it from everyday life, Wharton insists upon precisely that which Burke feared: that ethics, politics, and aesthetics are inseparable, and that human excellence resides in the capacity to engage the incalculable.[3] The following pages begin by examining the connection between speculation and the sublime as it appears both positively in Burke's aesthetics and negatively in his politics and then consider the ways in which Lily Bart's relation to risk and speculation suggests another version of sublimity.

If Burke rose to fame by defining himself as the theorist (or speculator) who speculated on the sublime, it is important to examine the ways in which Burke's discussions of sublimity are linked to questions about speculation, and we might begin by considering the diverse and contradictory meanings of that word. On the one hand, speculation entails interest: according to the *Oxford English Dictionary*, to speculate is "to engage in the buying and selling of commodities or effects in order to profit by a rise or fall in their market value; to undertake, to take part or invest in, a business enterprise or transaction of a risky nature in the expectation of considerable gain." On the other hand, a second definition of speculation implies disinterest and detachment, for to speculate also means to "theorize upon," "to observe or view mentally; to consider, examine, or reflect upon with close attention; and to engage in thought or reflection, especially of a conjectural or theoretical nature." The word's double meaning suggests that risk taking and theorizing are somehow related, as if contemplation were never quite so free of interest (or speculation) as one might prefer to believe.

The *Enquiry* is a speculative work in every sense of the word. Even Burke's consideration of the extremes of size links speculation, in the sense of a multitude of associations, to the sublime: vastness or littleness are both sources of sublimity because "they afford a large and fruitful field of speculation" (66). In this sense speculation is consistent with, if not a synonym for, sublime experience; in perceiving the magnitude or finitude of space we become "amazed and confounded," unable to distinguish the "extreme of littleness from the vast itself" (66). Speculation and the sublime both entail an experience in which objects that ordinarily are separate from one another become confused or "confounded." The shape of a "rotund," for example, produces a particularly "sublime effect" for in it "you can no where fix a boundary; turn which way you will, the same object still seems to continue, and the imagination has no rest" (68). But Burke invokes yet another meaning of speculation, for in writing the *Enquiry* he assumes a position of disinterest, as if the activity of theorizing demanded an observer who remains separate from that which he observes.

In this regard Lawrence Selden, who is fascinated by Lily Bart precisely because "it was characteristic of her that she always roused speculation" (3), but who nonetheless manages to keep her at a distance, enacts Burke's relation to the subject matter of the *Enquiry*: both present themselves as disinterested spectators who contemplate, or theorize about, a field upon which they exert no influence, preferring merely to observe the spectacles someone else creates.

Burke begins the preface to the first edition by stating his reasons for writing the *Enquiry*: he has "observed that the ideas of the sublime and the beautiful were frequently confounded" and that "such a confusion of ideas must certainly render all our reasonings upon subjects of this kind extremely inaccurate and inconclusive" (1). Burke intends to eradicate "confusion," a quality that will later emerge as one of the features that accompany sublime experience; his hope is that a "diligent examination of our passions in our own breasts" may provide "an exact theory of our passions" and thereby allow him to discover the "fixed or consistent principles" (1) that govern them. Burke's passion for "exact theory" is matched by his wish to "know the exact boundaries of their [the passions'] several jurisdictions. . . . It is not enough to know them in general . . . we should pursue them through all their variety of operations, and pierce into the utmost, and what might appear inaccessible parts of our natures" (48, 49). Indeed, in the "Introduction on Taste," he reemphasizes his wish to abolish the "uncertainty and confusion" to which "the term taste, like all other figurative terms . . . is therefore liable" (12): they are the impediments that might prevent him from proving that taste, which appears "indeterminate" and open to infinite "diversity," is in fact subject to principles, "so common to all, so grounded and certain, as to supply the means of reasoning satisfactorily about them" (13). Burke's goal is to reveal the certain and invariable laws that govern the imagination, to demonstrate that taste has "fixed principles" and that the imagination is "affected according to some invariable and certain laws" (12).[4]

Burke's desire to eradicate uncertainty and confusion is especially noteworthy because the *Enquiry* continually emphasizes their sublimity. Praising Milton's portrait of Death, for example, Burke writes that "in this description all is dark, uncertain, confused, terrible, and sublime to the last degree" (55). In great poetry, "the mind is hurried out of itself, by a crowd of great and confused images; which affect because they are crowded and confused" (57); a few paragraphs later he observes that "in nature dark, confused, uncertain images have a greater power on the fancy to form the grander passions than those which are more clear and determinate" (58). And when Burke remarks that "uncertainty is so terrible, that we often seek to be rid of it, at the hazard of a certain mischief" (76–77), he not only ascribes to it the very attribute of terror he has already described as "the ruling principle of the sublime" but implies that he will hazard "a certain mischief" in order to get rid of it.

Commenting upon his "method of proceeding" (4) in the preface to the second edition, Burke employs a word that was, in the eighteenth century, a synonym for the sublime. When it is a question of dealing with matters of great complexity, Burke emphasizes that "we must make use of a cautious, I had almost said, a *timorous* method of proceeding" (4; my emphasis). As Adam Phillips points out in his introduction to the *Enquiry*, the word "timorous" "fits accurately into an eighteenth-century discussion of sublimity, meaning, as it did then, 'causing fear or dread: dreadful, terrible' (*O.E.D.*)" (xvii). Phillips's gloss suggests that there is something terrible (or sublime) about Burke's own "method of proceeding," and that caution may be a quality he lacks. Burke believes that he can eradicate uncertainty and confusion in life even as he finds them productive of delight in art, but doing so depends upon a distinction between art and nature, or "imitation" and "the real," that his definition of the sublime calls into question.

If Burke's wager in the *Enquiry* is that theory can put certainty in the place of ambiguity and replace diversity with fixed and universal "principles in nature" (17), why does he choose to privilege that dimension of aesthetic experience in which uncertainty rules, a domain always in excess of any boundary or limit? If "clearness . . . is in some sort an enemy to all enthusiasms whatsoever" (56), Burke's discussion of the sublime serves to prove that "an exact theory of the passions" is a contradiction in terms. The sublime is never simply pleasure nor pain, but their confusion and combination—indeed, it is a pleasure "which cannot exist without a relation . . . to pain" (33); and delight is a "relative" rather than "positive" pleasure because it not only "accompanies," but also arises from, "the removal of pain or danger" (34). It is as if the *Enquiry*, which begins by deploring confusion, risk, and uncertainty, means to praise the very qualities it appears to despise. And although Burke maintains that "in an enquiry, it is almost everything to be once in a right road" (50), the sublime, in which "all is dark, uncertain, confused, terrible" (55), implies the probability of losing one's way.

The sublime demonstrates the capacity of one extreme to turn into the opposite. Its ruling principle resides in an incessant and infinite reversibility, a movement that destabilizes boundaries and undercuts the terms of any opposition. As W. J. T. Mitchell observes, Burke's sublime

> goes beyond the 'combination' of opposites in a single object, and involves the *transformation* of one into the other in the extremes. . . . This union of extreme opposites Burke will identify as itself a principle of the sublime: when 'two ideas as opposite as can be imagined' are 'reconciled in the extremes of both,' they concur in producing the sublime.[5]

Just as extreme light may be a source of the sublime because "by overcoming the organs of sight, [it] obliterates all objects, so as in its effects to resemble darkness" (74), so the sublime entails a merger or confusion of opposites in which light by its very excessiveness is transformed into darkness. The paradigmatic law of Burke's sublime, the principle of mutability or conversion by virtue of which one extreme turns into its opposite, imposes on its theorist the risk that disinterested speculation will also become that to which it is opposed. The diverse meanings at stake in the word "speculation" can never securely be divided, for the speculator is always part of the game she speculates about, or upon.[6] If, as Burke observes, in both nature and in art "we must expect to find the qualities of things the most remote imaginable from each other united in the same object" (114), we will see that the distinctions so dear to him mutate into one another according to the principle of transformation, or speculation, Burke underwrites as sublime. Burke's observations that "a true artist should put a generous deceit on the spectators" and that "no work of art can be great, but as it deceives" (70) lead us to speculate whether or not the theory of the sublime is not his own "generous deceit," for it produces the uncertainty and confusion he supposedly wishes to contain.

The early Burke can laud the sublime and the experiences of terror, confusion, and obscurity that accompany it because he believes he can keep them at a distance, confined within an aesthetic domain. But, as Donald Pease remarks, the sublime is "less a rhetorical or even an aesthetic category than a power to make trouble for categorizing procedures"; as such, it lays waste to binary (and inevitably hierarchical) distinctions.[7] The sublime cannot remain encased within an aesthetic domain because it is the force that undercuts the stability of boundaries, including those that divide masculine from feminine, politics from aesthetics.

I

Why, in the *Reflections on the Revolution in France* (1790), does Burke link speculation to the sublime, and what, in this context, might he mean by sublimity?[8] In his East Indian and counterrevolutionary writings, Burke describes the political events of his day in terms that echo the aesthetic categories of the sublime and the beautiful he had described some thirty years before in the *Philosophical Enquiry into the Origin of our Ideas of the Sublime and Beautiful.*[9] As his critics frequently observed, Burke in his later political writings employs the aesthetic constructs and vocabulary that were the explicit themes of the *Enquiry*. (Foremost among the critics, Ronald Paulson notes, was Mary Wollstonecraft, whose *Vindication of the Rights of Man*, published in the same month as the *Reflections*, points out that the categories Burke invokes in the *Reflections* derive from those he defined in the *Enquiry*.)[10] Among more recent critics, Neal Wood argues that Burke's concepts of the sublime and the beautiful "inform and shape several of his fundamental political ideas [and] are a unifying element of Burke's social and political outlook"; Steven Blakemore observes that Burke "reintroduces the sublime and the beautiful to explain, criticize, and control proliferating revolutionary forces at war with traditional meaning"; and Sara Suleri points out that "while Burke's treatise on the sublime predates his active involvement in the politics of the colonization of India, it constitutes a figurative repository that would later prove invaluable to the indefatigable eloquence of his parliamentary years."[11] It is as if Burke's encounter with the terrifying phenomenon of the French Revolution (which was already anticipated by his response to the East India Company's activities in India and his attempts to impeach Warren Hastings, its governor general, during the 1780s) was to assimilate it to the categories of the sublime and the beautiful he had first discussed in 1757.[12]

There is, however, a remarkable discontinuity between Burke's aesthetic and political positions. Indeed, Burke's politics appear to be the precise opposite of his aesthetics, for the very qualities he praises in the *Enquiry* he later condemns. As Mitchell observes, "When Burke confronted a historical event [the French Revolution] that conformed to his concept of sublimity, he could find it only monstrous and disgusting. His notion of the sublime remained safely contained in the realm of aesthetics."[13] We cannot account for the disparity between Burke's aesthetic and political preferences simply by emphasizing that for Burke terror can be a source of the sublime only because the affected subject is a spectator and not a participant in the terrifying event he observes. If "terror is in all cases whatsoever, either more openly or latently the ruling principle of the sublime" (54), it does not consist merely in the spectator's imaginary experience or observation of someone else's terror, for then it would not possess the mind-shattering effect of the sublime, which blurs the difference between observer and observed. Burke's definition of the sublime as a "great power" in which "the mind is so entirely filled with its object, that it cannot entertain any other, nor by consequence reason on that object which employs it" (53), undercuts those distinctions between spectator and event upon which his theory also relies. This is not to dismiss the role spectatorship plays in the production of the sublime, but rather to underscore its profoundly ambiguous status. For the experience Burke describes as sublime depends not only upon maintaining a certain distance from terror, but also upon an identification or merger between observer and observed that precludes the distance that supposedly is essential to sublime experience. Indeed, the originality of Burke's sublime is that it calls into question our belief in the "merely aesthetic" and unsettles the notion of an autonomous domain of human experience that exists independent of political, ethical, and social concerns.

Whereas in the *Enquiry* the sublime refers to the experience of "delight," a peculiar mixture of pain and pleasure that occurs when what would otherwise be dangerous "does not press too close" (42), by the end of his career the qualities that earlier had indicated aesthetic superiority become the focus of attack.[14] While the early Burke emphasizes that the experience of power, darkness, obscurity, astonishment, confusion, and terror not only are the source of the sublime but provide a standard of aesthetic excellence, in his counterrevolutionary writings the terror he had previously lauded as sublime instead evokes a vision of hell. In a speech delivered in Commons four years after the publication of the *Reflections*, Burke depicts "the condition of France" in terms that recall descriptions of the sublime in the *Enquiry*: "The condition of France at this moment was so frightful and horrible, that if a painter wished to portray a description of hell, he could not find so terrible a model, or a subject so pregnant with horror, and fit for his purpose."[15] In the *Enquiry*, we have seen, Burke considers terror to be "the ruling principle of the sublime" (54). Here, however, it functions as a metaphor for anarchy and political chaos: the sheer, undirected energy that the early Burke regarded as sublime is now envisaged as a dangerous threat to the social and moral order, linked to the dissolution of the monarchy and the unleashing of sexual passion. Through a bizarre reversal of sexual roles, the subject has become "pregnant with horror."

In *Letters on a Regicide Peace* (1796), his last work on the French Revolution, Burke continues to interpret the condition of France through recourse to the rhetoric of the sublime. As in the passage we have just remarked, Burke begins by ascribing to France the qualities of terror and vastness he had previously attributed to the sublime and ends by assigning a gender to "that hideous phantom" he has just described:

> Out of the tomb of the murdered monarchy in France has arisen a vast, tremendous, unformed spectre, in a far more terrific guise than any which ever yet have overpowered the imagination, and subdued the fortitude of man. Going straight forward to its end, unappalled by peril, unchecked by remorse, despising all common maxims and all common means, that hideous phantom overpowered those who could not be-lieve it was possible she could at all exist . . .[16]

The revolutionary sublime, it would appear, is a "she."

II

Burke's aesthetic categories are determined and shaped by prevailing assumptions about sexual difference; indeed, the success of his project depends upon eradicating the possibility that gender itself may be a form of speculation, a cultural role or performance and not a natural fact. I am not merely emphasizing that, as Terry Eagleton observes, "the distinction between the beautiful and the sublime, then, is that between woman and man," but rather that patriarchal assumptions about the nature of sexual difference are at the source, and provide the thematic value, of Burke's distinction between the sublime and the beautiful, which in turn provides a unifying structure for both his aesthetic and political ideas.[17] Burke's project in the *Enquiry* hinges upon assumptions about gender that give rise to the distinction between the beautiful and the sublime and offers the structuring principle that informs his subsequent political writings. It would, as Sara Suleri observes, "be too simple to read the *Enquiry* as a gendering of aesthetic categories, or to draw further attention to its masculinization of the sublime and the concomitant feminization of beauty." Presuppositions about an innate sexual difference supply the ground in which Burke's aesthetic and political categories take root and, especially in Burke's later political writings, become the rhetorical figure for their merger and confusion.[18] If gender lays the foundation for the distinction between the beautiful and the sublime, its instability also marks the necessity for their conflation.

In a footnote to "A Brief Appraisal of the Greek Literature" (1838), Thomas De Quincey observes that the idea of the sublime, "in contra-position to the Beautiful, grew up on the basis of *sexual* distinctions,—the Sublime corresponding to the male, and the Beautiful, its anti-pole, corresponding to the female."[19] Burke's understanding of the modes of aesthetic experience derives from assumptions about the nature of sexual difference and the proper relations between the sexes, commonly held preconceptions about the innateness and universality of sexual difference, which become the indispensable condition for the aesthetic theory he puts forward. Burke is able to argue that "the ideas of the sublime and the beautiful stand on foundations so different that it is hard, I had almost said impossible, to think of reconciling them in the same subject" (103) only because he has found that "foundation" in the apparent naturalness of the difference between the sexes.

Burke's distinction between the sublime and the beautiful rests upon an understanding of sexual difference in which the "masculine" passions of self-preservation, which stem from ideas of terror, pain, and danger, are linked to the sublime, while the "feminine" emotions of sympathy, tenderness, affection, and imitation are the preserve of the beautiful. The sublime amalgamates such conventionally masculine qualities as power, size, ambition, awe, and majesty; the beautiful collects the equally con-ventional feminine traits of softness, smallness, weakness, docility, deli-cacy, and timidity. The former always includes intimations of power, majesty, and brute male force—a storm at sea, a raging bull, a ruler or sovereign, greatness of dimension—while the latter connotes smallness, delicacy, and serenity: "it is the flowery species," such as, perhaps, a lily, "so remarkable for its weakness and momentary duration, that gives us the liveliest idea of beauty, and elegance" (105–6). Beauty, like femininity, is inseparable from a certain weakness. In part three of the *Enquiry* Burke observes that "the beauty of women is considerably owing to their weakness, or delicacy, and is even enhanced by their timidity, a quality of mind analogous to it" (106). He argues against the prevailing view that perfection is the cause of beauty:

> [Beauty] almost always carries with it an idea of weakness and imper-
> fection. Women are very sensible of this; for which reason, they learn
> to lisp, to totter in their walk, to counterfeit weakness, and even sick-
> ness. In all this, they are guided by nature. (100)

And although we may love weakness, imperfection, and the beautiful, we feel awe in the presence of paternal authority and imperial majesty; thus "we submit to what we admire, but we love what submits to us" (103). Burke's aesthetic categories hinge upon a presumed opposition between the masculine and the feminine that, in turn, generates the distinction between terror, power, sublimity and self-preservation on the one hand and pleasure, affection, beauty, and society on the other. The success of Burke's aesthetic project—the attempt to explain the universality of aes-thetic judgment through his distinction between the sublime and the beautiful—therefore depends upon assumptions about sexual difference whose validity is never put in question.

While in Burke's later writings the confusion of the sexes becomes a metaphor for the revolutionary forces that would destroy traditional distinctions and hierarchies, and parallels his critique of speculation, in the *Enquiry* he is not yet haunted by this specter and can privilege risk and chance as central to the experience of the sublime. A particularly inter-esting passage links the "confusion of ideas" with the "abuse of words," as if confusion were itself a kind of abuse, and does so specifically in descriptions of sexual difference:

> If beauty in our own species was annexed to use, men would be much
> more lovely than women; and strength and agility would be considered
> the only beauties. But to call strength by the name of beauty, to have
> but one denomination for the qualities of a Venus and Hercules, so
> totally different in almost all respects, is surely a strange confusion of
> ideas, or abuse of words. (96)

Already in the *Enquiry* there is a hint of impending confusion, and it is no accident that the feminine body figures the breakdown of the distinction between the sublime and the beautiful. In the following passage, the consequence of observing a beautiful woman, which ought to produce feelings of affection, sympathy, and a comforting sense of masculine superiority over weakness, instead gives rise to a dizzying mobility:

> Observe that part of a beautiful woman where she is perhaps the most beautiful, about the neck and breasts; the smoothness; the softness; the easy and insensible swell; the variety of the surface, which is never for the smallest space the same; the deceitful maze, through which the unsteady eye slides giddily, without knowing where to fix, or whither it is carried. (105)

Here the feminine body, supposedly the symbol of the beautiful, instead produces the effects of the sublime. Rather than securing boundaries and limits, its very "smoothness," "softness," and "variety" instill "unsteadiness": this body does not provide a site where distinctions can be fixed but rather represents the point at which they come apart, and the observer, seeking a resting place, "slides giddily." The absence of a fixed point of view or visual focus produces disorientation; unlike the male, the beautiful female body defeats our expectation of a center and instead becomes the occasion of a giddiness, or vertigo. Vertigo, of course, is a typically sublime feeling connected with the falling away of ground or center; it is what we feel when an abyss opens up before us. It is important to emphasize that feminine sexual difference, which provides the foundation for the distinction between the sublime and the beautiful, here becomes the figure for that distinction's instability, eliciting a moment of textual dizziness in which the beautiful takes on the characteristics of the sublime.[20]

III

In the *Reflections* Burke identifies the French Jacobins with the "vigorous and active principle" (44) that exemplifies the masculine spirit of ambition and boldness and, if unchecked by the tempering aristocratic principle, threatens to invert the social order. In *Remarks on the Policy of the Allies* (1793), Burke returns to this theme. After listing the features that make the Jacobins monstrous and dangerous, he asks what accounts for their success: "*One* thing, and *one* thing only—but that one thing is worth a thousand—they have *energy*."[21] By the time of the *Letters on a Regicide Peace* (1796), he believed that Britain was at war with a Jacobin conspiracy, a vast multitude possessing what he envisions as a "dreadful energy."[22] But what, we may ask, makes their energy so "dreadful"? Although J. G. A. Pocock suggests that "the 'dreadful energy' is that of the human intellect set free from all social relations, so that it is free to be constructive or destructive, and it frequently chooses the latter in sheer assertion of its own power," I argue that unchecked energy—one of the distinguishing features of Burke's sublime—is that of speculation itself, dreadful not only because of its metamorphic and transformative power, but because it implies a domain that, lying beyond our control, suggests the limits of human agency.[23]

Like the "dreadful energy" Burke regards with a mixture of fascination and horror, speculation brings us face to face with the incalculable, and Burke detests speculation of all kinds.[24] As early as the *Vindication of Natural Society* (1756), he emphasizes that abstract speculation endangered the status quo. Remarking upon the "extreme danger of letting the imagination loose upon some subjects," he underscores the riskiness of deducing practical policy from theoretical principle: metaphysical speculation, which presents the lure and charm of fiction, must not become confused with the brute reality of everyday politics.[25] But he also believes that financial speculation is a threat to the traditional social order and especially to the inviolability of landed property. As Christopher Reid points out, "it is precisely the new capitalist formations of France (and, of course, of England) which pose a threat. . . . For Burke, this urban capitalism, apparently controlled by individual speculators, seems to herald a complete social fragmentation."[26] In the *Reflections*, Burke's most vociferous attacks are directed at revolutionary finance. He condemns French legislators:

> the very first who have founded a commonwealth upon gaming, and infused the spirit into it as its vital breath. The great object in these politics is to metamorphose France from a great kingdom into one great playtable; to turn its inhabitants into a nation of gamesters; to make speculation as extensive as life. (169)

For Burke, metaphysical and financial speculation are dangerous, if not revolutionary activities: theorists and economists alike employ it to bring about the end of monarchy, landed property, and the "age of chivalry" (66) Burke so reveres. In his "Letter to the Sheriffs of Bristol on the Affairs of America" (1777), for example, Burke holds "abstract speculation," the

realm of pure theory, responsible for the demise of civil freedom, a
perilous threat to human liberty:

> There are people who have split and anatomised the doctrine of free
> government, as if it were an abstract question concerning metaphysical
> liberty and necessity . . . speculations are let loose as destructive to all
> authority, as the former are to all freedom. . . . Civil freedom, gentle-
> men, is not, as many have endeavored to persuade you, a thing that lies
> hid in the depth of abstruse science. It is a blessing and a benefit, not
> an abstract speculation.[27]

Philosophical and economic opposition to the revolution is fused in the
image of speculation and the speculator, the practices of revolutionary
thinking and revolutionary finance. In each case speculation is dangerous
because in producing an excess either of linguistic signs or of paper
currency, it threatens the loss of value. Just as the verbal excess that is a
by-product of abstract speculation interferes with the view that words
invariably have clear, distinct, and stable relations to the ideas for which
they stand, so financial speculation substitutes the symbolic, and therefore
shifting, contingencies of paper money, debt, and credit for guarantees of
economic value such as property or precious metals. In so doing, revolutionary finance, like revolutionary thinking, undermines the value and
prestige of landed property and the monarchic political configuration that
accompanies it. Metaphysical speculation has as its economic corollary
financial speculation, which becomes synonymous with social anarchy
and fragmentation.

Burke's fear that abstract speculation could, like financial speculation,
exceed control and proliferate to infinity suggests a reason why, in the
Reflections, he associates the sublime, which he revered, with speculation,
which he loathed. Language and money are each crucial modes of exchange, and the speculator, in the act of producing excess verbiage and/or
inflated currency, abuses both. By inducing proximity to excess, speculation enacts the very subject the *Enquiry* describes. But if the theory of
the sublime is intended to "investigate the springs and trace the course of
our passions" (5) and thereby to contain the excess it bespeaks, speculation
not only invites proximity to excess but produces more of it. In so doing
it foregrounds the subject's relation to the incalculable, to a domain that,
beyond the range of conceptual or economic stability, cannot be controlled.[28]

Soon we will look at the career of Lily Bart, who begins by attempting to personify the aesthetic of the beautiful Burke honored, and ends by risking her life in a version of the sublime she herself refashioned. In contrast, Burke's career revolved around the effort to keep sublimity at a distance. The British colonization of India and the French Revolution, events that he strenuously opposed, showed "the terrible god of chance" fully at work in the world, and Burke would spend the rest of his career attempting to reconcile the aesthetic values he had praised in the *Enquiry* with his own terror at what he perceived as the anarchy, cruelty, and tyranny unleashed by the major social and political events of his day. It is not, however, by chance that gender gives Burke his principal rhetorical strategy for keeping history at a distance: as we shall see, the moments when his distinction between the aesthetic and the political are most vulnerable are marked by recourse to metaphors of sexual difference, as if to invoke a solid ground that could ward off speculation, and with it the sublime.

IV

In one of the best-known passages in the *Reflections*, Burke remarks upon (and fictionalizes) what he believed to be the greatest crime of the French Revolution: the near-rape of Marie Antoinette on the sixth of October, 1798.[29] The *Reflections* reaches its affective and ideological climax in Burke's dramatic evocation of the Jacobin attack on the queen of France, whom he idealized as the personification of the beautiful. Viewing "the then dauphiness" at Versailles some "sixteen or seventeen years" earlier, he remarked that he had never seen "a more delightful vision . . . above the horizon, decorating and cheering the elevated sphere she just began to move in—glittering like the morning star, full of life and splendor and joy" (66). For Burke, Marie Antoinette embodied "the glory of Europe . . . extinguished forever," the aristocratic and feminine values that were being destroyed by the "sophisters, economists, and calculators" (66) whose success he witnessed with horror.

Reporting upon her attack, Burke employs the concepts of the beautiful and the sublime as a structural allegory not only for the proper relations between the sexes, but for political order itself. The passage acquires rhetorical force through the contrast between an active, boundless, and masculine sexual energy and the harmonious social order upon which it is unleashed. Burke relates that the queen was awakened from "a few hours of respite and troubled, melancholy repose" (62) by "a band of cruel ruffians and assassins" who, after killing her guard, rushed into her chamber "and pierced with a hundred strokes of bayonets and poniards the bed, from whence the persecuted woman had but just time to fly almost naked" (62). The queen escapes the mob and reaches the king's chambers, but the two are "forced to abandon the sanctuary of the most splendid palace in the world, which they left swimming in blood, polluted by massacre and strewed with scattered limbs and mutilated carcasses" (62). Despoiling the queen and piercing her bed become an analogue for destroying the aristocracy: sexual violation is a surrogate for political defilement, and the revelation of the queen's nakedness is a metaphor for the destruction of the social order itself.

Although, as Isaac Kramnick points out, Burke clearly identifies the revolutionary principle "with intrusive masculinity and the aristocratic principle with violated femininity," equally striking is the confusion of sexual difference that, in Burke's evocation of the royal captives' forced march to Paris, becomes a paradigm for the chaos unleashed by the revolution.[30] Although Burke's excessive rhetoric begins by emphasizing the mob's indeterminate composition—it is "a monstrous medley of all conditions, tongues, and nations . . . a mixed mob of ferocious men, and of women lost to shame" (59–60)—the figure of feminine evil becomes the vehicle that allows him to give the incalculable a form and thereby to keep it within bounds. In the description that follows, female mutation becomes a metaphor for the perversion of the feminine ideal of beauty and virtue represented by the fallen queen:

> Their heads [of the king's bodyguards] were stuck upon spears and led the procession, whilst the royal captives who followed in the train were slowly moved along, amidst the horrid yells, and shrilling screams, and frantic dances, and infamous contumelies, and all the unutterable abominations of the Furies of hell in the abused shape of the vilest of women. (63)

In this passage Burke is concerned to emphasize not only the sexual but also the peculiarly feminine nature of the violence, the better to stress the intensity of its departure from the natural social order. Noteworthy too is the fact that women and not men provide the concrete shape for "abominations" that otherwise would be "unutterable."[31] Sexual inversion, the confusion of genders, reflects social inversion; the distorted image of French women as "abused shapes" and "furies of hell" suggests a way of containing a perverted sublimity.[32] Although "the vilest of women" are not precisely equivalent to Burke's sublime, they have become the medium through which the unutterable and nameless can be made speakable, and thereby kept at bay.

Encountering Lily Bart, whom she finds alone and exhausted on a park bench one frigid winter's night, Nettie Struthers recalls meeting her in language almost reminiscent of Burke's vision of the queen:

> "You don't remember me . . . but I'd know you anywhere, I've thought of you such a lot. I guess my folks all know your name by heart. I was one of the girls at Miss Farish's club—you helped me to go to the country that time I had lung-trouble. My name's Nettie Struthers. It was Nettie Crane then." (312)[33]

Lily's beauty and grace has made so strong an impression that Nettie has named her infant daughter after an actress who, playing the part of Marie Antoinette, reminded her of Lily. Finding Lily too weak to walk to her boarding house, Nettie takes her home to rest in the warmth of her kitchen and to meet the baby named "Marry Anto'nette . . . after the French queen in that play at the Garden—I told George the actress reminded me of you, and that made me fancy the name" (314). Holding the little girl who is almost but not quite her namesake, Lily feels "as though the child entered into her and became a part of herself" (316). Later, falling into the drugged sleep from which she will not awake, she believes that she holds the sleeping child in her arms. What occurs when the woman who is meant to exemplify Burke's ideal of beauty instead prefers the sublime will be our concern in the pages that follow.

V

At the end of *The House of Mirth*, Lily Bart wants only to sleep. She is exhausted by poverty, loneliness, and insomnia; sleep offers her the sole respite from a life that has become unlivable, but she has come to depend upon the sedative chloral in order to obtain it and is already taking the maximum dose. Warned by her pharmacist that "the action of the drug was incalculable," Lily prefers to increase the dose and incur what she believes to be only "a slight risk" (322) rather than endure another sleepless night. She takes the risk and dies.

Lily's commitment to risk is the source of the ethical value she acquires in the course of the novel. When, for example, Rosedale proposes marriage on the condition that she use Bertha's letters to Selden to clear her name, Lily refuses in the name of a precept that links the possibility of freedom to the proximity of risk. Intrigued by the plan's certain outcome and "fascinated by this escape from fluctuating ethical estimates into a region of concrete weights and measures" (259), she nonetheless perceives that "the essential baseness of the act lay in its freedom from risk" (260) and declines. An action whose outcome can be calculated in advance is ethically inferior to one whose results are unknown. If an act is free of risk, its agent is no longer free, and to affirm risk means to enter into active relation with the realm of the "capricious and incalculable" (311). If, however, some actions are "base," what conditions might render them sublime?

The House of Mirth takes its title from the nickname of a firm on the New York Stock Exchange and from Ecclesiastes 7:3–4: "The heart of the wise is in the house of mourning; but the heart of fools is in the house of mirth." The novel suggests not only that the Exchange is the place where Lily, Trenor, and Rosedale (among others) win or lose, but that the world in which all these characters buy, sell, and place their bets is one of complete homogenization and commodification. Beauty too is a commodity where nothing remains outside the marketplace.[34] The novel's first scene underscores the diverse ways in which economic conditions shape and determine aesthetic judgments and presents art itself as a form of speculation. We first observe Lily Bart—whose name attests to the complicity between art and barter—through the eyes of Lawrence Selden, whose initial observations about her are couched in economic terms. Seeing Lily amidst the afternoon crowd at Grand Central Station, he notices that she looks as if "she must have cost a great deal to make, that a great many dull and ugly people must, in some mysterious way, have been sacrificed to produce her"; indeed, her contrast to "the dinginess, the crudity of this average section of womanhood" makes him feel how "highly specialized" (5) she is. The novel begins by emphasizing that beauty, be it that of a woman or of a work of art, is neither natural nor innate, as Burke would have it, but is rather a commodity that cannot be separated from economic determinations.

Lily has been trained from birth to fashion herself as a collectible object. To her mother, her beauty is "the last asset in their fortunes" (34): she has taught her daughter to see it as a "weapon," an "asset," a "property," and a "charge" (34); and Lily, who recognizes that she "had been fashioned to adorn and delight" (301), has learned to treat it as a commodity available for purchase by the highest bidder. Even the name "Bart," which contains the injunction to be art rather than produce it, attests to the "purely decorative" nature of her "mission" (301), for Lily "could not figure herself as anywhere but in a drawing-room, diffusing elegance as a flower sheds perfume" (100). Brought up to be ornamental, she has also learned to embody Burke's ideal of femininity as delicate, dependent, and submissive. Burke, however, was unaware that beauty requires money every bit as much as a pretty face and pleasing figure. As Lily explains to Selden, "a woman is asked out as much for her clothes as for herself. The clothes are the background, the frame, if you like: they don't make success, but they are part of it" (12). The custodian as well as the proprietor of her beauty, Lily knows that it is "only the raw material of conquest" (34): she requires clothes and jewels that display her beauty to advantage, servants to care for them, and careful attention to her hair and skin. Like any commodity, the value of her beauty fluctuates and her business is to market herself in order to increase its worth.

Lily's ability to construct herself as a work of art, to personify and incarnate Burke's notion of the beautiful, raises questions about the nature of beauty he never entertained. As we come to recognize, in the opening scene Selden's speculations about the relation between Lily's outer love-liness and her inner worth are symptomatic of his deeper concerns about the status of aesthetic value: he wonders, for example, if the qualities that distinguish Lily "from the herd of her sex" are merely external or if they signify her superiority to the realm of "the dull and ugly" (5)? Is beauty the visual counterpart of truth and goodness, as Selden would like to believe, or is it profoundly amoral, the result of calculation? (He wonders if her hair is "ever so slightly brightened by art" [5], and when she cries during their walk together he tells himself that "even her weeping was an art" [72]; it is helpful to recall that for Burke, feminine weakness and the need for protection are associated with the beautiful.) Although "as a spectator, he had always enjoyed Lily Bart" (4), the force of her beauty interferes with his predilection for detachment and causes him to indulge in exactly these sorts of "speculations" (5). Here, as in Burke's *Enquiry*, the feminine body functions as a "deceitful maze" whose initial beauty strangely passes into something sublime. Lily has the capacity to turn spectators into speculators, to transform the pleasures of Selden's "purely impersonal enjoyment" (10) into speculative interest and desiring activity; indeed, Selden can "never see her without a faint movement of interest" (3). Because Lily's beauty is something she both has and makes, and because she is herself the commodity she speculates upon, it—or she—is always on the verge of producing the excess, speculation, and confusion that characterize Burke's sublime.

At the beginning of the novel Lily's artistry lies in her ability to make the calculated and artificial appear uncalculated and spontaneous, the accidental seem intentional, and the cultural, natural. She conceals the labor that has gone into her own production and thereby upholds Burke's reassuring view that beauty just "is," a tribute to an ideal realm that does not require material support. In this sense Lily enacts Burke's precept that "a true artist should put a generous deceit on the spectators" (70), for she promotes his understanding of beauty as pure and uncontrived, a force that enhances social relations without being produced by them. In this regard it is important to emphasize the complicity between an industrialized (or capitalist) economy and Burke's notion of the beautiful, for the idealization of beauty is in fact an essential dimension of capitalist ideology: the marketplace requires a notion of beauty as extrinsic to and untrammeled by culture in order to augment itself. Capitalism needs art, which must appear to be outside the marketplace so as to command a higher price.

Like Selden's famous "republic of the spirit," Burke's notion of the beautiful is grounded in and dependent upon the market it appears to resist. When, for example, Lily displays herself as a *tableau vivant* at a fashionable party, she personifies the ideal of feminine beauty as eternal, timeless, and beyond price, and thereby augments her value. Beauty is valued in exact proportion to its uniqueness, rarity, and apparent detachment from the realm of commerce; the art object's worth increases to the extent that the potential purchaser is persuaded that it transcends individual, and therefore fluctuating, social norms and customs. Wall Street requires Park Avenue as commerce requires art, and the woman as *bel objet* actually enables a market economy. The successful entrepreneur needs to own a beautiful woman just as he needs to increase his capital; beauty is capital, and the beautiful woman allows the wealthy man not only to display his wealth but also to disseminate his power beyond the marketplace.

Lily inhabits a maddeningly contradictory position with respect to her beauty. She is at once the commodity upon which she encourages others to speculate, the object of their interest and desire, and the creator of that object, simultaneously her own author, director, producer, and publicist. Lily's relation to herself replicates that of the speculator to the marketplace: she must market her beauty in the same way that a successful entrepreneur markets a product, and this entails determining the optimum conditions for display, fixing a price, and negotiating the terms of her own purchase. Her labor reveals the kinship between art and the marketplace, for both artist and speculator must manipulate appearances and learn to read the signs of others' desire not only in order to fashion a product that will satisfy, but also to increase demand for the product.

There is, as Lyotard points out, "something of the sublime in capitalist economy," for its goal is to produce excess and expand infinitely, to generate capital out of all proportion to individual energy or merit.[35] In this sense, Terry Eagleton's description of "the restless, overweening movement of capitalism itself, its relentless dissolution of forms and commingling of identities," recalls Burke's emphasis upon the sublime's ability to confound specific and individual entities into one indeterminate and overwhelming force.[36] (In a speech during the impeachment trial of Warren Hastings, Burke himself said, "We dread the operation of money.")[37] The marketplace terrifies: it recalls the "lack of moderation and intemperance" that Marx describes as money's "true standard."[38] Immeasurable and beyond calculation, the force of its speculative energy and totalizing power transcends moral, political, or ethical precepts; like a tidal wave it engulfs whatever it encounters. Its power resides, as Wai-Chee Dimock points out, "in its ability to assimilate everything else into its domain"; in her view, the marketplace is as much "a controlling logic, a mode of human conduct and human assimilation," as an economic force, and Lily's position with respect to it is profoundly equivocal.[39] On the one hand, as the entrepreneur who seeks to manipulate the market and speculate upon her beauty, she is its exemplar and accomplice; on the other, as a single woman without influential family, friends, or capital, she is its victim and pawn. The question at stake in our reading of *The House of Mirth*, then, is whether we may find in Lily's resistance to the marketplace that she also personifies an alternative to Burke's notion of the sublime?

In the pages that follow I argue that Lily's encounters with and changing relation to contingency and the "terrible god of chance" also imply a counterpart to Burke's idealist account of the sublime. Like Burke's *Enquiry*, *The House of Mirth* raises fundamental issues about the nature of artistic activity and production in relation to political and economic concerns. Unlike the *Enquiry*, however, it suggests a radically different version of the relationship between aesthetics, ethics, and politics, one that emphasizes the very notions of risk and speculation Burke would prefer to repress. Consider, for example, the following scene, in which Selden's admiring proclamation "You are an artist" (66) reflects his perception of Lily as a mistress of deceit, able to manipulate appearances in order to make accidents appear to be "the result of far-reaching intentions" (3).

Lily, who is visiting the Trenors' country estate, takes an afternoon's vacation from the task of wooing the rich but stupefyingly boring Percy Gryce to walk with Selden, who has arrived unexpectedly. Observing her is, he says, the purpose of his visit: Lily is "a wonderful spectacle" and he always likes "to see what you are doing" (66). Selden, who prefers to occupy the observer's position, seldom buys or sells; relatively removed from economic activity, he can play the detached critic. He compares her walk with him to an artist making use of her material: "You are an artist and I happen to be the bit of colour you are using today. It's a part of your cleverness to be able to produce premeditated effects extempora- neously" (66). In Selden's view being "an artist" is equivalent to being an agent, connoting the ability to manipulate chance in order to further one's intentions and designs. Lily is an artist, then, because she avoids taking risks; Selden's view that Lily is "artist" as well as art object turns upon his awareness of her ability to make the accidental appear to be the expression of intent. Like the investor who takes calculated risks in order to maximize profit, the artist employs accident in order to minimize its effects; in both cases success lies in the possibility of mastering the un- predictable. The artist's business is to profit from the unexpected, not to indulge in speculation as an end in itself.

At the beginning of the novel the portrait of the artist as mistress of the calculated effect parallels Lily's profound inability to take uncalculated risks. Although the novel opens with a scene in which Lily, having met Selden accidentally, "takes the risk" (6) of visiting his bachelor apartment (and thereby acquires some helpful "points" about collecting Americana that will be useful in her pursuit of Gryce), she will not risk loving him. During their walk together Selden and Lily flirt with the idea of marriage by assuring one another of just how risky such an act would be. But, as if afraid of that which she cannot control, Lily withdraws when Selden declares himself ready to "take the risk" (73). She is not yet committed to what, as the novel progresses, will become an ethics of risk.

To make the calculated appear spontaneous and the accidental seem intentional: at the beginning of the novel, this is Lily's "art." The project of speculating upon her own beauty is predicated upon avoiding any unnecessary risk; indeed, the mark of her artistry is her ability "to use the accident . . . as part of a very definite effect" (66). In this view art distinguishes itself from non-art because it leaves nothing to chance, and the artist differs from the non-artist insofar as she is able to give accident the appearance of necessity. But if in her dealings with Selden Lily makes accidents look intentional, she can also make the premeditated seem impulsive. When, for example, she appeals to Gus Trenor for financial aid, "it was part of the game to make him feel that her appeal had been an uncalculated impulse, provoked by the liking he inspired" (85), and she allows him to convince her that "if she would only trust him . . . her modest investments were to be mysteriously multiplied without risk to herself" (85). Whether Lily is flirting with Selden or manipulating Trenor, however, her artistic practices reveal the complicity between the aesthetic of the beautiful and the economy of the marketplace. The artist and the speculator share an aversion to risk, for each seeks to maximize the possibility of artistic perfection (or the equivalent goal of financial profit) by minimizing the presence of chance. Lily's artistry makes explicit precisely what Burke's *Enquiry* conceals: that the domain of the beautiful exerts its own peculiar form of tyranny.[40] Nowhere is this more apparent than in the *tableaux vivants* scene, in which the attempt to resist the marketplace by invoking an alternative notion of the beautiful—one that would exist free from any form of speculation—serves only to reinforce and perpetuate it.[41]

In the *tableaux vivants*, in which fashionable women display themselves as famous paintings at an extravagant party, Lily chooses to present herself in the classical guise of Joshua Reynolds's portrait of Mrs. Lloyd, painted in 1766. This moment is perhaps the climax of her career: Selden, Trenor, and Rosedale, among others in the audience, see Lily, who "has shown her artistic intelligence in selecting a type so like her own that she could embody the person represented without ceasing to be herself" (134), revealed in pale draperies and flowing robes that accentuate rather than conceal the sensual lines of her body; she is captured in the act of writing her husband's name in the bark of a tree. Lily had feared "at the last moment that she was risking too much in dispensing with the advantages of a more sumptuous setting" (136), but nonetheless has chosen to display her beauty without the "distracting accessories of dress or surroundings" (134). She thus feels triumphant when the spectators' murmur of approval attests "not to the brush-work of Reynolds's 'Mrs. Lloyd' but to the flesh and blood loveliness of Lily Bart" (134). Reynolds's portrait brings to life Burke's notion of femininity as symbol of the beautiful par excellence, as does Lily's embodiment of it, and it is perhaps no accident that Burke and Reynolds were close friends.[42] The curtain that parts "on a picture which was simply and undisguisedly the portrait of Miss Bart" (134) shows not only that "the real" Lily Bart is the effect of a performance, but that that "self" is an aesthetic construct, an embodiment and imitation in which Lily appears as, and is identical to, the portrait she resembles.

Lily has taken a minor, but well calculated, risk. By "displaying her own beauty under a new aspect" she intends to present herself as a timeless work of art existing beyond the fluctuations of the marketplace, to show "that her loveliness was no more fixed quality, but an element shaping all emotions to fresh forms of grace" (131). And her successful evocation of an ideal realm finally touches "the vision-making" (133) faculty in Selden, who wants to believe that beauty has an essential value in and of itself and longs to see Lily's beauty allied with the "eternal harmony" (135) that his nature craves. As a *tableau vivant* Lily embodies this ideal, evoking a veritable "republic of the spirit" in which truth is beauty, and beauty, truth. Rather than mask the effects of chance, however, in portraying Reynolds's painting Lily actually appears to overcome it: here art attests to the absence of chance and Lily's genius lies in her ability to create an object, or self-representation, in which there are no accidents. Art testifies to the triumph of agency; god-like, the artist creates an ideal world in which every detail has meaning and nothing takes place by chance. In this notion of the aesthetic art does not so much imitate life as transcend it, and this aspect of Lily's artistry is supremely evident in her appearance as Mrs. Lloyd, for here outward beauty matches inner worth. Selden, her cousin Gerty, and even Lily are all convinced that they have seen "the real Lily Bart, divested of the trivialities of her little world" (135); Selden reflects upon "the noble buoyancy of her attitude, its suggestion of soaring grace, [which] revealed the touch of poetry in her beauty," and catches "a note of that eternal harmony of which her beauty was a part" (134–35).

For Selden, Lily's beauty is proof of a deeper, hidden meaning. In a fluctuating world of speculation, art takes on the function of religion, holding out the promise of abiding value and eternal truth.

Far from contesting the rule of the marketplace, this conception of aesthetic value instead reinforces it. The belief that art partakes of an ideal realm that is eternal, pure, and beyond price replicates the principle that underlies and regulates a capitalist economy: that of maximizing control and minimizing risk. Portraying what appears to be beyond price serves to increase Lily's value; becoming unique only makes her more collectible. The same attributes that make Lily seem ideal to Selden, and therefore finally worthy of marriage, also make her more desirable to the rest of her potential collectors, or acquirers. But whereas Selden views "the real Lily Bart" in Platonic terms, as a vision in which beauty and goodness are one, others perceive her as the commodity she is presumed to be. Seeing her so provocatively displayed, Van Alstyne remarks that Lily is "a deuced bold thing to show herself in that get-up; but gad, there isn't a break in the lines anywhere, and I suppose she wanted us to know it!" (135). And although Trenor finds her display in "damned bad taste" (138), the next day he lures her to his house, tells her the time has come to "pay up" (145), and almost rapes her. Embodying the priceless has served to increase her marketability, but Lily already owes much more than she can pay.

VI

Lily's visit to Trenor marks the novel's turning point. Before the visit it is still possible to imagine that she might marry well; after it, realizing that she owes Trenor nine thousand dollars and has acquired the reputation of being a woman who trades sexual favors for money, her downward spiral begins. The visit, however, also marks a shift from Lily's desire to embody the beautiful and market herself as an aesthetic object to a new definition of worth that resists the logic of barter and exchange. If for Burke beauty is aligned with social cohesion and the rather dubious "pleasures" of society, while the sublime induces a commitment to individuality and self-preservation, Lily's visit to Trenor signals the transition between the novel's beginning, in which Lily pursues beauty and avoids risk, and its conclusion, in which she becomes sublime by affirming it. *The House of Mirth* thus demonstrates not only Lily's commitment to a mode of self-preservation that, paradoxically, requires the cost of her own destruction; it suggests a version of the sublime that resists the economy of the marketplace and the aesthetic that accompanies it.[43]

While at the beginning of the novel Lily glorifies Selden's "republic of the spirit," whose ideality consists in freedom from risk and "all the material accidents" (68), by the end she recognizes that freedom becomes possible only when one recognizes risk's necessity and refuses to avoid it. The changes in Lily's relation to risk are accompanied by correlative shifts in her relationship to money and to art. At the beginning she accumulates debts she refuses to acknowledge and understands art to be the successful manipulation of appearances; at the end she pays her debt to Trenor, refuses Rosedale's offer of a loan, and burns the letters that represent her last bit of capital. The ethical injunction to live well takes on an aesthetic dimension that has nothing to do with beauty and the beautiful, for to live finely or nobly involves style in the sense of creating the kind of person one aspires to become and the kind of life one seeks to lead. In this case, the person Lily aims at becoming is one who takes unnecessary risks while refusing to speculate, one who is incomprehensible to the omnipresent measures of the world of exchange.

In *A Backward Glance*, written thirty years after *The House of Mirth*, Wharton observes that the central problem in writing the novel was how to extract "typical human significance" from the story of "a society of irresponsible pleasure-seekers." The answer, she explains, "was that a frivolous society can acquire dramatic significance only through what its frivolity destroys. Its tragic implication lies in its power of debasing people and ideals. The answer, in short, was my heroine, Lily Bart."[44]

Although the "frivolous society" Wharton depicts does in fact destroy Lily Bart, she nonetheless resists its power to "debase people and ideals," and her capacity for resistance is inseparable from her ability to engage the incalculable. In so doing she creates a kind of worth that defies the prevailing norms of her society, instilling ethical value where previously there was none. If significance is found only in what society destroys, Lily's acts of self-extinction become symbolic acts of self-creation. In *The House of Mirth* loss rather than gain becomes the fertile site from which significance is produced, and in this sense Lily's death is not so much an escape from the marketplace, but a way of passing judgment upon it.

Rather than epitomize the logic of capitalist exchange, Lily invents forms of resistance to it.[45] A capitalist economy depends upon accruing debts that remain unpaid, and is, as Dimock observes, a system that "has non-payment as its secret motto": successful exchange entails maximizing gain while minimizing loss and functions by sustaining imbalances of power.[46] In paying her debt to Trenor, however, Lily challenges the basis of exchange, which needs to maintain the very inequities she insists upon annulling. Here Lily asserts the power to define these terms, and the rate she determines—that of total payment—operates not to maintain exchange but rather to annul it. By reversing the implicit conventions of the marketplace and putting a different code of behavior in their place, Lily's behavior suggests an alternative mode of human interchange.

Paying her debt and refusing subsequent indebtedness defies the underlying structure of the marketplace. To reject, for example, Rosedale's proposed loan on the grounds that "a business arrangement between us would in any case be impossible, because I shall have no security to give when my debt to Gus Trenor has been paid" (299), is to insist that a loan can be free of obligation only if one has the means to repay it, that business and friendship cannot coexist. That her resistance to the market remains an integral part of the system's own internal strategies (Gus will reinvest the money she's repaid, and Rosedale has more profitable ways of investing it) in no way lessens the intensity of its effect, for Lily breaks the rules of the marketplace by the strictness of her adherence to them. Exorbitant dedication to the letter of the law makes evident its inequities. Taking its precepts at face value, her total obedience to the law becomes a parodic subversion of it.

Breaking society's rules by obeying them overscrupulously suggests the possibility of a different relation to the marketplace. The woman who at the beginning of the novel knows "very little of the value of money" (31) at the end has learned to create a kind of value that, while not transcending the logic of exchange, nevertheless presents an alternative to it. Unlike both the spectator and the investor, whose desire to avoid risk and ensure profit sustains the market, Lily wishes not to eradicate chance but to enhance it, and she finds in this desire an ethical precept: it is better to risk, to maximize accident, than to take advantage of a sure thing. Actively to seek risk implies the willingness to take one's chances, to employ agency neither to gain control nor to lose it, but to leave the outcome of an event up for grabs. To risk means to choose chance, that is, to choose an outcome one cannot predict or control. It implies a domain of constant fluctuation, a realm of "fluctuating ethical estimates" (259) that Lily's "tired mind" would prefer to, but does not, avoid. Here sublimity is shown to possess an ethical as well as an aesthetic component, one born out of proximity to the realm of accident and "the terrible god of chance." Whereas Marx believed that a commodity's value is a function of the labor that has gone into producing it, the kind of value Lily creates results from how much she is willing to risk. Lily's resistance to the market, which takes the paradoxical form of asserting her will in order to lose rather than produce capital, also affirms another criterion for determining, or creating, worth: her goal is not to avoid expenditure, but to pursue it.

Whereas at the beginning of *The House of Mirth* Lily is a mistress of the art of controlling accidents, at the end her artistry consists in embracing them. She acquires value by assenting to chance, with all the uncertainty and confusion it entails. She thereby sustains an aesthetic and ethical value that, existing within the culture of consumption, functions to resist it. Such an aesthetic would no longer be understood as the discovery of a preexistent harmony or the embodiment of a timeless, transcendent order, but would rather consist in insisting upon and inventing form in one's life.

Lily's most incisive act of resistance can be found in the moment when, visiting Selden in order to bid him goodbye before she confronts Bertha Dorset with their correspondence, she unexpectedly throws these letters into the fire and thereby destroys her last chance of saving herself. Burning the letters is Lily's gift to Selden, a gift that is all the more profound for remaining unobserved. If the power of the marketplace resides in its ability to define the value and position of those who inhabit it, here Lily assumes that power in order to produce a different worth. Affirming the principle of expenditure that, according to Bataille, the bourgeoisie detests, Lily not only draws attention to the ideology of the marketplace but demonstrates an alternative to it: she and not it will become the arbiter of her value, a value determined not by how much she has but by how much she is willing to lose.[47]

Lily affirms a form of "self-preservation" that both is akin to and deviates from that which Burke envisioned as the goal of the sublime, for it entails the desire to maintain "a moral attribute" (169) at any cost, even if doing so leaves her destitute, or dead. Fashioning a self whose value is established through its willingness to lose more than it can ever gain, she creates an alternative version of sublimity that, far from being synonymous with the marketplace, affirms the alterity it risks. At stake is a portrait of the artist who produces neither calculated effects nor beautiful objects, but rather enacts an aesthetic in which, in Jean–Paul Sartre's words, "art is a

ceremony of the *gift*, and the gift alone brings about the metamorpho-
ses."[48] What Lily resists is a notion of the aesthetic in which art is just
another form of barter; what she creates is a kind of value that cannot be
reduced to dollars and cents. If Lily's gift to Selden is to protect his
reputation without his ever knowing it was in danger, her gift to us is to
transform the Burkean sublime and enact a version of it in which ethics
and aesthetics, risk and art, have become inseparable.

3

Strange Bedfellows

Kant, Shelley, Rhys,
and the Misogynist Sublime

Culture is made by those in power—men. Males make the rules and
laws; women transmit them.

(Gloria Anzaldúa, Borderlands/La Frontera)

Is it to be expected that a *woman of education* and a *lover of forms* will
yield before she is attacked? . . . I must, therefore, make my first effort
by surprise. There may possibly be some *cruelty* necessary: but there
may be *consent in struggle*; there may be *yielding resistance*. But the first
conflict over, whether the following may not be weaker and weaker,
till *willingness* ensue, is the point to be tried. I will illustrate what I have
said by the simile of a bird new-caught. We begin, when boys, with
birds, and, when grown up, go on to women; and both, perhaps, in
turn, experience our sportive cruelty.

(Samuel Richardson, Clarissa)

As you see, you have sought counsel from a physician who is no flat-
terer and who does not seek to ingratiate himself. Were you wanting a
mediation between yourself and your beloved, you see that my way of
defining good conduct is not at all partial to the fair sex, since I speak
for your beloved and present him with arguments that, as a man who
honors virtue, are on his side and that justify his having wavered in his
affection for you.

(Kant, draft of a letter to Maria von Herbert)

Midnight too is noon; pain too is a joy; curses too are a blessing; night
too is a sun—go away or you will learn: a sage too is a fool.

(Nietzsche, Thus Spoke Zarathustra)

And now, once again, I bid my hideous progeny go forth and prosper.

(Mary Shelley, Frankenstein or,
The Modern Prometheus,
introduction to the 1831 edition)

Kant's sublime provides a paradigm in terms of which, and also against
which, narrative structures such as the novel operate, for it becomes a

prime strategy, perhaps even a requisite one, for plot making and character production. This is not to suggest that the Kantian sublime operates at a level from which fictional structures are exempt but rather that the *Critique of Judgment* is itself a narrative, and that it makes explicit in a theoretical register some of the processes through which identities, including novelistic ones, are formed. In so doing it brings to center stage the misogyny that lies at the heart of the sublime's theorization and remains implicit in so many novels. On the one hand, I show that in Kant's writings the imagination is gendered as feminine and that its sacrifice functions rhetorically to ensure the sublime moment, a sacrifice that is doubled in many novels—whether their authors are men or women—by scapegoating a feminine figure as a point of reference to guarantee discursive unity and the formation of autonomous, centered selves.[1] In both cases the operation requires violence directed against women or a feminine surrogate. On the other, I explore narrative strategies that women novelists have employed to represent and resignify their misogynistic inheritance. In the pages that follow, a reading of "The Analytic of the Sublime" points out gender-specific scapegoating mechanisms essential to Kant's sublime. In many instances feminine misogyny, one of patriarchy's most pernicious symptoms, becomes its thematic corollary, a pattern especially apparent in eighteenth-century popular women's fiction.[2] This complex configuration alters, but its basic structure persists in later writing. By looking at Mary Shelley's *Frankenstein* and Jean Rhys's *Good Morning, Midnight*, we see that it can take on the form of a fantastic and explicit production and sacrifice of an implicitly feminine monstrosity yet function to resist the misogyny it represents. Although these two novels by no means eradicate the misogyny so crucial to Kant's authoritative formulation of the sublime, they do articulate aspects of it that Kant himself could not admit and thereby allow the possibility of its critique.

I

From the outset, Kant's formulation of the sublime presupposes an interplay between two highly personified faculties of mind, the imagination and the reason. This dyad is in fact a barely disguised hierarchy that provides the grounds for debasing one half of the couple at the expense of the other. For the attainment of the Kantian sublime is dependent upon a sacrifice; its cause is the collapse of the imagination's capacity to connect empirical reality with the realm of abstract ideality, and reason's subsequent amplification occurs only because the imagination has been unable to comprehend reality. Indeed, Kant links the defeat of the imagination to the very possibility of representing what had belonged previously to the domain of the unrepresentable.

Throughout the "Analytic of the Sublime," Kant emphasizes that the true source of sublimity is a faculty of mind. The sublime is never produced by an object, but only by "the mental attunement in which we find ourselves when we estimate the object" (112, §26), and the pleasure that accompanies it is not a satisfaction in the object, as in the beautiful, but rather in the mind's capacity to comprehend an entity whose sheer magnitude had exceeded the imagination's grasp:

> we express ourselves entirely incorrectly when we call this or that *object of nature* sublime, even though we may quite correctly call a great many natural objects beautiful . . . all we are entitled to say is that the object is suitable for exhibiting a sublimity that can be found in the mind. (99, §23)

Sublimity is for Kant a certain intrasubjective relation stimulated but not caused by the external world, a moment of triumphant unity in which the mind, identifying with the law of reason, perceives its own capacity for abstraction as sublime.

Although Kant distinguishes two forms of the sublime, the mathematic and the dynamic, in each case the imagination's defeat is the key to reason's triumph. Kant insists that "the only way for this [the sublime] to occur is through the inadequacy of even the greatest effort of our imagination to estimate an object's magnitude" (112, §26), and that "this might actually reveals itself aesthetically only through sacrifice [*Aufopferungen*]" (131, §29). If in the sublime "even to be able to think proves that the mind has a power surpassing any standard of sense [*Maßstab der Sinne*]" (106, §25), it is important to emphasize that the imagination provides the "standard of sense" that is surpassed. Whereas in the mathematical sublime the imagination's confrontation with sheer immensity (an apparently infinite series or object of extreme magnitude) challenges it to an impossible attempt at comprehension and triggers its collapse, in the dynamical sublime the effect of brute nature—violent storms, earthquakes, waterfalls—makes the imagination aware of its inadequacy: the "idea of the supersensible . . . is aroused in us when, as we judge an object aesthetically, this judging strains the imagination to its limit [*dessen ästhetische Beurteilung die Einbildungskraft bis zu ihrer Grenze*], whether of expansion (mathematically) or of its might over the mind (dynamically)" (128, §29). In both forms, what is crucial is that the attempt to do reason's work forces the imagination to overextend itself: it takes on a task that exceeds its ability, stretches to the point where it can no longer function, and finally breaks down. Although ultimately Kant defines the sublime as a transcendent moment in which reason identifies with the supersensible, attaining that moment depends upon a prior narrative progression in which, as in the plots of eighteenth-century novels of seduction, feminine submission enhances and confirms masculine identity.

The position of the imagination may be likened to that of a surrogate victim whose sacrifice allows the restoration of order. Reason finds in the moment of chaos the opportunity to exercise its superior ability; amplified and strengthened, it steps in to represent the idea of magnitude that had precipitated the imagination's collapse. Reason's function is to comprehend a totality that the imagination cannot itself represent, and thereby to disclose a superiority over nature that the mind could not otherwise achieve:

> Though the irresistibility of nature's might makes us, considered as natural beings, recognize our physical impotence, it reveals in us at the same time an ability to judge ourselves independent of nature, and reveals in us a superiority over nature that is the basis of a self-preservation quite different in kind from the one that can be assailed and endangered by nature outside us. (120–21, §28)

The imagination's failure has been required so that a higher order of meaning can become accessible. And its expulsion gives rise both to the perception of a continuity and the formation of an identity far greater than that which had preceded it, for as Steven Knapp points out, "the self whose stability is served by the sublime is a self *produced* in the moment of the sublime."[3]

So far I have suggested that Kant's account of the sublime is a story of sacrifice through which identities (and by extension, texts) are constructed. To a certain extent this schema might seem applicable to a wide variety of literary situations where a substitute victim first makes a grand attempt, proves unequal to the challenge, and whose defeat or death then prepares the way for the entry of the authentic, truly masterful agent. But

I argue that there is a more specific connection between Kantian aesthetics and the discourse of misogyny and that gender has a crucial role in the construction of the sublime. In both cases what is at stake is a certain violence that imposes a hierarchical relation whose paradigm is achieved through a self-sacrifice by the putatively weaker partner: in the theory of the sublime the imagination must yield itself to reason, while in many novels women, or a feminine surrogate such as Frankenstein's monster, challenge but ultimately submit to powerful, dominating men. Here questions of linguistic and sexual difference overlap, for a certain scapegoating, most frequently directed against feminine figures or an aspect of the self gendered as feminine, plays a crucial role in the formation of characters and also in the construction of narrative unity and coherence. In the next section of this chapter I emphasize a number of eighteenth-century female writers who enact this process and pay for their ascendancy in the literary marketplace by portraying women as weak and as complicit in their own domination by men.

In the context of eighteenth-century aesthetics, the idea that beauty is feminine and sublimity masculine is something of a cliché; it occurs explicitly, for example, in Burke's *Enquiry* as well as in Kant's relatively early *Observations on the Feeling of the Beautiful and the Sublime* and in his later *Anthropology*. In the *Observations* he writes: "the fair sex has just as much understanding as the male, but it is a *beautiful understanding*, whereas ours should be a *deep understanding*, an expression that signifies identity with the sublime."[4] The stock of discourses from which Kant drew in constructing his theory of aesthetic judgment was, on the whole, that of English writers who provide their own versions of such eighteenth-century commonplaces.[5] While by the time of the magisterial third *Critique* Kant suppresses these explicit concerns, the sublime does not occupy a domain outside the laws of sexual difference; to focus upon the place and function of the imagination in producing it is to become aware that the process elaborated by Kant and disseminated by most classical theorists of the beautiful and sublime is not sexually neutral.[6] Indeed, the interaction between the reason and the imagination in the sublime is itself an allegory of gender relations within patriarchy.

If, as W. J. T. Mitchell observes, "sublimity, with its foundation in pain, terror, vigorous exertion, and power, is the masculine aesthetic mode," I suggest that the reason woman is for Kant always associated with the beautiful, and never with the sublime, is that her subjugation is its very precondition.[7] Kant's account of the ordeal of the imagination resembles eighteenth- and nineteenth-century depictions (or constructions) of sexuality, particularly those by Sade and Freud. So perfectly does Kant's description of the imagination's role conform to the notion of woman as a sexually passive vehicle who awaits a violent penetration and whose "pleasure" consists in a certain adaptation to pain, we might conclude that this model of gender relations has occasioned, if not in fact determined, the very parameters in which Kant conceives of its trajectory. In an account strikingly congruent with Freud's view of feminine castration—in which the achievement of normal sexuality depends upon the woman's recognition that she lacks what men have and that the clitoris is merely an inferior version of the penis—the imagination's perception of its own inadequacy precedes the recognition and acceptance of its subordinate position.[8] No matter how painfully the imagination extends itself in its efforts "to estimate an object's magnitude [*Größenschätzung eines Gegenstandes*]" (112, §26), it "proves its own limits and inadequacy [*ihre Schranken und Unangemessenheit*], and yet at the same time proves its vocation to [obey] a law, namely, to make itself adequate to that idea [*Bestimmung zur Bewirkung der Angemessenheit mit derselben als einem Gesetze*]" (114, §27).

Kant's description of the imagination's role reproduces the same view that Western religions transmit: that the relation of male to female is one of dominance to submission. Kant emphasizes that the idea of sublimity occurs only "through the inadequacy of even the greatest effort of our imagination [*in Schätzung desselben*] to estimate an object's magnitude" (112, §26), and that in the attempt at comprehension "we perceive the inadequacy of the imagination—unbounded though it is as far as progressing is concerned—for taking in and using, for the estimation of magnitude, a basic measure that is suitable for this with minimal expenditure on the part of the understanding" (112, §26). This insistence both reiterates biblical notions of the woman's place in which, as Patricia Parker suggests, "woman is not just *after* man, but *of* and *for* man," and reenacts the marriage formula in the text of Ephesians 5:22: "Wives, be subject to your husbands, as to the Lord. For the husband is the head of the wife, as Christ is head of the Church."[9] Attempting a task too big for it forces the imagination to recognize that its role is to submit itself to reason as to a husband: to receive, not penetrate; stay within boundaries, not generate them; and be the object, not the perpetrator, of a certain violence.

For the violence done to the imagination is the very condition of the sublime moment:

> if something arouses in us, merely in apprehension and without any reasoning on our part, a feeling of the sublime, then it may indeed appear, in its form, contrapurposive for our power of judgment, incommensurate with our power of exhibition, and as it were violent [*gewalttätig*] to our imagination, and yet we judge it all the more sublime for that. (99, §23)

Kant emphasizes that violence, the experience of pain, and a peculiar kind of pleasure are each bound up with one another: indeed, the notion of sublimity as an aesthetic category is put forward in order to explain the "negative pleasure" that has pain as one of its principal constituents, for how is it that "the object is apprehended as sublime with a pleasure that is possible only by means of a displeasure [*einer Lust . . . die nur vermittelst einer Unlust möglich ist*]" (117, §27)? The inadequacy of the imagination is crucial to Kant's explanation. Simultaneously, the feeling of the sublime generates pain, which arises from the imagination's inability to estimate magnitude, and awakens pleasure, which is "aroused by the fact that this very judgment, namely, that even the greatest power of sensibility is inadequate, is [itself] in harmony with rational ideas, insofar as striving toward them is still a law for us" (115, §27). The imagination's violation and failure are necessary to the sublime precisely because its pain gives rise to the reason's pleasure, which is not "a liking for the object (since that may be formless), but rather a liking for the expansion of the imagination itself [*an der Erweiterung der Einbildungskraft an sich selbst*]" (105, §25). Here reason requires and delights in the imagination's defeat as the occasion for its own aggrandizement:

> For he has the feeling that his imagination is inadequate for exhibiting the idea of a whole, [a feeling] in which imagination reaches its maximum, and as it strives to expand that maximum, it sinks back into itself, but consequently comes to feel a liking [that amounts to an] emotion [*in ein rührendes Wohlgefallen versetzt wird*]. (109, §26)

Kant's account of aesthetic pleasure not only represents a view of sexual difference that it subtly reinscribes but is strikingly congruent with the view of feminine sexuality Freud will inherit and transmit.[10]

If the Kantian sublime is marked and engendered by a certain crucial misogyny, its precise kind requires further clarification. For the imagination is not tormented wholly against its wishes but is rather a somewhat willing victim that assents to and even participates in its own violation:

> a liking for the sublime in nature is only *negative* (whereas a liking for the beautiful is *positive*): it is a feeling that the imagination by its own action is depriving itself of its freedom [*Beraubung der Freiheit*], in being determined purposively according to a law different from that of its empirical use. The imagination thereby acquires an expansion and a might that surpasses the one it sacrifices [*aufopfert*]; but the basis of this might is concealed from it; instead the imagination *feels* the sacrifice or deprivation [*Aufopferung oder die Beraubung . . . fühlt*] and at the same time the cause to which it is being subjugated. (129, §29)

The imagination is the victim of superior forces in that it receives the orders for its sacrifice from a law that is not its own. Yet it also becomes the agent of its self-mutilation: it gives up its unbounded activity of perception and deprives itself of freedom by its own act. The imagination can have a meager share in the reason's power, if not perhaps its pleasure, only by identifying with its oppressor and thereby consenting to its own subordination. In this way it gains "an expansion and a might that surpasses the one it sacrifices," and may participate, at least up to a certain point, in the mind's apprehension of its own supersensible vocation. The sole activity for which it is not punished, then, is that of self-victimization, and it can have access to the sublime moment on the condition that it scapegoats itself.

If, as I have suggested, the imagination is in the position of and behaves in ways traditionally required of women, then Kant's sublime tells the story of internalized oppression, one of the principal strategies through which patriarchy reproduces itself. In particular, however, it describes a specifically *feminine* misogyny, for what it narrates are the conditions under which women learn to do to themselves and other women what society has done to them. As is so often the case in scenarios of violence directed against women, what is dramatized is the question of consent, and it is this, particularly in the context of misogyny, that Kant's sublime invites us to consider. For although at the end of its encounter with reason the imagination has agreed to its own sacrifice, what is the status of this consent if its only choice is to say "yes"? Instances of feminine agency in eighteenth-century British women's fiction respond to precisely this question.

II

It is perhaps no accident that the entry of women during the mid to late eighteenth century into the British literary market place as writers of commercial fiction coincides with the rise of the sublime in aesthetic theory.[11] The genre of the novel and the theory of the sublime both reflect a new emphasis on the primacy of the individual and curiosity about the processes that form individual identities.[12] For perhaps the first time in history, middle-class women were beginning to achieve recognition as individuals and acquire correlative political and legal status. Among their new, if limited, prerogatives was the right to authorship: a new market had opened up to women and, barred from other forms of employment, they were quick to take advantage of it.[13] Women needed the money that writing novels could provide and could actually support themselves by producing them.[14] To give some examples of the extent of feminine productivity of commercial fiction throughout the century, between 1720 and 1730 Eliza Haywood authored thirty-eight works, mostly novels; Penelope Aubin wrote seven novels between 1721 and 1728; and Charlotte Smith wrote ten between 1788 and 1798.[15] The literary historian F. G. Black estimates that between two-thirds and three-quarters of epistolary novels between 1760 and 1790 were written by women.[16] As the century progressed, the novel, at first considered a vulgar and lowly genre, gained literary prestige and women writers also rose in status. The success of Jane Austen, Fanny Burney, Sarah Fielding, and Ann Radcliffe (to name but a few) is evidence that the emergence of the novel as a literary genre was accompanied by a difference in the gender of those producing it.

At first glance it would appear that, as the successful producers of commercial fiction, women were rapidly attaining a new authority and that their novels portray them as beginning to employ agency in precisely the way that the Kantian sublime defends against. The role of the imagination in the Kantian sublime might seem to reflect the notion that an act of writing, as Jane Spencer observes, "might seem to be challenging received notions of womanhood." The following pages, however, emphasize the parallel structure of female sacrifice essential to both eighteenth-century women's fiction and the Kantian sublime.[17] Female authorship, though prevalent, was not for all that seen as legitimate nor, as we shall see, did it necessarily resist the status quo. Women frequently prefaced their work with advertisements that proleptically disclaimed any literary merit, ambition, or ability. As the following prefaces to Elizabeth Boyd's *The Female Page* (1737) and Susannah Rowson's *Charlotte Temple* (1790) make painfully clear, writing was something for which the woman writer needed to apologize:

> As I never was ambitious of the Name of Author, nor even design'd to indulge in writing any Thing of this Nature, none than for my own Amusement. I have printed this Transcript (which otherwise I would never have done) with a View to settling my self in a Way of Trade; that may enable me to master those Exingencies of Fortune, which my long illness had for some time past reduc'd me to suffer . . .[18]

> Convinced that I have not wrote a line that conveys a wrong idea to the head or a corrupt wish to the heart, I shall rest satisfied in the purity of my intentions and if I merit not applause, I feel that I dread not censure.[19]

It is important to emphasize that the defensive tone so prevalent in the prefaces to many women's novels, their almost eager affirmation of supposedly inherent feminine inadequacies, is emblematic of the fictional situations their fictions all too frequently describe.[20]

Much eighteenth-century fiction by women reinforces stereotypes of women's innate inferiority and although the majority was written by women, their female protagonists frequently enact the very self-scapegoating Kant's imagination undergoes. In order to win her personal and financial independence, then, the woman writer had to create a heroine whose chief interest lay in relinquishing it. In two of the era's most popular genres of women's fiction—novels of feminine seduction and feminine reform—the heroine undergoes a series of trials to ascertain whether or not virtue can control passion. In each case feminine weakness provides the basis for narrative structure, but the scenarios differ in offering multiple versions of feminine disempowerment. In the standard plot of seduction novels (established in the early 1700s by Delariviere Manley and Eliza Haywood, and drawn upon by later writers), the use of feminine agency is almost exclusively reactive: a woman's forbidden passion overrides both her reason and her chastity, and she suffers accordingly. As Ruth Perry points out, in the plots of seduction novels "women are imprisoned, seduced, abducted, raped, abandoned, and their passively outraged responses to these developments are carefully detailed."[21] And as Patricia Spacks observes, the message therein is that "for women to combat their natural and necessary inadequacies in life amounts to a full-time occupation."[22] Eliza Haywood's novels, for example, typically warn "how dangerous it is to transgress, even the least Bounds of that Reserve which is enjoined by Virtue for our Guard."[23] A heroine can become a heroine only by suppressing desire, remaining "virtuous," and thereby subordinating herself to prevailing social norms and customs.

Novels of reformed heroines tell the story of a mistaken but unfallen heroine who learns from her mistakes—usually through accepting the authority and tutelage of the man who will become her husband. Novels such as Fanny Burney's *Evelina* (1778), Charlotte Smith's *Emmeline* (1788), and Elizabeth Inchbald's *A Simple Story* (1791) differ from the seduction tale in that an initially spoilt young woman is saved, rather than ruined, by the man who becomes her lover-mentor-husband. Tales of feminine reform show that, in Spencer's words, novels could "become fictional illustrations of the female conduct-book precepts, recommending modesty, gentleness, and obedience to parents and guardians."[24] Like seduction novels, they put forward a message that is fundamentally congruent with that conveyed by the Kantian sublime: the only acceptable form of feminine agency is that the female protagonist employ it to sacrifice herself.

Although by the middle of the eighteenth century women's fiction had gained wide acceptance, the terms of its acceptance were that it conform to a view of woman as naturally subordinate to man. As Spacks points out:

> Women—eighteenth-century women—employ the writing of novels to affirm the social order that limits them. They characteristically define a heroine by her weakness, showing how weakness and passivity became social resources, but they acknowledge the cost of weakness, either in terms of the diminishment a woman allows herself to endure or the anger induced in her by social necessities.[25]

It would appear that the only way in which a woman author could gain both financial reward and literary commendation was by creating characters who learn to agree to their own victimization. If in the third *Critique* the imagination wins reason's approval only by displaying her weakness and sacrificing herself, so eighteenth-century women wrote novels that consented to and perpetuated the very conditions that contributed to their oppression.

The rise of women's fiction must be understood both as a crucial sign of the exertion of feminine agency and, at least in part, as a reinscription of the structures of oppression that form women's social and cultural inheritance. The vast majority of eighteenth-century women's fiction puts forward a deeply conservative, if not misogynistic, message: by upholding an ideal of feminine passivity, it reinforces patriarchal views of women's innate inferiority.[26] The feminine protagonist's victimization is crucial for narrative closure as well as the triumph of masculine authority, and the feminine subject female novelists create is by no means exempt from the misogynistic structures that shape it.[27] Women's fiction of the period represents precisely the view of woman-as-victim that the Kantian imagination personifies, suggesting that feminine authorship must be understood not only as a crucial sign of women's rise to power but also as helping to instantiate the very ideology its authors were beginning to resist. The emergence of women's fiction and that of Kant's sublime tell much the same story: that of the successful repression of feminine agency. In Shelley's *Frankenstein*, however, this repression assumes the shape of an allegedly masculine, and hence representable, monstrosity that begins to resignify the misogynist tradition it also inherits and transmits.

III

Shelley's representation of monstrosity in *Frankenstein* may also be read as an enactment and, at least to some extent, a parody of the Kantian sublime.[28] For although misogyny is everywhere apparent in the novel it resides not so much in Victor Frankenstein's (or the reason's) triumph over a victimized and monstrously excessive imagination as in its representation of maternity as simultaneously monstrous and sublime. Here I expand Gilbert's and Gubar's claim that "*Frankenstein* is a version of the misogynistic story implicit in *Paradise Lost*" and argue that it is also a version of the misogynistic narrative implicit in the "Analytic of the Sublime."[29] Kant's depiction or construction of the sublime both portrays and defends itself against monstrosity, and *Frankenstein* dramatizes the very aspects of the sublime that the third *Critique* needs to repress.[30]

Kant's definition of the sublime is caught up in a system of encasements, injunctions, and imperatives that function to protect the sublime from the monstrous potential inherent in it, for the sublime's identity is dependent upon a series of negations that constitute and frame it. From paragraphs

26 to 29, the principal sections in which he discusses the mathematical and dynamical sublime, Kant presents four pairs of oppositions, each of which is crucial to his definition of sublimity. Every couple functions to split the sublime in two, separating what in it is moral and good from what is marginal, excessive, or destructive. At stake is Kant's need to keep the sublime within its aesthetic encasement, so that, like the beautiful, it too may remain "the Symbol of Morality" (225, §59).

Sublime states of mind must be produced by *colossal* but not *monstrous* representations of nature (109, §26), and should provoke *religious* sentiments that give rise to "reverence," as opposed to *superstition* that instills "fear and dread" (123, §28). The sublime can include "an affect of the *vigorous kind* (i.e., that we have forces to overcome any resistance)" but not "an affect of the *languid kind*," which has "nothing *noble* about it" (133, §29). Finally, it may induce *enthusiasm*, even though in it "the imagination is unbridled" (136, §29), but not *fanaticism*, "which is the *delusion* [Wahn] *of wanting to see something beyond all bounds of sensibility*" (135, §29). In each case, Kant briefly describes the negative quality that might, if he did not quickly exclude it, become identified with the sublime and prevent it from being an aesthetic, hence legislatable, category.

Although each pair has its own fascination, let us consider only the distinction between the colossal and the monstrous, since it is the most germane to a reading of *Frankenstein*. Kant defines the colossal as "the mere exhibition of a concept if that concept is almost too large for any exhibition" (109, §26). The difference between the colossal and the monstrous is a matter of degree: the colossal, although it "borders on the relatively monstrous" (109), is never quite identical to it. Whereas the colossal involves "the intuition of the object *almost* too large for our power of apprehension" (my emphasis), an object is "monstrous" only "if by its magnitude it nullifies the purpose that constitutes its concept" (109, §26). By aligning the sublime exclusively with the colossal, Kant attempts to protect it from monstrosity, which has the power to annihilate or nullify. Sensitive to the possibility of confusing "natural things *whose very concept carries with it a determinate purpose* (e.g., animals with a known determination in nature)" with "crude nature" (e.g., nonpurposive natural objects), Kant next cautions that the former, precisely because of its proximity to the monstrous, must never be allowed to "point to the sublime" (109, §26). Yet since "crude nature contains nothing monstrous (nor anything magnificent or horrid)" and will thus always yield purely colossal representations, Kant insists the sublime be exhibited only "insofar as crude nature contains magnitude" (109, §26). The negative and extrinsic, in this case identified with the "monstrous," functions as a boundary line that gives definition to the positive, intrinsic, or "colossal." And although these divisions enclose the sublime within a theory of the beautiful that fits into a theory of taste itself encased by a theory of judgment, an extremely fragile line divides the positive aspect of the sublime from its negative, destructive side. The sublime can never be contained because part of what has been removed and put outside still remains within, and what has been excluded may always return, as if from without. In this case, its name is Frankenstein, for between them Victor and his Monster stage everything Kant is careful to say the sublime isn't but secretly is.

As Derrida remarks in another context, "the frame fits badly."[31] In *Frankenstein* his comment applies literally: as Victor observes the first time he sees what has turned out to be a monster, "His yellow skin scarcely covered the work of muscles and arteries beneath."[32] The fit of the Monster's skin is comparable to the encasement of the sublime within Kantian theory: *Frankenstein* demonstrates that the frame in which Kant encloses the sublime is too tight.[33]

Victor has tried expressly to create a "being of gigantic stature," one whose size, "about eight feet in height, and proportionally large" (49), would reflect Victor's lofty ambition and the magnitude of his task. And it is supremely important that his creation be *beautiful*. Initially, the Monster's monstrosity is an effect of how he looks and not what he does. As soon as Victor sees the creature take its first breath and "agitate its limbs," he can barely find words adequate to convey his distress at the creature's ugliness: "How can I describe my emotions at this catastrophe, or how delineate the wretch whom with such infinite pains and care I had endeavored to form? His limbs were in proportion, and I had selected his features as beautiful. Beautiful! Great God!" (52). And Victor proceeds to chronicle the Monster's various atrocities: "his watery eyes, that seemed almost of the same colour as the sunken white sockets in which they were set, his shriveled complexion, and straight black lips" (52). Victor had intended to create something colossal and instead gives birth to monstrosity. *Frankenstein* can be read to invert the *Critique of Judgment*, for in it everything Kant identifies as sublime, including the products of sublimation, yields precisely that which Kant prohibits: monstrosity, passion, fanaticism, and femininity.

At the very moment of his birth the Monster is already gendered as and associated with the feminine.[34] Indeed, as Barbara Johnson observes, *Frankenstein* is "the story of a man who usurps the female role by physically giving birth to a child."[35] On the night that Victor first "infuses a spark of being" into his creation and confronts the "catastrophe" (52) he has wrought, not only has "the beauty of the dream [of producing life] vanished," but this transformation is doubled by "the wildest dreams" in which his sister Elizabeth is transformed:

> I thought I saw Elizabeth, in the bloom of health, walking in the streets of Ingolstadt. Delighted and surprised, I embraced her; but as I imprinted the first kiss on her lips, they became livid with the hue of death; her features appeared to change, and I thought that I held the corpse of my dead mother in my arms; a shroud enveloped her form, and I saw the grave-worms crawling in the folds of the flannel. I started from my sleep with horror; a cold dew covered my forehead, my teeth chattered, and every limb became convulsed; when, by the dim and yellow light of the moon, as it forced its way through the window shutters, I beheld the wretch—the miserable monster whom I had created. (53)

The dream is prophetic. After the Monster's creation, the narrative moves inexorably toward the misogynistic goal of eradicating all the feminine figures in the novel.[36] The monstrosity of incest and of female beauty transformed into rotting flesh is the oneiric reflection of the monster, who is said to "mutter" and is compared to "a mummy again endued with animation" (53). Victor has not only become a male mother who is indirectly responsible for the deaths of all the mothers and potential mothers in the novel; he gives birth to, or creates, a monster who is also a mummy. Both Victor and his monstrous double figure a certain femininity, for Shelley does not so much "exchange a woman for a monster" (131), as Mary Jacobus puts it, as conflate maternity with monstrosity.[37] The ultimate misogyny in *Frankenstein* is not so much the scapegoating and victimization of the mother-monster, as the representation of mothers as monsters.

It is important to emphasize the parallel between the inception of Victor's passionate "thirst for knowledge," a quest that leads ultimately to the Monster's production, and the maternal body for which the Monster is the substitute. Just as the novel *Frankenstein* was conceived on a rainy evening when Shelley's party amused themselves "with some German stories of ghosts which happened to fall into our hands" (7), so Victor's passion for natural philosophy commences when, in search of a book to read while confined by inclement weather at an inn, he comes by chance upon the work of Cornelius Agrippa, whom he reads with great enthusiasm. Victor's ambition to discover the secret of life originates in a scene of forbidden reading: he enthusiastically conveys his discovery to his father who dismisses the book with the words, "My dear Victor, do not waste your time upon this; it is sad trash" (32). The father's warning against knowledge that would promise access to the origins and secrets of life not only increases Victor's desire for "natural philosophy"—after reading Agrippa's collected works he consumes the texts of Paracelsus and Albertus Magnus—but also parallels the father's prohibition of the son's access to the mother. The knowledge Victor craves, to "penetrate into the recesses of nature, and shew how she works in her hiding places" (42), is the symbolic equivalent of communion with the prohibited maternal body. The analogy between forbidden bodies and books is heightened by the fact that, although his mother's death postpones Victor's departure for the University of Ingolstadt, what he finds there becomes a substitute for her, an *alma mater*. Shortly after he arrives Victor sets out to find a way of making mothers irrelevant: he responds to her death by attempting to become a mother himself and eventually finds in "natural philosophy" the means "to found a new species" that he believes will bless him "as its creator and source" (49). Just as the knowledge Victor pursues in the hope of gaining access to the secrets of life brings him into intimate proximity to death, so the sublimation of Victor's desire for the mother produces a monstrous "mummy" who is responsible for the death of mothers. In this case the fruits of reason serve not merely to scapegoat the feminine but to destroy it.

Kant's theory of the sublime is a defense against the threat of formlessness, a way of keeping materiality and excessive magnitude at bay in much the same way that Victor's obsessive "thirst for knowledge" functions as a substitute for and a defense against the maternal body he attempts to ward off and become. But although both narratives may be read as parables of male misogyny, Shelley's differs from Kant's in that, as a parodic reversal of the Kantian sublime, it makes explicit its misogynistic subtext.

All the things Kant's sublime intends to be and do, for example, "raise the soul's fortitude above its usual middle range" (120, §28) and produce a conviction of the mind's "superiority over nature itself in its immensity" (120, §28), the vision of the sublime in *Frankenstein* systematically inverts. Even the topography of the novel—full of mountain heights, elevated vistas, and crashing thunder—sounds like Kant's description of a sublime landscape. The reader might encounter the following topos, "thunder-clouds piling up in the sky and moving about accompanied by lightning and thunder claps . . . the horror and a sacred thrill" that seizes the spectator who beholds "massive mountains climbing skyward, deep gorges with raging streams in them, wastelands lying in deep shadow and inviting melancholy meditation" (120, §28; and 129, §29) in one of Victor's accounts of a journey to Mont Blanc, among "the sublime shapes of the mountains" near his home in Geneva.[38]

But whereas in Kant "the irresistibility of nature's might . . . reveals in us at the same time an ability to judge ourselves independent of nature, and reveals in us a superiority over nature" (120–21, §28), in *Frankenstein* an identical geography produces neither peace of mind nor aesthetic pleasure, but rather a vision of and encounter with monstrosity. Each depiction of a sublime landscape is linked to the Monster's appearance. After the Monster's birth at Ingolstadt, Victor's meetings with him take place only at the tops of mountains, on glaciers surrounded by fields of ice, or during violent storms, amidst echoing thunder and repeated, dazzling flashes of lightning. The landscape is the same as Kant's—that of Nature in all her might and majesty—but its effect (and affect) is not.

In Longinus, as in Kant, the lightning flash is one of the most privileged examples of the sublime. Longinus even posits an equivalence between them: sublime oratory, which exhibits a "genuine power over language," is like "a flash of lightning" in that both "strike the hearer," "rend everything before them," and in so doing "reveal the full might of the orator."[39] In *Frankenstein* lightning illuminates the sky and does indeed reveal the orator's full might, but the Monster is the one who possesses the gift of eloquence; and the sublime flash of lightning, even while it yields a moment of sheer luminosity, also brings with it utter devastation.

When Victor is fifteen he watches a "terrible thunder-storm" in the security of his home "with curiosity and delight" (35). But lightning strikes a nearby "old and beautiful oak" (35), and a stream of fire issues from the tree that tears it to ribbons. Nature's sublime and dazzling lightning flash destroys the beautiful oak and thus foretells the future's shape: the lightning destroys the tree as the monster will destroy Victor's family. Nothing remains but a "blasted stump." From the very outset the sublime in *Frankenstein* lays waste to the beautiful. "I never beheld anything so utterly destroyed" (35), Victor says. The next flash of lightning brings him face to face with monstrosity. Walking in the Alps on the way home after the murder of his brother William, Victor watches lightning "play on the summit of Mont Blanc in the most beautiful figures" (70) and continues the ascent while "vivid flashes of lightning" dazzle his eyes and illuminate the lake, "making it appear like a vast sheet of fire" (71). But again a naturally beautiful form, or "figure," is blasted away by the sublime, for here Victor meets the Monster for the first time. "I perceived in the gloom a figure which stole from behind a clump of trees near to me. . . . A flash of lightning illuminated the object and discovered its shape plainly to me; its gigantic stature, and the deformity of its aspect, more hideous than belongs to humanity, instantly informed me that it was the wretch, the filthy daemon, to whom I had given life" (71). Moments of pure vision indeed illuminate "the truth," but its shape is as monstrous as it is sublime.

What the lightning in *Frankenstein* shows is that the intellectual tradition's faith in vision as an adequate index of the truth is misplaced. The belief, or bias, that vision is an accurate judge of the truth, which is also presumed to be both good and beautiful, is reflected both by Kant's conviction that beauty is the ultimate symbol of the good (paragraph 59 of the third *Critique* is appropriately titled "On Beauty as the Symbol of Morality"), and by Victor's assumption that, because his progeny's shape is monstrous, so must be his spirit. That Kant's sublime figures in the mind's response to an object or event that unsettles its representational faculties explains why Kant must at all costs demonstrate that reason can master and comprehend an uncircumscribable excess that surpasses the imagination's grasp. The novel tests the premise that truth is something that can be *seen*: no one questions the supposition that the true is identical to the good (which has a beautiful, or at least a pleasing, form), or that eyes and vision have a closer proximity to "the truth" than ears and hearing. The only human who ever says a kind word to the Monster is the old blind man De Lacey (whose name contains the word for what he cannot do, i.e., see), and even he trusts the evidence of his family's eyes rather than his own ears: when the family returns and sees the Monster clinging to their father's knees, Agatha faints, Safie flees, and Felix beats him. The Monster's voice is his only pleasing attribute: "although harsh," it has "nothing terrible in it" (128), but his very eloquence makes him suspect. At the end of the novel Victor warns Walton not to be seduced by the Monster's rhetorical power when they meet: "He is eloquent and persuasive; and once his words had even power over my heart: but trust him not . . . hear him not" (206). By aligning the lightning, the Monster, and sublime, the novel shows that Longinus' "genuine power" may as easily produce devastation or beauty, and that the sublime has a power beauty lacks.

In the Western tradition, as Heidegger has pointed out, notions of vision and theory are closely linked.[40] "Theory" comes from the Greek *theorein*, which combines *thea*, the visible aspect of things, and *horao*, which means to look at something closely or view it attentively. Their relation suggests that, at least in the West, the sense of sight has become a metaphor for knowledge itself. The etymology of the word "theory" is particularly interesting because Victor calls natural philosophy "the genius that has regulated my fate" (32), while for Kant the provinces of natural philosophy and theory are almost identical: "Hence," he tells us, "we are right to divide philosophy into two parts that are quite different in their principles: theoretical or *natural philosophy*, and practical or *moral philosophy*" (introduction, 10). Victor, whose inquiries are "directed to the metaphysical or, in the highest sense, the physical secrets of the world" (32), may be said to personify metaphysics' desire for transparent meaning, showing the ways in which the theorist's very desire for mastery must also lead to a certain blindness.

Victor represents Kant's "natural philosopher" or "theorist" to the letter. According to Kant, the province of "theoretical philosophy" is precisely the "laws of nature," for "legislation through concepts of nature is performed by the understanding and is theoretical" (introduction, 12–13); and it is precisely to the study of natural philosophy, or metaphysics, that Victor, in his "fervent longing to penetrate the secrets of nature" (34), turns. From the day that he hears Professor Waldman lecture on the advances modern natural philosophy has made and the improvements it can be expected to accomplish, "natural philosophy and particularly chemistry in the most comprehensive sense of the term" become his "sole occupation" (45).

Victor, like Kant, wants knowledge of the foundations and ultimate causes of things. His belief that metaphysics can give access to "the secrets of heaven and earth" is similar to Kant's faith that knowledge is built upon stable foundations that reason can locate, and, independently of experience, use "as the basis for the unity of all empirical principles under higher though still empirical principles, and hence [as] the basis that makes it possible to subordinate empirical principles to one another in a systematic way" (introduction, 19).[41] Kant's topographical, and territorialistic, view of knowledge as a geographical realm that reason can chart, divide, bridge, and then connect to other domains is of a piece with his faith in the stability of its foundations; his certainty that knowledge has an unchanging ground on which the theorist can construct an edifice reflects the extent to which metaphysics, albeit unconsciously, is committed to, if not constituted by, the thematics of sight. The desire that pervades the *Critique of Judgment*, that is, to demonstrate that there is "a basis that determines the feeling of pleasure a priori and validly for everyone" (introduction, 27), and utter confidence in the attainability of such an end are congruent with Victor's certainty that the acquisition of knowledge can give him insight into the nature of nature itself, and that metaphysics will yield a moment of pure, unmediated vision.

The ways in which Victor provides a portrait of Kant, or mirror of metaphysical desire, allow us to ask two crucial questions. First, what is the logic that links the theorist's desire for truth to a wish for the sublime and the construction of monstrosity? And second, might the monstrosity of a being that, like the maternal body, is a collectivity of parts neither totally separate nor totally merged, also be a figure for theory?

The diverse meanings of the word "monstrosity" help to explain the connections between the sublime on the one hand and theory on the other. Just as Kant's most general definition of the sublime is bound up with magnitude ("We call *sublime* what is *absolutely large . . . that is sublime in comparison with which everything else is small*" [103 and 105, §25]), so the word "monster" is defined most frequently as something of huge and often unmanageable proportions. An initial rapport between sublimity and monstrosity, then, consists in their enormity, their almost unnatural size. In this both resemble a misogynistic conception of the pregnant female body, which is viewed as unsightly and distorted when its customary borders are stretched and displaced. That it also contains a baby that, simultaneously the same and the other, is not yet differentiated from its mother, bears mute witness to the terrifying condition of radical dependence and confusion of boundaries that precedes and accompanies human life. Here the maternal body not only is the very incarnation of monstrosity but supplies a vision of what theory itself might become did its authors not struggle successfully to keep it within bounds. And Frankenstein's monster-mother, composed of parts that, loosely sutured and stitched together, bear no inherent or organic relation to one another, threatens (or rather promises, depending upon one's point of view) to interfere with the project of Kantian theory as such.

The affinity between sublimity, monstrosity, and maternity resides in a certain relation to, and definition of, the theoretical enterprise itself, for a "monster" is also something shown, proven, or demonstrated—like an idea or argument. According to the *O.E.D.*, the word derives from the Latin *monstrum*, which originally meant a divine portent or warning. Just as significantly, the French *monstre* (a relative of *montrer*, to show) was once in English an obsolete form of monster, something huge or enormous, and a demonstration or proof, something shown or exhibited. A whole family of English words reflects this conjunction: *monstrable* means capable of being shown; *monstrance* means demonstration or proof; *to monstrate* is to prove; a *monstration* means a demonstration; and the archaic verb *to monster* meant to exhibit or point out. Theory, the showing or demonstrating of an argument or concept, is not only bound up with vision, but the very notion of showing itself is related to, if not a synonym for, monstrosity. This conjunction suggests that an investigation of monstrosity might yield a theory of theory and that, correlatively, an investigation of theory might demonstrate something about demonstration, about that which purports to contain the sublime and prohibit the monstrous, while exhibiting the differences between them. The etymology of "monster" (or of the French *monstre*, since in *Frankenstein* the Monster's mother tongue is French) allows an elaboration of theory as a form of monstrosity, and an exploration of sublimity as a form of, even a figure for, theory. The word "monster" also means "a threatening force, an engulfing power," which describes both negative representations of maternity and what the Monster in *Frankenstein* does. In this regard it is perhaps worth noting that the word "frank" once meant "free from bondage or restraint," and that Kant's sublime "can also be found in a formless object, insofar as we present *unboundedness*" (p. 98, §23). If being "free from bondage" is a condition for "unboundedness," Frankenstein's name contains the word that is synonymous to, and one of the properties of, the sublime. The very name *Frankenstein* is emblematic of this movement, for the title, once intended to name only the Monster's progenitor, now refers to the Monster instead. Indeed, "frankenstein" has become a word in its own right: according to *Webster's Third New International Dictionary* it means a monster in the shape of a man; a work or agency that proves troublesome to or destroys its creator; and a law unto itself, interested largely in its own perpetuation and expansion. "Frankenstein" is an example of a word that monsters, for the Monster has appropriated not only the novel's title, but his creator's very name.

Writing about monstrosity in a review of a special issue of *Yale French Studies* edited by a collective who describe themselves as "a seven-headed monster from Dartmouth," Jane Gallop speaks of "the monstrosity of a being whose boundaries are inadequately differentiated . . . such a being is terrifying because of the stake any self as self has in its own autonomy, in its individuation, in its integrity."[42] Like Shelley, Gallop associates mothers with monsters: if the two are not quite equivalent, she implies that, at least from a certain perspective, maternity has its monstrous aspects. For the qualities that make monsters seem monstrous—their terrifying capacity to call into question the fundamental difference between self and other—applies not only to misogynistic representations of mothers but to the extraordinary powers of Kant's sublime that, itself of incommensurable proportions, threatens to engulf and incorporate whoever would merely stand outside and observe. While Kant's unintentional conflation of monstrosity and the sublime does have the effect of successfully defending against formlessness and indeterminacy, it is important to observe that, as Jacobus points out, "the function of the female 'victim' in scenarios of this kind is to provide the mute sacrifice on which theory itself may be founded."[43] While in Kant the threat of sheer magnitude triggers reason's identification with powers that it cannot comprehend (albeit only at the imagination's expense) and perpetuates the illusion that theory, and the theorist, can master the instability and impenetrability of excess itself, as an invented form of Kant's sublime *Frankenstein* makes explicit the misogyny that is responsible for envisioning maternity as monstrous. In so doing it offers a critique of a tradition in which, as Gilbert and Gubar observe, "women have seen themselves (because they have been seen) as monstrous, vile, degraded creatures, second-comers, and emblems of filthy materiality."[44] In the process Shelley also demonstrates that "filthy materiality" and the monstrosity that accompanies it have more to do with the sublime than its theorists would like to think.

IV

> Good morning, Midnight!
> I'm coming home,
> Day got tired of me—
> How could I of him?
>
> Sunshine was a sweet place,
> I liked to stay—
> But Morn didn't want me—now—
> So good night, Day![45]
> (Emily Dickinson)

> Impasse. 1 A position from which there is no escape, a deadlock.
> 2 A road etc. without an outlet, a blind alley.
> (O.E.D.)

Good Morning, Midnight (1938) raises many of the issues we have seen in Shelley and in Kant, but with one crucial difference, for the story is told from the point of view of the monster or sacrificial victim and not from that of the enhanced and reconstructed (male) self. The poem by Dickinson that gives the novel its title addresses one of Kant's central concerns, that of the mind's "super-sensible vocation," but in this case the protagonist is a woman whose destination is exile. Just as the poem's speaker longs for a masculine Day who no longer wants her and seems eager to return to Midnight as to her proper place, so the heroine's voyage ends in an impasse that culminates a long series of failures. Sasha Jansen is, as Mary Lou Emery has pointed out, an outsider to women's traditional domestic sphere and an intruder on masculine public territory; she lives on the edges of respectability, sanity, and dignity, and the "home" to which she returns does not offer a refuge from rejection but is rather the site of its repetition.[46] If in the Kantian sublime the mind turns inward and discovers itself afresh in an attitude of awe, the feminine protagonist's moments of self-reflexivity are marked by self-abuse and abjection, revealing that she has learned to do to herself what others have done to her and to find in auto-mutilation her sole creative enterprise.

The novel concerns a woman who, like Kant's imagination, is at an impasse. It takes place in late October 1937 and begins with a description of the large, dark room at the top of a cheap Paris hotel in which the protagonist has been staying for five days:

> There are two beds, a big one for madame and a smaller one on the opposite side for monsieur. The wash-basin is shut off by a curtain. It is a large room, the smell of cheap hotels is faint, almost imperceptible. The street outside is narrow, cobble-stoned, going sharply uphill and ending in a flight of steps. What they call an impasse. (9)

From the very first sentences Rhys foregrounds the issue of boundaries. Without any intervening building in between, the room expands into the street and, as the reader will shortly learn, the "flight of steps" that ends in an impasse is also within, for the steps both duplicate the staircase that leads to Sasha's room and dramatize her position inside of it. "Flight" is precisely what's impossible: she waits in a room at the top of the stairs that overlooks an impasse with nowhere to go. The impasse is both without and within, and what is at stake in the novel is the complexity of the difference between them.

The meaning of the impasse, particularly the fact of its social construction, is amplified by Rhys's treatment of the room as a surrogate for the protagonist herself. Sasha's continuing meditation upon and relation to rooms—what they are, do, and have not done for her—illustrates not only the extent to which her fate is already determined; when placed within the context of Rhys's literary inheritance it may be read both as an ironic commentary upon Virginia Woolf's somewhat idealistic view of the role of private property in ensuring feminine happiness and as a demonstration that the identity of authors as well as the fictional characters they construct may be produced by and inextricably bound up with a monstrous attack upon an imaginary or unknown other.

In the essay "Women and Fiction" and the brilliant *A Room of One's Own*, both written in 1929, Woolf emphasizes that economic independence is the condition for the development of autonomous female authorship. She concludes "Women and Fiction" by looking forward to "that golden, that perhaps fabulous, age when women will have what has so long been denied them—leisure, and money, and a room to themselves."[47] In *A Room of One's Own*, Woolf's narrator illustrates this point by describing the difference an aunt's legacy of five hundred pounds a year has made. The gift has not only changed her life: "Indeed my aunt's legacy unveiled the sky to me"; it has brought about a shift in her attitude toward the male sex as well:

> It is remarkable, remembering the bitterness of those days, what a change of temper a fixed income will bring about. No force in the world could take from me my five hundred pounds. Food, house and clothing are mine for ever. Therefore not merely do effort and labour cease, but also hatred and bitterness. I need not hate any man; he cannot hurt me. I need not flatter any man; he has nothing to give me. So imperceptibly I found myself adopting a new attitude towards the other half of the human race.[48]

Woolf quite rightly emphasizes the importance of economic factors in creating the very possibility of human happiness. But in *Good Morning, Midnight* a room of one's own does not quite provide the benefits Woolf believed would follow automatically, and Rhys implies that Woolf's views have been shaped by assumptions about class and privilege of which she herself was unaware. Like Woolf's narrator, Sasha is also preoccupied with "leisure, and money, and a room to oneself," but she lives in a world very different from that depicted by Woolf, one that opposes and undercuts the most cherished values of the upper-class milieu to which Woolf belonged. Although she too has inherited a small legacy from a distant aunt (£2 10s every Tuesday, the capital not to be touched), which allows her minimal financial security and a small room in London, far from empowering her, the room becomes the site of absolute withdrawal. Economic independence offers a place in which to bury herself: "Well, that was the end of me, the real end. Two-pound-ten every Tuesday and a room off the Gray's Inn Road. Saved, rescued and with my place to hide in—what more did I want? I crept in and hid. The lid of the coffin shut down with a bang" (42). Rather than unveil the sky, Sasha's room is the place in which she seeks refuge from it. She sets out to drink herself to death, and has almost accomplished it when Sidonie, an English acquaintance whose name contains the French word for gift (*don*), "swooped down" (12) upon her, insists that she needs a change, lends her the money for a fortnight in Paris (where Sasha used to live), and promises to find her a hotel room when she visits Paris the following week.

Woolf assumes what Rhys does not: a protagonist who has remained unmarked despite oppressive social circumstances. But unlike Woolf's, Rhys's characters have been shaped by living in an environment in which they are outsiders by virtue of class as well as gender, and their experiences of self-mutilation are, as Judith Kegan Gardiner points out, "the specific historical result of social polarizations about sex, class, and morality. Her heroes are women alienated from others and themselves because they are female, poor, and sexually active. They are also misdefined by a language and literary heritage that belongs principally to propertied men."[49] Sasha Jansen, the oldest of Rhys's heroines and her quintessential "lady in the dark," might be understood to typify Alice Walker's notion of the "suspended woman," women whose "life choices are so severely limited that they cannot move in any direction."[50] Sasha's history of friendlessness, poverty, and dispossession have made her too knowing to attempt to belong in a world she despises, but also too wounded to contest a society she cannot accept.

From her perspective there is indeed a certain truth "about this business of rooms" (38), but it contradicts Woolf's assumption that rooms are synonymous with creativity and self-containment. For Sasha, rooms are good for only one thing: they provide a place in which to hide.

> All rooms are the same. All rooms have four walls, a door, a window
> or two, a bed, a chair and perhaps a bidet. A room is a place where
> you hide from the wolves and that's all any room is. (38)

The rooms' four walls are supposed to provide a barrier that will keep the oppressive wolves at bay and protect the person inside from what is without. But *Good Morning, Midnight* demonstrates that a room of one's own cannot be counted upon to perform even this modest goal because the wolves that appear to be only external are, like the impasse, also within. A fierce wolf lives inside Sasha's head and "walks by [her] side" (52), but before discussing the ways in which Sasha's very self-construction depends upon her relation to a persecutory other, let us note the extent of the interplay between wolves and rooms, for Sasha's wolf is perhaps also Rhys's Woolf.

In *Orlando* (1928), written the year after *A Room of One's Own*, Woolf gives the name Sasha to a character who barks and behaves like a wolf. Before becoming a woman, the young Elizabethan courtier Orlando falls in love with a visiting Russian princess whom he affectionately calls Sasha because "it was the name of a white Russian fox he had had as a boy—a creature soft as snow, but with teeth of steel, which bit him so savagely that his father had it killed."[51] But Sasha barks like a wolf, not a fox: "Seldom would she talk about her past life, but now she told him how, in winter in Russia, she would listen to the wolves howling across the steppes, and thrice, to show him, she barked like a wolf."[52] Sasha also acts as wolves are said to act: she deserts Orlando the day they are to elope, and he never loves again.

Sasha perhaps names both Woolf's and Rhys's wolf-woman, but what is particularly intriguing is the persecutory relay-system her name appears to set off. For if Rhys's protagonist is attacked by wolves, so in her pointed recasting of some of Woolf's major themes does Rhys attack Woolf: she is the influential literary predecessor in whose terms Rhys must define herself and from whom she must distinguish herself in order to establish a separate authorial identity. Just as Sasha's sense of self is constituted in part by internal persecution as she does to herself what society has done to her, so a persecuting and persecutory relationship with Woolf is perhaps one condition of Rhys's literary identity. In each case, self-definition is achieved through the scapegoating of a feminine figure. As Sasha ironically remarks, "Sacrifices are necessary . . ." (29).

Throughout the novel feminine misogyny is particularly manifested by Sasha's self-scapegoating. Rhys gives us access to Sasha's consciousness by depicting the two opposed voices that are in constant dialogue within her. As in the Kantian sublime, identity is generated through a process of victimization. (Trying to remember a few phrases of German, Sasha repeatedly comes up with the Latin saying *homo homini lupus* [man is a wolf to man]) (24). Sasha's impasse reproduces that of the imagination's just before its collapse: for both the only possible movement is that of self-sacrifice. But while in Kant the imagination's surrender was a necessary stage on the way to the achievement of a higher unity, here the impasse produces a different version of identity, one that is generated by self-victimization. Rhys records an internal dialogue between agencies that are remarkably similar to that of the imagination and the reason: there is a wishful, imaginative Sasha whose "film-mind" (176) can still imagine the possibility of happiness, and the voice of reason, a well-socialized voice Sasha calls "the other" (184) that criticizes her relentlessly. The plot turns upon the conflict between the Sasha who is still capable of desire and the critical "other" who believes her very survival depends upon no longer wanting:

> But careful, careful! Don't get excited. You know what happens when you get excited and exalted, don't you? . . . Yes . . . And then you know how you collapse like a pricked balloon, don't you? (15)[53]

Rhys continually emphasizes the extent to which the self is socially constructed. "The other" that mocks from within replicates the world that taunts and condemns from without: Sasha's wolf-woman, a composite of external voices, mirrors that of society. A hyperconventional, middle-class Englishwoman who always knows best, she calls Sasha "dear" or "dearie," and speaks most frequently from within the security of parentheses: "(Let it pass, dearie, let it pass. What's it matter?)" (78). She mocks the wishful Sasha who is still capable of desire; knowing that for Sasha to feel is to fail, she tries to keep her from feeling.

The visit to Paris poses a particularly intense threat, for here Sasha begins to remember what "the other" would prefer her to forget: the brief moments of happiness ("the street, blazing hot, and eating peaches. The long, lovely, blue days, that lasted for ever, that still are. . . ." [132]), and the miserable failures. The reasonable voice of "the other" especially wants Sasha to stay away from the streets, cafes, and restaurants that might intensify her memories (" 'I told you not to come in here,' scolds the voice, 'I told you not to' " [50]). And she is full of advice. According to her, "The thing is to have a programme, not to leave anything to chance—no gaps" (15). But Sasha can't live according to the plan. She wanders into the wrong places, buys a hat, has her hair colored ash blond ("At it again, dearie, at it again!" [61]), goes to the Dôme in her old fur coat, and meets a young man who mistakes her for a wealthy woman of a certain age. It is the imaginative Sasha who remakes herself by having her hair colored, spends three hours selecting a new hat, and searches for just the right lighting to apply her makeup; and it is this Sasha who must be sacrificed. "The other," sensing danger, tries to avert Sasha's impending involvement and certain humiliation:

> Her voice in my head: 'Well, well, well, just think of that now. What an amazing ten days. Positively packed with thrills. The last performance of What's-Her-Name And Her Boys or It Was All Due To An Old Fur Coat. Positively the last performance. . . . Go on cry, allez-y. Encore. Tirez, as they say here. . . .' (184–85)

The voice despises Sasha. Like an excessively critical, punitive mother, she can't forgive Sasha for being a victim and punishes her with bitter self-hatred.

When at the end of the novel Sasha finally silences the voice ("I have another drink. Damned voice in my head, I'll stop you talking. I am walking up and down the room. She has gone. I am alone" [187]), we discover that her attacks have had a self-preservative function. Just as her speeches, enclosed by parentheses, were securely divided from the text proper, so her oppression helped define Sasha; like a room's four walls, her presence separated inside from outside. Her persecution was necessary because it created borders that enhanced, or allowed, the identity of the persecuted: imitating the wolves outside helped keep them away. And Sasha's self is constructed from these self-inflicted wounds, for once "the other" is gone, all the boundaries collapse. Another wolf enters the room, who, like Shelley's Monster, represents the fantasy of a male, or phallic, mother.

From the outset, a white-robed, ghostly figure who reminds Sasha of "the priest of some obscene half-understood religion" (34) has haunted both her dreams and the landing outside her door. The novel even begins with a dream about a wounded man in a white nightshirt who insists that he is her father. In the dream Sasha is trapped in a crowded passage in a London tube station. The sign announcing an invisible exhibition takes the place of a nonexistent exit. We are still inside the impasse, but the appearance of a little, bearded man who wears a long white nightshirt and insists that he is her father adds another dimension to it. "'I am your father,'" the man repeats, "'remember that I am your father'" (13). Blood streams from a wound on his forehead and he screams, "Murder." Helplessly she watches, too frightened to speak. Sasha finally wakes up to hear herself shouting, "Murder, murder, help, help" (13).

The white nightdress suggests that the dream has been occasioned by her sinister next-door neighbor, a man who hangs around the landing outside her room and habitually wears a long, white dressing gown that reminds Sasha of a priest's robes. She finds him frightening and repulsive. He is "thin as a skeleton," and has a "bird-like face and sunken, dark eyes with a peculiar expression, cringing, ingratiating, knowing" (14). Perhaps because he lurks about waiting for her, she is always running into him. Sasha names him "the ghost of the landing"; she imagines that he is a "commis voyageur" (14), a commercial traveler who is temporarily unemployed. But the fact that she dreams he is her father suggests that he is already familiar to her, and that his appearance next door is an externalization of something, or someone, who has been there all along, yet another embodiment of the wolf who "walks by her side."

One evening she returns to find him on the landing, this time wearing a flannel nightshirt that barely reaches his knees. When he sees Sasha he grins, comes to the head of the stairs, and blocks her way. She walks past him and slams the door to her room, but that doesn't stop him: he believes that women living alone in cheap hotels want only one thing, and he intends to give it to her:

> I have just finished dressing when there is a knock on the door. It's the commis, in his beautiful dressing-gown, immaculately white, with long, wide, hanging sleeves[. . . .] He stands there smiling his silly smile. I stare at him[. . . .]
>
> At last I manage: 'Well, what is it? What do you want?'
> 'Nothing,' he says, 'nothing.'
> 'Oh, go away.'
> He doesn't answer or move. He stands in the doorway, smiling. (Now then, you and I understand each other, don't we? Let's stop pretending.)
> I put my hand on his chest, push him backwards and bang the door. It's quite easy. It's like pushing a paper man, a ghost, something that doesn't exist.
> And there I am in this dim room with the bed for madame and the bed for monsieur and the narrow street outside (what they call an impasse), thinking of that white dressing-gown, like a priest's robes. Frightened as hell. A nightmare feeling. . . . (35)

This ghostly, even paternal figure provides the opportunity for Sasha's final self-sacrifice; in the book's concluding passage, when the female "other" has disappeared, Sasha welcomes the commis into her bed. He is her final destination, the "home" to which Dickinson's poem alludes. But if in Kant's sublime the imagination's failure is the key to reason's enhancement and provides the way out of its impasse, here what is staged is the ambiguity of its consent. For the novel's conclusion articulates both the complexity of Sasha's abjection and the power of her assent.

On the evening she visits the Dôme, a handsome young man approaches her. His name is René but, although never completely certain he is one, she calls him "the gigolo." Sasha intends to enjoy his mistake: she will lead him along, let him make his pitch, and then "be so devastatingly English that perhaps I should manage to hurt him a little in return for all the many times I've been hurt" (73). But there is something between them. Like her, he's foreign, homeless, down on his luck, and looking for comfort. He says he doesn't want money, just to "put my head on your breast and put my arms round you and tell you everything[. . . .] I could die for that" (75). When she is with him she sometimes feels "natural and happy, just as if I were young (I've never been that young)" (155). She almost believes him. Briefly it seems that they might become lovers, but after a series of complex interactions she becomes increasingly mistrustful; after a second evening together Sasha says good night at the door of her hotel. He follows her and when they meet in the darkness outside her door, Sasha throws her arms around him: for a moment she believes that he does really want her. Unfortunately, the hoped-for love-making turns into a near rape. The gigolo accuses Sasha of "playing a comedy" (179). How did she know who was on the landing? Hasn't she just been pretending all along? If she was so sure he'd follow her that she'd kiss him without being able to see him, why didn't she say yes right away? René wants to be paid to have sex while maintaining the pretense that money has nothing to do with it, but pretends not to be a gigolo in a way that makes him impossible to believe.

Their argument escalates, and he tries to rape her. Sasha thwarts him by calmly pointing out that he can have the money without the bother of sex. "I'm just trying to save you a whole lot of trouble," she says. "You can have the money right away, so it would be a waste of time, wouldn't it?" (183). She asks him to take a thousand francs from her dressing case, but begs him to leave the rest. "Yes, you're right," he says. "It would be a waste of time" (184). She watches him take some money before he leaves, but once he is gone, she weeps. The voice inside her head taunts her for crying and suggests that Sasha see how much, if any, money remains. When Sasha discovers that the gigolo has taken only 150 francs, she begins to cry again: "I appreciate this, sweet gigolo, from the depths of my heart." The other Sasha mocks her: "'Well! *What* a compliment! Who'd have thought it?'" "Not used" to such "courtesies," she toasts the "chic gigolo," the "sweet gigolo" (186), and falls into a stupor. Her subsequent dream recalls the previous nightmare and predicts the novel's conclusion: all the gods—Venus, Apollo, even Jesus—are dead, and in their place is a monstrous machine with "innumerable flexible arms, made of steel" (187). This monster has arms instead of hands; its image merges with the "damned voice" that echoes in her head, and the dream ends when Sasha silences "the other" once and for all. She wakes up alone longing for René's return and decides that visualizing his every step will bring him back: the sheer force of her imagination can make him return to her. She turns on the light, leaves the door ajar, undresses, gets into bed, and tries to imagine every step of his return: "This is the effort, the enormous effort, under which the human brain cracks. But not before the thing is done, not before the mountain moves" (188). She tracks his every step until, certain that he has followed her directions, she sees him turn into the end of her street, come to the hotel, enter the lobby, and climb the stairs:

> Now the door is moving, the door is opening wide. I put my arm over my eyes.
>   He comes in. He shuts the door after him.
>   I lie very still, with my arm over my eyes. As still as if I were dead. . . . (190)

It will come as no surprise that her imagination fails.

The door opens and a man comes in. She knows his identity without having to look. All that matters is his choice of apparel: is it the blue or the white dressing gown? The commis enters to find her lying naked on the bed. Sasha sees him looking down at her, "his mean eyes flickering":

> He doesn't say anything. Thank God he doesn't say anything. I look straight into his eyes and despise another poor devil of a human being for the last time. For the last time. . . .
>   Then I put my arms round him and pull him down on to the bed, saying: 'Yes—yes—yes. . . .' (190)

The novel ends with Sasha's assent to the man she despises.

Many critics have remarked that *Good Morning, Midnight* concludes with a phrase that echoes Molly Bloom's last words in *Ulysses*, but unlike Molly's unambiguous affirmation of sexuality, it is not clear precisely to whom, or what, Sasha is saying "yes." Although critics have interpreted Rhys's reference in distinctly different fashions, those of Elizabeth Abel, Judith Kegan Gardiner, and Thomas F. Staley are representative. Whereas Gardiner argues that Rhys's ending refutes Joyce's stereotypic and polarized views of women, in which "a woman's voice signals both her creator's fantasy of total female responsiveness and his ironic use of a woman's voice to affirm the value of man's existence," and finds that "when Rhys ends her novel 'yes—yes—yes' she says *no* to Joyce's ideas of women," Staley and Abel hold the more prevalent view that Rhys reinforces and underscores Joyce's message.[54] Staley, for example, thinks that in each ending "feminine consciousness" achieves release "after a crisis" and believes that Molly's and Sasha's "yeses" affirm "the possibility of union between men and women in which both natures are in harmony and love," while Abel agrees that Sasha's final "yes" is "a sign that she has achieved a portion of Molly's wholeness and simplicity."[55]

But even while critics disagree regarding Rhys's intentions as an interpreter of Joyce, they are in accord in their assessment of its conclusion, a concordance that is particularly surprising given that the end of the novel has produced more commentary than any other event in the Rhysian canon. Even while noting Sasha's humiliation in taking into her bed a man who has verbally and physically abused her, they are anxious to offer a redemptive reading of it. Elgin W. Mellown, for example, postulates that with her last words Sasha "overcomes the drift toward death that obsesses the earlier manifestations of the Rhys woman (and the earlier Sasha) by finding . . . compassion"[56]; for Carole Angier, "in accepting the commis as her lover, Sasha accepts into herself, as equal to herself, what is mean and contemptible and mad" and is finally able "to admit her identity with even the most hopeless of the human race";[57] Elizabeth Abel refers to Sasha's "psychic triumph,"[58] while Arnold E. Davidson finds Sasha's act "transcendent."

> She thereby judges her own previous judging to see that she and the commis are equally . . . 'another poor devil of a human being.' It is a simple enough recognition, but under the circumstances it is also transcendent. . . . Her immediately subsequent 'yes' . . . is 'yes' to a different kind of love, one that depends entirely on her. She will now define, for herself, what her love—or whatever it is—is.[59]

Judith Gardiner also concludes on a remarkably optimistic note. According to Gardiner, Sasha finally is able to "accept the burden of a full humanity possessed of the ironies of having been incarnated female in a patriarchal society. . . . She has returned from the 'wrong bed,' the position of monsieur, to her own more capacious bed, and there she regains the power of speech, the power of the last word."[60]

Her critics' unanimously positive interpretation is perhaps symptomatic of their wish to discover a way out of Sasha's impasse, for they transform an extremely complex moment of abjection into an expression of triumphant wholeness. Such a reading duplicates the structure of the Kantian sublime in which the imagination's scapegoating is the condition for reason's success and its sacrifice occasions resurrection or rebirth. Even more important, it reinscribes the Kantian notion of transcendence Rhys calls into question.

Sasha's consent is neither an act of "supreme charity," nor a "relationship" into which she "actively enters," as Davidson and Abel would have it, but a final manifestation of her own desire, this time in erotic form.[61] In assenting to the commis Sasha relives the nightmare with which the novel began and enacts the wish it conceals: her "yes" is at once a consent to the priest, the skeleton, the ghost, the traveling salesman, wounded father, and steel-armed man, for the metaphor of the white dressing gown condenses all these associations. Sex with the commis is perhaps an incestuous ritual consummated with a priestly figure who reminds her of her father; but his feminine garments, tentacle-like arms, and appearance immediately after Sasha has finally silenced the voice of the maternal "other" also suggests that "he" is also a surrogate for the mother. (If this is indeed the case, Rhys succeeds in representing the act of maternal incest Shelley kept at bay.) Saying "yes" to the commis is, in any event, an assent to her own degradation at the hands of a man she detests: the mean-eyed "lover" despises her and uses sex to demonstrate it, and she, with full awareness of his feelings, welcomes them. It is as if she might reach the exhibition, the unattainable destination in her dream, only by becoming an exhibition herself. If, as Weiskel maintains, the sublime recapitulates the (male) Oedipus complex, perhaps the feminine sublime depicts its transformation.[62]

The novel's conclusion demonstrates the fictionality of the notion of choice that the majority of Rhys's critics would wish to maintain. For Sasha cannot, as Davidson would have it, simply "define, for herself, what her love . . . is," nor is it the case that "the kind of love" to which she says yes "depends entirely on her(self)."[63] To endorse such a view of individual choice is both to deny the extent to which the self is socially shaped and constrained and to ignore the extent of the misogyny Rhys so meticulously depicts. Sasha is not free to decide, independently of society and its judgments, what sex with the commis will mean.[64] Her welcome does not change his assessment; from his perspective the woman lying naked on the bed is worse than a whore, and her consent alters neither his loathing nor her awareness of it. Like Kant's imagination, Sasha is free to choose only her own violation: just as the imagination has no choice but to will its own destruction, all she can do is sacrifice herself. The one act to which she can consent is her own rape, and the commis is the agent who enables it.

Understanding Sasha's "yes" as an enactment of the sublime told from the imagination's perspective nonetheless contributes to our understanding of oppression, for it makes explicit the strategies that bring about what looks like consent. Audre Lorde's perceptive analysis of internalized oppression as the technique par excellence to perpetuate sexism and racism fits both the issue of feminine misogyny and the problematic status of Sasha's consent. Lorde describes the internalization of patriarchy's values as the royal road to the continuation of oppression, so that, like Sasha, the victim becomes incapable of choosing anything else:

> The way you get people to testify against themselves is not to have police tactics and oppressive techniques. What you do is build it in so people learn to distrust everything in themselves that has not been sanctioned.[65]

Because the victim's identification with the desires of the other is the operation that best maintains the status quo, Lorde emphasizes that "the true focus of revolutionary change" must never be only external:

> never merely the oppressive situations which we seek to escape, but that piece of the oppressor which is planted deep within each of us, and which knows only the oppressor's tactics, the oppressor's relationships.[66]

Such a view exposes the superficiality of Margaret Atwood's famous injunction: "This above all, to refuse to be a victim," for it shows that the victim is defined by the fact that she cannot refuse to be victimized.[67] As Lorde reminds us, effective resistance is possible only when we recall that, like Sasha's wolf, the oppressor is within as well as without and does not necessarily appear in masculine form.

If *Good Morning, Midnight* does not offer a way out of the impasse it presents a meticulous exploration of it, and in so doing suggests a version of the sublime that at last makes explicit the extremity of feminine misogyny, implicit within and securely contained by the Kantian formulation. Here we see the sublime as the wish for and affirmation of a moment of utter self-loss, but one in which feminine sacrifice does not ensure reason's aggrandizement. If the imagination can participate in and have access to the mind's supersensible vocation only by laying waste to itself, Sasha assents to a sacrifice that is at once sheer abjection—her bitter recognition of the fact that "sacrifices are necessary"—and a defiant resistance to the forces that have determined it. That she becomes the agent and not merely the recipient of her own destruction is a perhaps dubious victory. But I would like to imagine her final "yes" as a moment of self-mutilation that wounds the self not only to nullify but perhaps also to sustain it, albeit in fragmented form. Unlike the Kantian version, this sublime calls into question the efficacy of the dividing line as such. For at the end of the novel self-shattering and self-constitution have become one and the same, and if Sasha finally embraces negativity itself, the condition is that feminine self-hatred has, for perhaps the last time, not been denied.

We might read Sasha's "Yes—yes—yes. . . ." as the subversive rather than compulsive repetition of a woman's assent to her own violation. Sasha does not see the entrance of the commis as the invasion of an external force that would demonstrate her own weakness. Rather, once she knows that it is he (and not René) who has entered her room, she scripts the event as a performance. The commis must wear the white dressing gown, perhaps so he can appear as priest-like and remind her of her father (and her mother); he must be silent, so that she can speak. If the costume were different, if he were to talk, there is no reason to suppose that Sasha would embrace him with her parody of Molly Bloom's "yes." But as it is she takes the opportunity to transform her room from a hiding place, one that she's just successfully defended against René, into a theater where she can perform, imitate, and therefore transform the narrative of female subjugation that haunts the entire novel. As Judith Butler has argued, we can see the resemblance between behavior by lesbians and gays that contests the norms of heterosexual conduct by demonstrating that the norm exists only insofar as it is performed and (compulsively) reiterated.[68] Sasha, too, transforms what might appear to be her fate in a certain novelistic genre into a performance; an affirmation of the exertion of her own agency that has the paradoxical effect of transforming the very event she performs/repeats, for she says "yes" to the possibility of taking her own pleasure in a scene with incestuous overtones. In the Kantian sublime the affirmative moment is reserved for masculine reason, which insists on its transcendent validity at the expense of the imagination; here Sasha performs and parodies that role, and in doing so she not only transgresses sexual norms but subverts and displaces them. Her "yes" is indeed excessive with respect to the norms that have made her a marginal and outcast figure; but it is also excessive in respect to the excess acknowledged by the theory of the sublime and the narrative of female sacrifice with which it is complicit.

4

Love's Labor

Kant, Isis, and
Toni Morrison's Sublime

"It's gonna hurt, now," said Amy. "Anything dead coming back to life hurts."

(Toni Morrison, *Beloved*)

Well, we've got a ghost story on our hands all right. But we should wait until there are more than two of us before we start.

(Jacques Derrida, *The Truth in Painting*)

So the beginning of this was a woman and she had come back from burying the dead.

(Zora Neale Hurston,
Their Eyes Were Watching God)

In "Unspeakable Things Spoken: The Afro-American Presence in American Literature," written in 1988 shortly after completing her novel *Beloved*, Toni Morrison demonstrates how issues of race and representation intersect; she ascribes to race the very quality of unrepresentability that we have seen to be the hallmark of the Kantian sublime. According to Morrison, "in spite of its implicit and explicit acknowledgment, 'race' is still a virtually unspeakable thing."[1] Suggesting that the "presence" of Afro-American literature within the American canon is itself an "unspeakable thing unspoken," she compares the quest for it to a search for "the ghost in the machine":

> Another [focus on the study of African-American literature] is the examination and re-interpretation of the American canon, the founding nineteenth-century works, for the "unspeakable things unspoken"; for the ways in which the *presence* of Afro-Americans has shaped the choices, the language, the structure—the meaning of so much American literature. A search, in other words, for *the ghost in the machine*. (11; my emphasis)

Afro-American literature is present within American literature as a ghost is within a haunted house. And the search for it, for that which is uncannily both dead and alive, absent and present, is akin to the search for a ghostly presence that, repressed, improperly buried, or ignored, comes back to haunt.[2] "Are there," Morrison asks, "ghosts in the machine? Active but unsummoned presences that can distort the workings of the machine and can also *make* it work?" (13). Morrison's use of the word "ghost" raises the question of color—for how do we envision a *black* ghost?—just as she uses the word "presence" to signify self-contradiction. For the figure of the ghost, which becomes Morrison's metaphor for the "presence" of Afro-American literature within the American literary canon, symbolizes a particular and crucial absence, one that too often remains unheard and unseen.

Morrison invites us to look for this "presence" in contemporary literature that is within or outside the canon, "regardless of its category as mainstream, minority, or what you will," to undertake, in other words, a search for "absences so stressed, so organic, so planned, they call attention to themselves" (11). A ghost represents a very particular kind of "presence," and the pages that follow suggest that the search for "the ghost in the machine"—for "the informing and determining Afro-American presence in traditional American literature" (18)—not only describes Morrison's project in *Beloved* but may also become a commentary upon precisely those aspects of the sublime that Kant finds it necessary to combat.

Playing in the Dark: Whiteness and the Literary Imagination (1992) returns to these issues, for in it Morrison argues that "a dark, abiding, signing Africanist presence" is the unacknowledged other that shapes, if not produces, American identity.[3] Here Morrison examines the strategies through which a certain "knowledge" disowns the African-American presence in American culture and literature by insisting that it has no place:

> For some time now I have been thinking about the validity or vulnerability of a certain set of assumptions conventionally accepted among literary historians and critics and circulated as "knowledge." This knowledge holds that traditional, canonical American literature is free of, unformed and unshaped by the four-hundred-year-old presence of first, Africans and then African-Americans in the United States. It assumes that this presence—which shaped the body politic, the Constitution, and the entire history of the culture—has no significant place or consequence in the origin and development of that culture's literature. Moreover, such knowledge assumes that the characteristics of our na-

tional literature emanate from a particular "Americanness" that is separate from and unaccountable to this presence. (5)

Such "knowledge" also refuses to question matters that Morrison's fiction
and criticism persistently interrogate: the nature of the boundary that
divides absence from presence, container from contained, or black from
white.[4] And, as we shall see, it is this borderline to which the third *Critique*
attests.

In *Playing in the Dark* the very strategies of identity formation we have
seen at work in Kant and some of his recent critics are shown to exist in
the formation of American national and cultural identities. Here Morrison
examines the ways in which "Africanism"—"the fetishizing of color, the
transference of blackness to the power of illicit sexuality, chaos, madness,
impropriety, anarchy, strangeness, and helpless, hapless desire" (80)—has
helped to establish white identity. Procedures familiar to us from the third
Critique elaborate the construction of black and white identities, for in each
case they define identity by what opposes it. Black identity functions as
the obverse of American, or white, identity; according to Morrison,
"American means white" (47) because it provides the background that
allows the foreground to emerge. Indeed, the black figure becomes a con-
venient receptacle for all that needs to be denied. As Morrison puts it:

> Africanism is the vehicle by which the American self itself knows itself
> as not enslaved, but free; not repulsive, but desirable; not helpless, but
> licensed and powerful; not history-less, but historical; not damned, but
> innocent; not a blind accident of evolution, but a progressive fulfill-
> ment of destiny. (52)

The coherence and self-definition of American literature is achieved at the
expense of "a distancing Africanism" (8) in which African people come
to signify "denotative and connotative blackness" (6). And Morrison
likens the darkness of Africanism to a shadow that accompanies and is a
companion to whiteness, a presence that "haunts" American literature,
but from which it is unable to extricate itself (33).[5]

The position of African-American literature within American literature
is thus akin to that of the sublime within the third *Critique*. While in Kant
the sublime is secondary and marginal, an appendage that frames the
"Analytic of the Beautiful" and gives it a border, for Morrison African-
American literature is the repressed body of writing that "helped to form

the distinguishing characteristics of a proto-American literature" (38). The Africanist presence that hovers "at the margins of the literary imagination" (5) replicates the place of the sublime with respect to the beautiful: like Kant's sublime that, relegated to the margins, contests the authority and universality of the beautiful, so African-American literature is at once inside and outside the canon, both its border and its frame. If Africanism is "the quite ornamental vacuum" (11) that provides "the staging ground and arena for the elaboration of the quintessential American identity" (44), its function mirrors that of the Kantian sublime: to contain the fear of boundlessness and primal terror; to give the unnameable a name and thereby defend against it; to aggrandize (or create) identity, but only at the expense of a scapegoated other; and to keep the fear of unrepresentability at bay.

The following pages explore the presence of another sublime, one that does not eradicate alterity but rather seeks to articulate and bear witness to it. Of more than casual interest is an inscription on the temple of Isis, the Egyptian goddess of mourning, that gives Kant an example of the most sublime "thought ever expressed" (185, §49), at the same time that it appears only as a footnote to his text. In the figure of Isis we encounter the combined threat of women and mourning that Plato, and the tradition he inaugurates, genders as feminine, and holds in contempt:

> "So then," I said, "we won't allow those whom we claim we care for and who must themselves become good men to imitate women . . . either a young woman or an older one . . . or one who's caught in the grip of misfortune, mourning and wailing. And we'll be far from needing one who's sick or in love or in labor."[6]

In the third *Critique*, however, that which Plato kept out of the *Republic* returns, if only in the margins. This chapter proposes that Isis embodies those aspects of the sublime Kant excludes, and that *Beloved* enacts the very sublime to which her name attests.

I

The most important sentence in Kant's *Critique of Judgment* occurs in a footnote halfway through the "Analytic of the Sublime." Discussing what he calls an "aesthetic idea," that is, "a presentation of the imagination which prompts much thought, but to which no determinate thought whatsoever, i.e., no [determinate] concept can be adequate" (182, §49), Kant argues that such ideas are unique. They produce an excess of signification: since "no language can express it completely and allow us to grasp it" (182), they "quicken the mind by opening up for it a view into an immense realm of kindred presentations" (183–84). He cites as an example a few lines from a poem by Frederick the Great: "The sun flowed forth, as serenity flows from virtue," and his commentary—that the consciousness of virtue "spreads in the mind a multitude of sublime and calming feelings, and a boundless outlook toward a joyful future" (184–85)—gives rise to this extraordinary footnote: "Perhaps nothing more sublime has ever been said, or a thought ever been expressed more sublimely, than in that inscription above the temple of *Isis* (Mother Nature): 'I am all that is, that was, and that will be, and no mortal has lifted my veil'" (185). The sentence inscribed on Isis' temple functions as an "aesthetic idea" because it gives rise to an impression of limitlessness and occasions "so much thought as can never be comprehended within a determinate concept" (183), thereby producing the impression of unrepresentability Kant defines as the sublime. Even more relevant is the complex web of questions and associations that the footnote engenders. Unraveled, the web may open up a space for, and tell us something instructive about, another version of the Kantian sublime.

Why does Kant make such a significant instance of the sublime only an addendum to the main body of the text? How does the footnote's position dramatize Kant's description of the sublime as itself "a mere appendix" (100, §23) to the primary subject of the third *Critique*, "the Analytic of the Beautiful"? What logic links the sublime both to the question of feminine sexual difference, here personified by the goddess Isis, and to the territory of the belated and excluded, to what arrives and can be symbolized only after the fact? And how does *Beloved* enact just those aspects of the sublime that, in Kant, appear only in the margins?

I respond to these questions by dwelling in some detail upon what may seem to be only an accessory: the identity of the goddess Isis. Her story is emblematic of the sublime, although perhaps not in the way Kant had in mind, for she names an ethic and aesthetic of attachment that resists the economy of detachment he upholds. And if she presents an exemplary, if quite literally marginal, instance of the sublime, it becomes imperative to know at least something about who she was and what her name implies.

II

According to Wallis Budge's *Osiris and the Egyptian Resurrection*, the divine couple Isis and Osiris (sister and brother, and also wife and husband) are not native to Egypt; rather their cult is "of purely African origin and existed long before the Dynastic period in Egypt."[7] Whether or not Budge is correct regarding their homeland, for our purpose what matters is Isis' position as a goddess of burial and mourning and as a protector of the dead. Plutarch, the myth's most influential transmitter (*De Iside et Osiride*, first century A.D.), relates that she is best known for her role in recovering and burying Osiris' body after Seth, his jealous brother, trapped him in a coffin and threw it into the Nile.[8] When Isis heard the news of his death she uttered a lament that became the prototype of all Egyptian lamentations for the dead:

> Come to thy house, thou who hast no foes. O fair youth, come to thy house, that thou mayest see me. I am thy sister, whom thou lovest; thou shalt not part from me. . . . Come to thy sister, come to thy wife, to thy wife, thou whose heart stands still. I am thy sister by the same mother, thou shalt not be far from me. Gods and men have turned their faces toward thee and weep for thee together. . . . I call after thee and weep, so that my cry is heard from heaven, but thou hearest not my voice; yet I am thy sister, whom thou didst love on earth; thou didst love none but me, my brother, my brother.[9]

There follows the story of her wanderings. Disconsolate, Isis travels up and down the banks of the Nile until she finds the coffin containing Osiris' body and returns it to their son Horus for proper burial. But Seth finds the coffin, tears the body into fourteen pieces, and throws them back into the Nile. Only Isis is able to recover the dismembered body: sailing among the marshes she finds and buries the missing fragments, leaving sepulchers to mark their place. Plutarch tells us that there is only one part of Osiris' body that Isis cannot find: his male member. She therefore makes a replica to take its place and consecrates it as holy. Isis replaces the member that is irretrievably lost with its simulacrum and thereby symbolizes an attachment that resists death. She does not try to resurrect the body or put the scattered pieces back together, but rather memorializes them through the ritual of burial. To know where a beloved body lies is perhaps one condition of its remembrance.[10]

Not only is Isis learned in the arts of mourning; she is also a mistress of signs and symbols, and what interests me is the complexity of the relation between them. Her name and the legends surrounding it attest to connections between mourning and naming. According to Robert Graves, Isis is named for her ability to mourn Osiris, for "Isis" derives from an onomatopoeic Asian word, *Ish-ish*, meaning "she who weeps."[11] But she is also known as the one "who is mighty with words" and "whose words maketh the dead live."[12] Isidore, archbishop of Seville (ca. 600–636 A.D.), believes that Isis brought the Egyptians their alphabet: "As for the Egyptian alphabet, Queen Isis, daughter of King Inachus, coming from Greece to Egypt brought them [*sic*] with her and gave them to the Egyptians."[13] And Budge relates that among the Egyptians of the Middle and New Empires, Isis was regarded as a great magician, for she knew how to weave spells and possessed knowledge of the secret and hidden names of all the gods. Papyri contain frequent allusions to her magical powers and relate in great detail how Isis gained possession of the secret name of Ra, the sun god, thereby acquiring for herself the power of the gods.[14] The goddess whose love for her husband-brother is so great that her lamentations do not cease until she finds and buries the fragments of his body also has an intimate relation to language; she who builds monuments to mark the sites of loss also knows how to call the gods by name. We will want to explore the nature of the alliance between the act of mourning and that of storytelling, between the ability to bury the dead and to keep them alive in symbolic form.

If, as Kant would have it, Isis' inscription gives rise to thoughts of the ineffable, her story, of which he was apparently unaware, attests to a capacity for limitless attachment even in the face of traumatic loss. As trauma does, the sublime occasions a crisis of representation such that what is lost can never be found whole or in one place. It is recoverable only as a series of disconnected fragments—a search for the pieces of a dis-membered or, in Morrison's words, "disremembered" body. Isis' quest for Osiris' body stages the scene of writing as a search for what language witnesses but cannot say.

Isis mourns and buries Osiris, but no one mourns for her. Her in-scription lies unnoticed in a note at the bottom of Kant's page, just as the sublime it epitomizes is buried within the third *Critique*. And what returns as the signifier of something missing also appears in belated form: as a footnote, in the case of Isis, and as "a mere appendix" in that of the sublime. Isis' position within the third *Critique*—appearing in the margins, as a footnote or afterthought—is a metaphor for not only the sublime's relation to the beautiful, but for the third *Critique*'s relation to its two predecessors. As we shall see, it marks an abyss that even Kant cannot bridge.

For Kant the aesthetic is the third term that will resolve the breach between nature and freedom, or theoretical understanding and practical reason, that was set up by the first two *Critiques*. Nature appears on the basis of the *Critique of Pure Reason* as a world of phenomena strictly subject to our forms of intuition (in space and time) and to our categories of understanding (including cause and effect). But the moral world that is the subject of the *Critique of Practical Reason* is one that presupposes the freedom of the rational agent. The architectonic goal of the *Critique of Judgment* is to exhibit the possibility that we do in some sense live in one world where freedom can be actual within the natural. If there is a ground for our aesthetic judgments, in which we suppose that the experienced world is constituted as if freedom were expressing itself in what we perceive as natural beauty, then we have some justification for thinking (if not knowing) that the realms of freedom and nature are compatible. Kant's aim in the third *Critique* is to provide an absolute foundation for judgments of taste, to supply the a priori principle through which aesthetic judgments can claim universal validity. If aesthetic judgments rest on a ground that is independent of experience, they not only become the objects of a necessary "liking" but also provide a missing link, supply "the concept that mediates between the concepts of nature and the concept of freedom" (36). Charged with bridging "the great gulf [*Kluft*] that separates the supersensible from appearances" (35), aesthetic judgments have a specifically reparative function: their task is to make it possible "to throw a bridge from one domain to another" (36).

But, not surprisingly, the bridge doesn't quite work. Just as the third *Critique* supplements the lack opened by the first two *Critiques*, so the "Analytic of the Sublime" supplements the strangely inadequate theory of the beautiful, which cannot explain the complex form of "negative pleasure," or mixture of pain and pleasure, that distinguishes the sublime. Isis' footnote, then, testifies to something excluded from the "Analytic of the Sublime." Kant relegates Isis to a footnote and in doing so he shows what must be barred from the *Critique of Judgment*: an ethics and aesthetics of attachment rather than detachment. This exclusion operates in the same way that the sublime frames and supplements the "Analytic of the Beautiful," displacing the emotions from the realm of beauty; the third *Critique* itself attempts to repair the breach between the two preceding it. Yet every attempt to bridge the gap produces more gaps to be bridged, just as the attempt to excise what has been repressed only gives rise to more of it. (We will return to bridges in connection with *Beloved*).

If, in the sublime, borders disappear and the subject is overwhelmed by a magnitude she can neither control nor represent, the notion of *parerga* (ornaments or frames) haunts discussion of the sublime and even fore-shadows its appearance.[15] *Parerga* are said to distinguish those elements that are internal to the work of art; their use for Kant is to lend credence to the view that only an object's formal properties may contribute to judg-ments of taste. His definition of *parerga*—"what does not belong to the whole presentation of the object as an intrinsic constituent, but [is] only an extrinsic addition, does indeed increase our taste's liking, and yet it does so only by its form, as in the case of picture frames, or drapery on statues, or colonnades around magnificent buildings" (72, §14)—occurs just be-fore he mentions the sublime for the first time, and "emotion [*Ruhrung*]" is the intermediary term that links them. Immediately after his remark about *parerga* Kant describes emotion as "a momentary inhibition of the vital force followed by a stronger outpouring of it," adding that it "does not belong to beauty at all" (72).

Kant's definitions of emotion and the sublime are almost interchange-able. In the first section of the "Analytic of the Sublime" he describes the sublime as a pleasure that is "produced by the feeling of a momentary inhibition of the vital forces followed immediately by an outpouring of them that is all the stronger" and remarks, "hence it [the sublime] is an emotion" (98, §23). Emotion and the sublime are alike in that both entail a rapid alternation between extremes of feeling, a moment of inhibition that leads to an intense outburst of the "vital force," and neither allows detachment. Like pent-up water rushing from a dam, this "outflow" bursts boundaries; it cannot be bordered. But if we have begun to account for the connection between emotion and sublimity, we have yet to explain how they are related to the *parergon*.

To respond to this question it is necessary to look a bit more closely at paragraph 14, in which Kant enumerates the conditions that allow "pure [*rein*] judgments of taste," that is, those judgments whose "uniformity [is] undisturbed and uninterrupted by any alien sensation [*fremdartige Emp-findung*]." (Sensations of color, for example, can be regarded as beautiful only insofar as they are "pure"; "mixed colors do not enjoy this privilege, precisely because, since they are not simple, we lack a standard for judging whether we should call them pure or impure" [71].)[16] Since "sensation [*Empfindung*]" has nothing to do with determining "a pure judgment of taste" (72), qualities such as "charm [*Reiz*]" and "emotion" do not belong in the beautiful. In order to produce "a pure judgment of taste," Kant is required to show that materiality is irrelevant to the aesthetic experience described in the "Analytic of the Beautiful." Because nothing will be allowed to disturb the purely formal beauty of the work of art, Kant feels the necessity to excise emotion, and with it, the sublime. Kant mentions the sublime in the last sentence of the "Analytic of the Beautiful," asserting that it has no place in the beautiful and requires its own standard of judgment: "But sublimity (with which the feeling of emotion is connected [*verbunden*]) requires a different standard of judging from the one that taste uses as a basis. Hence a pure judgment of taste has as its determining basis neither charm nor emotion, in other words, no sensation which is [merely] the matter of an aesthetic judgment" (72). My point is not that the sublime is an emotion, but that Kant describes them in the same terms. The qualities that define emotion also define the sublime and both need to be ejected not only from our aesthetic judgments of the beautiful, but from the "Analytic of the Beautiful" itself. Both involve an experience of attachment that threatens aesthetic judgments and with them the working of Kant's aesthetic. The "Analytic of the Sublime" thus contains everything the "Analytic of the Beautiful" cannot admit and must reject. Whatever has no place in the beautiful—emotion, charm, and the sublime itself—must be relegated to the margins and treated in an aftermath that Kant describes as "a mere appendix" to the main body of the work.

If a judgment of taste is "pure only insofar as no merely empirical liking is mingled in with the basis that determines it" (69), we must distinguish the "pure" from the "empirical," divide the thing itself from what is merely extrinsic to it, and discern what in the art work is foreign or impure. Aesthetic judgment presumes a knowledge of the difference between inside and outside, form and matter, that Kant takes for granted. But, as Derrida so astutely observes in *The Truth in Painting*, it requires a distinction between container and contained, extrinsic and intrinsic, or emotion and detachment, that the notion of *parerga* calls into question.[17] Because a *parergon* is both inside and outside the work of art it belongs to the work by not belonging to it, and is thus neither intrinsic nor extrinsic to that which it seems to adorn. By disclosing the presence of the outside within the inside, the *parergon* undermines the possibility of universally valid judgments of taste, which depend upon keeping the difference between them intact. It thereby cancels the success of Kant's aesthetic project.

Kant's Isis, whose inscription provides an example of the most sublime thought ever expressed, also provides a perfect example of a *parergon*. Placed in the margins, the footnote defines the main body of the text by marking its difference from it. The note, however, is not simply adjacent to and outside the text proper, for it is also part of and intrinsic to it. The footnote seems to be both subordinate to the text, a *mere* supplement to it, and also a *necessary* supplement. Its position at the bottom of the page suggests the former, but the fact that it deals with what Kant thinks is probably the most sublime thought ever expressed suggests the latter. Like Morrison's view of the Africanist presence within American culture, the *parergon*, which supposedly happens after the fact, is the "alien sensation" (71, §14) that enhances, if not produces, the identity of that to which it is subordinate. And the footnote's subject matter also exemplifies its *parergonal* status. The inscription (but isn't an inscription itself a *parergon?*) that adorns Isis' temple attests to a veil no mortal can lift—and veils, like footnotes, are supposedly extrinsic, an accessory or ornament to the body they are said merely to cover. What, however, is the basis for deciding where, or if, the veil ends and the body inside it begins? For the veil is not merely extrinsic to the goddess but is an integral and nondetachable part of her representation, and rather than illustrate the difference between inside and outside, primary and secondary, or disinterest and emotion, it occupies the very point at which the differences between them dissolve.

What is true of the *parergon* is also the case for the sublime: both name that moment within Kant's system at which the distinctions that are essential to judgments of taste break down. And the *parergon*, whose position marks it as adjacent to or outside the work of art, is also a metaphor for the sublime that, as a "mere appendix to the beautiful," functions as a supplement. Wherever they appear we find the attempt to fill in for something missing, a gulf that cannot be bridged, a place where aesthetic judgments threaten to collapse. The *parergon* reveals at the level of structure what emotion and the sublime reveal at the level of affect and theme: the complexity of the connection between the two terms of any opposition, be they form and content, intrinsic and extrinsic, or "pure" and "alien." Just as the *parergon* demonstrates the impossibility of discerning where the "inside" begins and the "outside" ends, so the sublime, like emotion, demonstrates the inextricability of borders. Hence it testifies to what Isis' story affirms: the impossibility of detachment, and to what Morrison in *Beloved* calls "the join."

Two very different responses to loss are at issue here. A vocabulary of emotion and attachment, of bondage and boundarylessness, attends that of the sublime; the beautiful brings with it a wish for disinterest, independence, and autonomy. The beautiful conveys a notion of mourning as detachability, of losses effaced and covered up. The sublime, on the other hand, is the place where boundaries come apart and boundarylessness is at issue. It is the "ghost in the machine" that disturbs Kant's aesthetic—or anaesthetic—project, for the sublime not only usurps the priority of the beautiful but exposes the fragility of its claim to totality and disinterestedness. If for Kant aesthetic judgment requires an absolute lack of interest in the existence of the work of art (taste, he tells us, "is the ability to judge an object, or a way of presenting it, by means of a liking or disliking *devoid of all interest*" (53, §5) and if, as Derrida reminds us, a "disinterested attitude is the essence of aesthetic experience," the sublime marks the failure of any judgment of taste based upon an aesthetic of detachment.[18]

And it indicates a crucial absence. As "the concretization of a missing presence, the sign of what is there by not being there," the sublime is like a ghost in that it marks what has been excluded from the main body of the work and returns in an attempt to make up for its loss.[19] Jacques Lacan reminds us of the commonly held belief that ghosts appear "when someone's departure from this life has not been accompanied by the rites that it calls for."[20] They come back to keep us in touch with a history we can neither remember nor forget, with a past that refuses to die. And can be laid to rest only when the labor of mourning begins to transmit the silence they signify into speech. If the sublime appears to mark a trauma that exceeds language, it simultaneously impels and disables symbolization, and its effect is that we can never relinquish the attempt to find words for some of the unspeakable things that remain unspoken.

III

Kant loves Isis for her una*vail*ability. She is the totality of all that was, is, and will be: no one can lift her veil and that is what makes her sublime. Isis appears (veiled) a second time in Kant's writing. In "On a Newly

Emerged Noble Tone in Philosophy" (1796), a polemic against romantic philosophers of feeling, he describes the veiled goddess as "the inner moral law in its inviolable majesty," and while Kant says that both he and the romantics (or "mystagogues") must "bend our knees" before her, he is suspicious of their claims to immediacy and of the danger that representation in images will displace philosophical principles.[21] It might appear that these two manifestations of Isis present her under very different aspects, or with more than one veil. In the note to the *Critique* she becomes "Mother Nature" and stands for the ultimate truth of things, while in the later essay she personifies the moral law. If Kant were an ultimately dualistic philosopher we might wonder how she could play both roles. Yet as the *Critique of Judgment* makes clear, he wants to bridge the apparent gap between cognitive and moral domains. Isis can figure as an aesthetic idea for the truth of nature, for the moral law, or finally, for the very tentative connection between them that Kant wants to effect.

Derrida's parodic response to Kant's essay "Of an Apocalyptic Tone Recently Adopted in Philosophy" (1983) shows in part how Isis functions there. For although in *The Truth in Painting* Derrida never comments upon Isis' appearance in the third *Critique*—an extremely interesting omission given her *parergonal* position within the text and the centrality of this concept to Derrida's reading of it—in "An Apocalyptic Tone" he remarks in some detail upon "the intrigue of a certain veil of Isis."[22] Derrida understands Isis exclusively as a "matter of the veil and of castration" (15) and even appears to link murder, castration, and femininity: he calls Isis "the universal principle of femininity and murderess of Osiris" (19). "Faced with Isis," he says, "I am going to expose myself to taking (and tying) up again with the threads of this intrigue and with the treatment of castration" (15).[23] Faced with Isis, Derrida looks the other way.

In Kant's "On a Newly Emerged Tone," as in Derrida's "Apocalyptic Tone," Isis has neither existence nor interest apart from her veil. This veil plays a surprisingly large role in Kant's flirtation with Isis, given that he explicitly includes "drapery on statues" under the category of *parerga* (72, §14). In the case of Isis Kant would seem to insist, contrary to his more explicit aesthetics, that the *parergon* or frame cannot be eliminated from the figure or work. Indeed, Kant's criticism of the romantic philosopher of his day, whom he calls the "philosopher of intuition" (284) or "philosopher of vision" (285), is elaborated in terms of the latter's rapport with the veiled goddess. "The term 'Philosophy,'" Kant tells us, has "lost its

first meaning as a 'Scientific Wisdom of Life'" and "now implies the
revelation of a mystery" (283). The "Philosopher by Inspiration" (283)
refuses mediation and seeks direct contact with what the true philosophers—"those 'schoolmen' who proceed slowly and cautiously through
criticism to knowledge" (284)—know to avoid. Believing himself in
immediate and intuitive relation with the mystery, the romanticist tries
to attain an intimate rapport with the goddess without the aid of con-
scientious, diligent labor. In the futile attempt to see directly into the
unseeable, he hopes "to come so near to the goddess Wisdom that [he]
can hear the rustling [*Rauschen*] of her garment" (285). For although "the
Platonic sentimentalist . . . 'cannot remove the veil of Isis, [he tries] to
make it so thin [*so dunne*] that one can divine the goddess beneath it' [*unter
ihm*]. How thin? Presumably still dense enough to make of that *phantom*
[*Gespenst*] whatever one likes" (285; emphasis mine).

The true philosopher, however, should place the law above and beyond personification, even that represented by the veiled goddess; recognize the difference between the moral law and the mystery of vision
and contact; and realize that, as Derrida says, "the moral law never gives
itself to be seen or touched" (13). Kant concludes: "the veiled goddess
before whom both of us bend our knees is the inner moral law in its
inviolable majesty. What we ought to do remains the same. Only: to
reduce the moral law to logical conceptions is the philosophical procedure, to personify it in a veiled Isis is an aesthetic representation" (285).
But Kant himself comes close to deviating from properly "philosophical
procedure" through recourse to what he says distinguishes the "philosopher of intuition" from the "schoolmen": he personifies the sublime
moral law (which may itself be the veiled truth of nature) as a veiled
goddess.

Isis and her inscription are sublime because they manifest a certain
reserve and distance: because she is past, present, and future, no one can
lift her veil, that is, directly apprehend the totality she represents. Kant's
Isis is impenetrable, and therein lies her power. She is herself the enigma
she exhibits and she ensures the place of the unknowable by placing a
frame around it, thereby giving its supposed inaccessibility limit and
definition. But, as we have seen, Isis' veil raises the same questions that
haunt the *parergon* and the sublime: is there a "real" ghost behind the veil
or sheet that adorns it? Is the ghost identical with the veil that seems to
conceal it; does anything lie beneath the veil? And what if Isis, exemplar

of the sublime, were indeed a ghost? Would the anonymous spectator really be able "to make of that phantom whatever one likes?" Kant and Derrida both assure us that it is dangerous, if not in fact a serious error, to get near enough to find out, that we should keep a proper distance and leave the veil intact.

Like Kant's notion of Isis, ghosts are (as Marjorie Garber reminds us) "often veiled, sheeted, and shadowy in form . . . a cultural marker of absence, a reminder of loss," and they appear in the place where they have not been acknowledged or admitted. Ghosts "always come back, but they are always already belated when they come—it is only when they return, *re-venant*, that they are ghosts, and carry the authority of their own belatedness."[24] For example, in the numbers of a certain address: 124 Bluestone Road, the house in which *Beloved* takes place and for which, as for the third *Critique*, we sense a third term it cannot possess.[25] For the number three simultaneously names what the house on Bluestone Road does not contain and signifies the return of that which renders detachment impossible. It also announces that, since there are definitely a lot more than two of us now, the ghost story can begin. Again.

IV

Written while *Beloved* was nearing completion, Morrison's "Site of Memory" has something very different to tell us about the subject of veils, one that has nothing to do with notions of lack and castration or the question of veiled or unveiled truth. It is concerned not with the unspeakably good, but with the unutterably inhuman: The "veil" to which Morrison refers calls attention to those aspects of the slaves' experiences that their writing could not address. Morrison points out that eighteenth- and nineteenth-century slave narratives do not describe the most unspeakable aspects of their history. And it is striking that the need to appear disinterested and objective, that is, to conform to a Kantian aesthetic, informs that omission. Morrison explains:

> American slaves' autobiographical narratives were frequently scorned as "biased," "inflammatory," and "improbable." These attacks are particularly difficult to understand in view of the fact that it was extremely important for the writers to appear as objective as possible—not to offend the reader by being too angry, or by showing too much outrage, or by calling the reader names. As recently as 1966, Paul Edwards, who

edited and abridged Equiano's story, praises the narrative for its refusal to be "inflammatory."[26]

Although the slaves' narratives had ample reason to maintain Kantian aesthetic standards, their motivation had perhaps more to do with survival than with the desire to adhere to established criteria of taste. Because black writers "knew that their readers were the people who could make a difference in terminating slavery," a great deal depended on "using their own lives to expose the horrors of slavery" (107), on doing so in a way that, as Edwards writes of Equiano, "puts no emotional pressure on the reader other than that which the situation itself contains" (106). And Morrison cites an 1836 review of Charles Bell's *Life and Adventures of a Fugitive Slave* that celebrates the narrative precisely for its objectivity: "We rejoice in the book the more, because it is not a partisan work . . . it broaches no theory in regard to [slavery], nor proposes any mode or time of emancipation" (106). Morrison emphasizes that slaves in their writing perforce not only demonstrated their ability to reason but also described their experiences while maintaining the very standards of taste Kant advocates in the third *Critique*. Even while they wrote of events that erode the possibility of trust in human reason and judgment, good taste required them to uphold it.

Although the slaves wrote thoughtfully and in great detail about their enslavement, Morrison hears the silence that lies at the heart of their narratives. The "monstrous features" of slavery, the most traumatic aspects of their experiences, went unwritten and unsaid. As in Kant, emotion needed to be excised, or in this case, kept under wraps. For Morrison, the narratives exhibit a profound reticence, a need to draw a veil over "proceedings too terrible to relate":

> Whatever the level of eloquence or the form, popular taste discouraged the writers from dwelling too long or too carefully on the more sordid details of their experience. . . . Over and over, the writers pull the narratives up short with a phrase such as, "But let us *drop a veil* over these proceedings too terrible to relate." In shaping the experience to make it palatable to those who were in a position to alleviate it, they were silent about many things, and they "forgot" many other things. There was a careful selection of the instances that they would record and a careful rendering of those that they chose to describe. Lydia Maria Child identified the problem in her introduction to "Linda Brent's" tale of sexual abuse: "I am well aware that many will accuse me of in-

decorum for presenting these pages to the public; for the experiences of this intelligent and much-injured woman belong to a class which some call delicate subjects, and others indelicate. This peculiar phase of Slavery has generally *been kept veiled*; but the public ought to be made acquainted with its monstrous features, and *I am willing to take the responsibility of presenting them with the veil drawn* [aside]."

But most importantly—at least for me—there was no mention of their interior life. (109–10; my emphasis)

A veil had to be drawn over tales of monstrous, often overtly sexual abuse, as if survival depended upon keeping a veil, however fragile, between what could and could not be said. Thus what Morrison finds missing from the narratives is any trace of the slaves' "interior life." The monstrous and the evil need to be spoken, somehow, but they cannot be approached directly, any more than Kant's Isis can become present without an intermediary. The sublime re-emerges in this context through the metaphor of the veil, but here it is a border that overflows, exceeds, and refuses to stay within bounds. Like a sepulcher, it marks the place of traumas that can be symbolized only after the fact. For what remains veiled in one era comes back, as a ghost, to haunt us in another.

Morrison's sublime is not, like Kant's and Derrida's as well, conditioned and maintained by reserve, distance, or the need to keep the veil intact but refers instead to the other Isis, to the goddess of mourning that Kant's Isis veils. Here, in Lyotard's phrase, writing devotes itself "to marking on its body the 'presence' of that which has not left a mark."[27] Morrison is also willing to find the traces and testify to the loss of a beloved body, however mutilated. "For me," she says, "a writer in the last quarter of the twentieth century, not much more than a hundred years after Emancipation, a writer who is black and a woman . . . my job becomes how to rip that veil drawn over 'proceedings too terrible to relate'" (110). Ripping aside the veil does not reinstate the difference between "interior" and "exterior," but rather shows their interrelation, for what is "within," "the unwritten interior life of these people," cannot be separated from what is "without," those collective memories Morrison calls "the subsoil of my work" (111). In this case, the work of unveiling discloses the intensity of the connection that binds them. Like Lydia Maria Child, Morrison assumes the responsibility for encountering and trying to find words for "proceedings too terrible to relate." And it is this act of witnessing—in which language undertakes the work of mourning that an earlier epoch had left undone and begins, in Morrison's words, to "properly [and] artistically" bury the "unburied, or at least unceremoniously buried"—to which *Beloved* attests.[28]

V

So the beginning of this was a woman who had not been able to come back from burying the dead. Unlike Hurston's protagonist Janie Woods, who at the beginning of *Their Eyes Were Watching God* has just returned from burying her husband, at the beginning of *Beloved* Sethe Suggs has not yet laid to rest her infant daughter.[29] Her body lies beneath a headstone on which the word "Beloved" is engraved—because Sethe had no money she paid with her body for the headstone; the engraver said "You got ten minutes I'll do it for free" (one word was all he had time for)—and the grave is still open.[30] If to leave unburied is, as Morrison suggests, to be buried "unceremoniously," without the proper rituals and observances, in *Beloved* writing becomes a funeral rite in which Morrison performs the labor of mourning that Isis enacts.

"Sixty Million / and more." A written number, with words below it that attest to that number's incalculability, appears on *Beloved*'s dedication page. Morrison begins by confronting the reader with a phrase that signifies excess: the number of slaves who died as a result of the Middle Passage. *Beloved* is dedicated to "more," to an unquantifiable surplus, a number that cannot be known. Asked in an interview in *Time* magazine if the number sixty million had been "proved historically," Morrison emphasizes the historian's uncertainty regarding the exact figure:

> Some historians told me 200 million died. The smallest number I got from anybody was 60 million. There were travel accounts of people who were in the Congo—that's a wide river—saying "we could not get the boat through the river, it was choked with bodies." That's like a logjam. A lot of people died. Half of them died in those ships. . . . I thought this has got to be the least read of all the books I'd written because it is about something that the characters don't want to remember, I don't want to remember, black people don't want to remember, white people don't want to remember. I mean it's national amnesia.[31]

As Mae G. Henderson points out, Morrison's "accomplishment in this novel is precisely *not* to allow for the continuation of a 'national amnesia' regarding this chapter in America's history."[32] Dedicated to the unnamed dead, the phrase "sixty million / and more" presents itself as an epitaph on a nonexistent tombstone, commemorating the incalculability of black suffering and loss. At the heart of the novel lies a project familiar to us from discussions of the sublime: the process of translating and figuring events that exceed our frame of reference, and the need to attest to emotions that can be experienced only after the fact of their occurrence. Morrison's "and more" both denotes the impossibility of knowing just how many died as a result of slavery and refers to the surplus of "dead negroes' grief" (5) that, in part, is the subject of the novel. At issue is an aesthetics of the incalculable.

"124 was spiteful. Full of a baby's venom" (1). *Beloved* begins with a sentence that is not one. As Morrison observes in "Unspeakable Things Unspoken," the novel's second sentence "is a phrase that properly, grammatically belongs as a dependent clause with the first" (32). The novel commences by insisting upon a disconnection between phrases that should be joined. Putting a period in the place of a comma, Morrison activates a gap that she refuses to fill. Rather than mark a point of entry that would secure the differences between the work's lobby and its main body, the house and those it contains, Morrison's opening sentences are meant to confront "the reader with what must be immediately incomprehensible" (32). The sentences do to the reader what the house does to those who seek to inhabit it: just as the narrative frame is meant to be "incomprehensible," so Sethe and Denver live in a house that, disrupted by "a baby's venom," is full of an incomprehensible presence it cannot contain. In each case the frame does not secure differences but rather calls into question the mere possibility of containment.

In her commentary upon *Beloved*'s first sentences in "Unspeakable Things Unspoken," Morrison compares the house into which the reader is propelled to the body of a slave ship. We are meant to confront something that lies beyond our comprehension: the suffering of those who were "thrown into an environment completely foreign":

The reader is snatched, yanked . . . and I want it as the first stroke of the shared experience that might be possible between the reader and the novel's population. Snatched just as the slaves were from one place to another, from any place to another, without preparation and without defense. No lobby, no door, no entrance—a gangplank, perhaps (but a very short one). And the house into which this snatching—this kidnapping—propels one, changes from spiteful to loud to quiet, as the

sounds of the body of the ship itself may have changed. . . . Here I
wanted the compelling confusion of being there as they (the characters)
are; suddenly, without comfort or succor from the "author," with only
imagination, intelligence, and necessity available for the journey. (32–
33)

Morrison's wager is on the possibility of a "shared experience" between
the reader and the "novel's population," the recently freed slaves who
live in and around 124. But if, like Kant, she links the experience of pain
to a certain kind of aesthetic pleasure, unlike Kant she ensures the reader's emotional involvement in what she reads. Rather than maintain
distance from personal or political trauma, the novel from the outset
insists upon our proximity to it. While we are "preoccupied with the
nature of the incredible spirit world," Morrison supplies us with "a
controlled diet of the incredible political world" (32), thereby calling
attention to the intricacy of their connection. Rather than detach ourselves from a chapter of our history so horrendous as to be "unspeakable," Morrison insists that we encounter it. But how? The question
Beloved addresses is the same as that which motivates the discourse of the
sublime: how do we symbolize events that are defined by their very
unrepresentability?

VI

It is fundamental that the novel is set in Cincinnati in 1873 and takes place
after the Civil War, during the period of its alleged reconstruction.[33] It
is not by chance that the story of what took place in "the interior life"
of the slaves can be told only in its aftermath, nor is it by chance that a
novel that treats events that, as Morrison says, "no one wants to remember" could begin to be written only more than one hundred years after
their occurrence. Certain stories can be remembered only after the fact.
As Dori Laub remarks of Holocaust testimonies: "these testimonials—
even if they were engendered during the event—become receivable only
today . . . it is only now, *belatedly*, that the event begins to be historically
grasped and seen." Traumatic events create what Laub describes as an
"historical gap" in the collective witness.[34] And Cathy Caruth points
out, "in trauma the greatest confrontation with reality may also occur as
an absolute numbing to it, [so] that immediacy, paradoxically enough,
may take the form of belatedness": thus at the beginning of *Beloved* its

protagonists, years after their escape from slavery, are still numb from its effects.[35] They are haunted by an excess of the past that can be neither forgotten nor clearly articulated in memory. There is no way for them to tell the "story" of events that not only have been omitted from history but that, owing to their traumatic nature, may be too terrible to be told; and what is crucial to the novel's narrative structure and plot is the way that it deals with that which lies beyond the threshold of representability.

The phenomenon of what is currently known as "post-traumatic stress disorder" was first studied after World War I.[36] Faced with the onset of "war neuroses" in returning soldiers, in 1920 Freud defined trauma as "excitations from outside which are powerful enough to break through the protective shield," and remarked upon the compulsive reliving of the traumatic experience in the form of a memory that returns, often in the form of repetitive nightmares or flashbacks, against the victim's will:

> [People] think the fact that the traumatic experience is forcing itself upon the patient is a proof of the strength of the experience: the patient is, one might say, fixated to his trauma. . . . I am not aware, however, that patients suffering from traumatic neuroses are much occupied in their waking lives with memories of their accident. Perhaps they are more concerned with not thinking about it.[37]

As in Lyotard's famous remarks about the sublime, trauma also attests to the fact that something unpresentable exists.[38] At the beginning of the novel, 124 is consumed by a history that it cannot contain. The house is "so full of strong feeling" and "spite" that "there was no room for any other thing or body" (39), and Sethe's main concern—that of "keeping the past at bay" and protecting Denver "from the past that was still waiting for her" (42)—gives weight to Freud's conviction that the chief activity of trauma victims lies in "not thinking about it." The novel commences by linking "the unspeakable" to a past of such immeasurable horror that it cannot pass away: "every mention of her past life hurt. Everything in it was painful or lost. She and Baby Suggs had agreed without saying so that it was unspeakable" (58).

If the sublime refers to a magnitude that leaks out of any container that would "keep it at bay," so in *Beloved* the past shatters narrative and characterological frames; it bursts into the present and plunges protagonist

and reader backwards, preventing a straightforward, chronological se-
quence of events. Unwanted memories of "unspeakable" events surge
involuntarily into Sethe's consciousness. Living in a house constantly
disrupted by the presence of the past, Sethe is also haunted by what she
calls "rememory": spontaneous re-experience of occurrences so traumatic
she can neither forget nor escape their effects. "Past errors" take "possession of the present" (256), and what returns like a ghost is history itself.
Sethe tells Denver:

> Some things go. Pass on. Some things just stay. . . . It's when you
> bump into a rememory that belongs to somebody else. Where I was
> before I came here, that place is real. It's never going away. Even if the
> whole farm—every tree and grass blade of it dies. The picture is still
> there and what's more, if you go there—you who never was there—if
> you go there and stand in the place where it was, it will happen again;
> it will be there for you, waiting for you. (35–36)

The past is permanently inscribed in the present and it appears suddenly,
in unexpected times and places. Denver replies: "If it's still there, waiting,
that must mean that nothing ever dies." And Sethe answers: "Nothing
ever does" (36). Like Kant's sublime, in which an encounter with sheer
magnitude shatters ordinary perceptions of space and time, the traumatic
event also disrupts temporal boundaries. Because the past is always present,
there is no future: the novel's protagonists are possessed by a past so
catastrophic they can neither articulate its effects nor forget its scars. In this
case, what cannot be remembered or forgotten is the history of a specific
people, the untold tale of a tribe.

If, as Freud said, hysterics "suffer from reminiscences," trauma victims
suffer from flashbacks.[39] The symptoms of post-traumatic stress disorder
differ from those of neurosis in that they do not involve repression or
distortion. Rather, against the wishes of those it possesses, the trauma
reappears in all its literality. According to the *Diagnostic and Statistical
Manual of Mental Disorders*, traumatic events are "persistently re-experi-
enced" in the form of "recurrent distressing dreams of the event," as
"recurrent and intrusive distressing recollections of the event," and/or as
"feeling as if the traumatic event were recurring."[40] Laub points out that
trauma survivors live "with an event that could not and did not proceed
through to its completion, has no ending, attained no closure, and therefore, as far as its survivors are concerned, continues into the present and

is current in every respect" (69). Like the symptom of a trauma, Sethe's "rememory" is always present. In the following scene, perceptions of the present trigger flashbacks from the past:

> She might be hurrying across a field, running practically, to get to the pump quickly and rinse the chamomile sap from her legs. Nothing else would be in her mind. . . . And then sopping the chamomile away with pump water and rags, her mind fixed on getting every last bit of sap off . . . then something. The splash of water, the sight of her shoes and stockings awry on the path where she had flung them; or Here Boy lapping in the puddle near her feet, and suddenly there was Sweet Home rolling, rolling, rolling out before her eyes, and although there was not a leaf in that farm that did not make her want to scream, it rolled itself out before her in shameless beauty. It never looked as terrible as it was and it made her wonder if hell was a pretty place too. (6)

We will return to the question of hell's aesthetic status. For the moment, it is important to explore the effects of trauma upon symbolic processes. Like the sublime, which is defined by its capacity to overwhelm the subject and entails an experience for which there is no adequate form of presentation, trauma produces, in Robert Jay Lifton's phrase, "an impairment in the symbolization process itself."[41]

After the First World War, Freud began to study war's psychological consequences. Responding to the same event and the failure of narrative that emerged from it, Walter Benjamin's "Storyteller" describes its impact upon speech. He observes that men returned from battle unable to speak about their experiences: "with the [First] World War a process began to become apparent which has not halted since then. Was it not noticeable by the end of the war that men returned from the battlefield grown silent—not richer, but poorer in communicable experience?"[42] Some experiences instill silence, not speech, and the legacy of traumatic events is to render problematic the possibility of their narration. Laub points out that "massive trauma precludes its registration; the observing and recording mechanisms of the human mind are temporarily knocked out, malfunction" (57), and emphasizes that the psychic numbing that accompanies trauma is actually required to survive the experience. Trauma has the capacity to obliterate its own witness, for survival depends, at least in part, upon absenting oneself from the event even as one experiences it. The representation of trauma thus raises at the level of history the issue raised in aesthetics by the sublime: that of symbolizing an event whose magnitude impedes its very symbolization. The traumatic events to which *Beloved* bears witness are defined by the fact that they require a particular kind of narration that will find a way to metabolize the repression of a terrible event. Sethe can no more simply "tell her story" than Morrison can represent the largely "unspeakable and unspoken" events of slavery. But how can we tell not only a story "no one wants to remember," but one that "nobody thinks about" and "nobody knows"?[43]

The problem at the heart of the novel is knowing how to read the traces of a people whose death left no trace, who, "disremembered and unaccounted for" (274), left no story to be told. In an interview entitled "In The Realm of Responsibility," Morrison uses the phrase "nobody knows" while referring to the silence that surrounds the Middle Passage:

> Nobody knows their names, and nobody thinks about them. In addition to that, they never survived in the lore; there are no songs or dances or tales of these people. The people who arrived—there is lore about them. But nothing survives about . . . that.[44]

Like Benjamin, she emphasizes that "nothing survives" simply because survival depends upon not telling about, or dwelling upon, this event:

> I suspect the reason [that nothing survives] is that it was not possible to survive on certain levels and dwell on it. People who did dwell on it, it probably killed them, and the people who did not dwell on it probably went forward. I think Afro-Americans in rushing away from slavery, which was important to do—it meant rushing out of bondage into freedom—also rushed away from the slaves because it was painful to dwell there, and they may have abandoned some responsibilities in so doing. It was a double-edged sword, if you understand me. There is a necessity for remembering the horror, but of course there's a necessity for remembering it in a manner in which it can be digested, in a manner in which the memory is not destructive. The act of writing the book, in a way, is a way of confronting it and making it possible to remember. (5)

The story of the slaves who died in the Middle Passage is inaccessible not only because the event left no survivors, but because the experience of trauma entails a crisis in representation: as in the sublime, we encounter that which imperils, or impedes, speech. In assuming the responsibility for making it possible to remember a history "nobody thinks about,"

Morrison cannot simply tell the story of events that are available but forgotten, but rather must reconstruct, or invent, events that are accessible only as an omission and a gap. It is not a matter of simply substituting memory for forgetfulness or putting speech in the place of silence, for what has been "forgotten" was never fully present to begin with. The challenge at stake in *Beloved*, then, is not to recover a repressed or forgotten past, but rather to represent an absence, reconstruct a past that had no witnesses, and read the traces of a history that in fact may be unreadable.

Trauma may impede storytelling yet nonetheless impel it. On Sethe's back the anesthetized becomes the site of an aesthetic that has nothing whatever to do with the beautiful. If, according to the *O.E.D.*, the aesthetic pertains not only to interpretive activities but also (as in the Greek *Aisthesis*) to "things perceptible by the senses," in *Beloved* the realm of the aesthetic cannot be perceived: it is figured by "a clump of scars" (18) that mutely bear witness to an unspeakable past. Sethe's "back skin had been dead for years" (18), a result of the savage beating she endured under slavery, and like Sethe herself at the beginning of the novel, it is incapable of feeling. In this case the unspeakable, that which cannot be told, is encoded in the scars on Sethe's back, which bears the traces, or marks left behind, of a history that announces its own unreadability. Here scars, a moment of the past made permanent, are inscriptions that take the place of stories, images of an illegible writing that nonetheless calls for interpretation. As Valerie Smith observes, "their symbolic power is evident in the number of times that others attempt to read them."[45]

Just as Isis symbolizes "the inner moral law in its inviolable majesty" ("On a Noble Tone," 285), the marks on Sethe's back signify both the law's capacity to harm and the immorality of aesthetic or political judgments based solely upon perceptions of "the beautiful." That hell might be beautiful, a "pretty place" just like the ironically named Sweet Home, means that beauty cannot, as Kant would have it, be the symbol of "the morally good" (228, §59).[46] The scars on her body attest to the inextricability of political and aesthetic domains, for they function both as the permanent reminder of Sethe's legal status as a slave, the visible sign that she was once a white man's property, and as an aesthetic site that calls for symbolic reconstruction by her friends and family.

That which consciousness cannot register is inscribed upon Sethe's body. This inscription, bearing the traces of an event that challenges and disrupts the powers of memory, calls for an aesthetics that no longer centers on the experience of the beautiful. Any approach that would deal with the horror and meaning of these marks would imply a critique of the beautiful and the aesthetic ideologies that flow from it. As Morrison says, "the concept of physical beauty as a *virtue* is one of the dumbest, most pernicious and destructive ideas of the Western world, and we should have nothing to do with it."[47] In "Behind the Making of *The Black Book*," Morrison criticizes the slogan Black Is Beautiful as an example of "instant and reactionary myth-making" (88) and remarks upon the political and ethical consequences of the reification of beauty:

> I remember a white man saying to me that the killing of so many Vietnamese was "of course wrong, but worse was the fact that they are so beautiful." I don't know if there is a white mind; if there is— this is it. *Too bad such beautiful people had to die.* A mere question of aesthetics! . . . Physical beauty has nothing to do with our past, present or future. Its absence or presence was only important to them, the white people who used it for anything they wanted—but it never stopped them from annihilating anybody. (88–89)

Reading the marks on Sethe's back offers an alternative version of the aesthetic, one that refuses beauty as a criterion for judgment. For the scars, a sign of gratuitous brutality, also function as an aesthetic site in that they become the focus of interpretation and reconfiguration by three successive readers: a white girl, a black man, and a black woman.

If writing takes root in a wound, who will be able to read it? The novel proposes several scenes of reading the traces that remain from an unrepresentable past. Here reading is a means of refiguring history and allows the reader to interpret marks that are, strictly speaking, unreadable. Whereas the intention of her masters was to create a lasting sign of ownership, the scars on Sethe's back function as an aesthetic space for Amy, Paul D, and Baby Suggs, each of whom reads it in a different way. The aesthetic activity of reading calls the master's meaning into question by turning the significance of the event against the intentions of those who imposed it. Sethe's owners wished to leave her back a bloody mess as a reminder of her powerlessness and their power, yet her readers are able to find aesthetic form in the marks they leave and thus to rewrite the master's "text."

In the eyes of Amy, the white girl who helps Sethe escape, ministers to her wounds, and helps to deliver her daughter Denver, the whipped and bloody back is "a chokecherry tree":

> See, here's the trunk—it's red and split wide open, full of sap, and this
> here's the parting for the branches. You got a mighty lot of branches.
> Leaves, too, look like, and dern if these ain't blossoms. Tiny little
> cherry blossoms, just as white. Your back got a whole tree on it. In
> bloom. What God have in mind, I wonder. (79)

Amy's reading of Sethe's wounds shows the connection between healing and interpretation. Envisioning the cluster of marks as a tree in full bloom provides a way of symbolizing the unspeakable. If the primal scene of trauma is itself unrepresentable, reading its traces creates the possibility of an alternative reality; turning the marks on Sethe's back from a bloody mess that reflects the white man's cruelty admits the possibility of change and makes it possible to survive the past. Aestheticizing wounds that have nothing whatever to do with beauty serves a political end: because Amy can find the outline of a tree in bloom in the wounds Sethe bears, the master's meaning need not be dominant. Amy's reading alludes to the unpresentable and in doing so transforms it.

Baby Suggs and Paul D offer alternative interpretations. For Baby Suggs, who cares for Sethe while the wounds are still open, Sethe's "flowering back" is a pattern of "roses of blood" (93), as if the signs of her brutal treatment can be endured and made communicable only by endowing them with an aesthetic form. For Paul D the marks are also open to interpretation: before he and Sethe make love for the first time he rubs "his cheek on her back and learned that way her sorrow, the roots of it; its wide trunk and intricate branches. . . . And when the top of her dress was around her hips and he saw the sculpture her back had become, like the decorative work of an ironsmith too passionate for display, he could think but not say, 'Aw, Lord, girl'" (17). (The next day, however, he feels different: "the wrought-iron maze he had explored in the kitchen like a gold miner pawing through pay dirt was in fact a revolting clump of scars" [21], and it will take the rest of the novel for him to change his mind.) In these scenes of reading, an aesthetic (perhaps we should call it a poetics of the unspeakable) comes into play that has nothing to do with disinterested pleasure. The reading that must be done here is one that is constantly brought back to the reality of trauma and loss. Interpretation opens up a passage to the unsymbolizable; by refiguring Sethe's scars it provides access to powerful affects that otherwise would be unknowable. In *Beloved* the function of the aesthetic of reading is to de-anesthetize the terrible inscriptions and bring dead feelings back to life. Morrison's poetics, while not eradicating trauma, nonetheless bears witness to its horrifying and ineluctable facticity.

If trauma can turn people into ghosts, perhaps only a ghost story has the capacity to symbolize trauma. In *Beloved* the ghost that returns, first as a spirit that haunts the house at 124 and then as a young woman who appears to be Sethe's murdered, nameless daughter, is also a survivor of the Middle Passage, a representative of "the people of the broken necks, of fire-cooked blood" (181). She speaks "a traumatized language" that combines the experience of death with that of the Middle Passage. In "In the Realm of Responsibility," Morrison describes "the levels on which I wanted *Beloved* to function":

> She is a spirit on the one hand, literally she is what Sethe thinks she is, her child returned to her from the dead. And she must function like that in the text. She is also another kind of dead which is not spiritual but flesh, which is, a survivor from a true, factual slave ship. She speaks the language, a traumatized language, of her own experience, which blends beautifully in her questions and answers, her preoccupations, with the desires of Denver and Sethe. So that when they say "What was it like over there?" they may mean—they do mean—"What was it like being dead?" She tells them what it was like being where she was on that ship as a child. Both things are possible. And there's evidence in the text so that both things could be approached, because the language of both experiences—death and the Middle Passage—is the same. (5)

Morrison makes the dead return as an ambiguous presence who, both ghost and flesh, has a name that is not a name. And she gives Beloved a voice—broken, incoherent, fractured—that testifies to what it cannot tell.

VII

While some wounds impel interpretation, storytelling begins with an act of mourning. Benjamin chooses the story of the Egyptian King Psammenitus, related in Herodotus' *Histories*, to illustrate "the nature of true story-telling" (90), and it is perhaps not by chance that the story describes the conditions in which a vanquished king begins to mourn. Beaten by the Persian King Cambyses and forced to watch the Persian triumphal procession, Psammenitus sees his daughter pass by as a slave and his son about to be executed. In the midst of other Egyptians lamenting the spectacle, Psammenitus is unmoved. "But when afterwards he recognized one of his servants, an old, impoverished man, in the ranks of the prisoners, he beat his fists against his head and gave all the signs of deepest mourning" (90). Herodotus does not explain why Psammenitus begins to mourn only when he sees his servant, nor does Benjamin explain why he chooses a story of mourning to illustrate the idea of a story's immortality. Instead, he compares the story of Psammenitus to a seed that, enclosed within a pyramid, remains fruitful and alive: "it resembles the seeds of grain which have lain for centuries in the chambers of the pyramids shut up air-tight and have retained their germinative powers to this day" (90). Unlike "information," which "does not survive the moment in which it was new," a true story "preserves and concentrates its strength and is capable of releasing it even after a long time" (90).

The seed, like the story, may live forever. And if the seed attains immortality through its entombment, the story's power also results from its proximity to death. "Death," according to Benjamin, "is at the very source of the story" (90): it sanctions "everything that the story teller can tell. He has borrowed his authority from death" (94). For Benjamin, the pyramid is to the seed as Herodotus' *Histories* is to the story of King Psammenitus: the book is a monument that preserves the story's life and ensures its transmission. The pyramid encloses the seed in the same way that a story encases those about whom it tells, for a pyramid, monument to death, is also the site where life is retained. A story, then, may function as the linguistic counterpart of a pyramid or tombstone: both ensure that someone, although dead, also remains alive. In both cases an intimate connection to death is the condition for longevity.

In *Beloved*, as in the myth of Isis, the act of mourning parallels that of storytelling. Sethe cannot begin to let go of the past until she is able to tell stories about it, and Beloved's return allows that process to begin. As a silent figure from another time and place, neither wholly alive nor wholly dead, Beloved provokes in others both the desire to tell and the need to enact what they cannot recall. She is the medium through which, in Shoshana Felman's phrase, "what is not available in words, what is denied, what cannot and what will not be remembered or articulated, nonetheless gets realized" (267). Her ability to listen helps create the possibility of narrative. And her presence at 124 enables Sethe to move from the position of the one about whom stories are told to the active position of speaker and storyteller.

Marks give rise to stories and to trauma, although in different ways. In a community of slaves, however, they may also function as the only available symbols of identity. In *Beloved* marks substitute for names and sometimes supply the sole means of recognizing blood kin. In response to Beloved's questions, Sethe suddenly remembers her mother and the circumstances in which she learned how to recognize her: she remembers the brand, "a circle and cross burnt right in the skin" (61), that signifies her mother's position as a slave. And the first story she tells is of how her mother transformed the mark on her body into a name that allowed Sethe to know her. Pointing to the brand, her mother says: "I am the only one got this mark now. The rest dead. If something happens to me and you can't tell me by my face, you can know me by this mark" (61). Behind one scar are the traces of another. In Beloved's presence, Sethe begins to tell her daughters about the marks that have made her who she is. She remembers another story, told to her by Nan after her mother's death. In a language Sethe had forgotten she ever knew, Nan tells her how she received her name:

> She told Sethe that her mother and Nan were together from the sea. Both were taken up many times by the crew. "She threw them all away but you. The one from the crew she threw away on the island. The others from more whites she also threw away. Without names, she threw them. You she gave the name of the black man. She put her arms around him. The others she did not put her arms around. Never. Never. Telling you. I am telling you, small girl Sethe." (62)

Nan's narrative links the act of naming to that of marking, as if to tell, or name, were to imprint one's intentions upon the body of another. "Telling," in this context, implies the power to name rather than be named, the ability to give meaning to scars rather than merely bear them.

Sethe's name, Nan says, is "the name of the black man," and in an interview Morrison explains what bearing such a name implies: "If you come from Africa, your name is gone. It is particularly problematic because it is not just *your* name but your family, your tribe. When you die, how can you connect with your ancestors if you have lost your name?"[48] If one consequence of coming from Africa is that "your name is gone," the name "Sethe" carries with it a specific legacy, for instead of signifying identity and familial relation it points to the loss of connection and the destruction of family ties. Receiving "the name of the black man" is to bear a name that signifies absence and loss. Continuing her discussion of the problem of having, or writing about, an African name, Morrison remarks that in *Song of Solomon* she used "biblical names to show the impact of the Bible on the lives of black people, their awe and respect for it coupled with their ability to distort it for their own purposes," and also "used some pre-Christian names to give the sense of a mixture of cosmologies."[49] It appears that she has employed this technique in choosing Sethe's name as well, for Sethe signifies the novel's relation to a variety of religious and mythic subtexts.[50] Mae Henderson points out that Sethe "recalls the Old Testament Hebrew name of 'Seth,' meaning 'granted' or 'appointed' . . . (Eve named her third born Seth, saying 'God has granted me another child in the place of Abel.') In this instance, it would seem that Sethe signifies the child whose life was spared or 'granted' by her mother, who did not keep the offspring of the white men who forced themselves upon her."[51] In addition, Sethe recalls the Greek river *Lethe*, which signifies forgetfulness and rhymes with "death." Perhaps most importantly, however, the name links Sethe's story to that of Isis, for Seth is also the name of Osiris' brother and murderer. But if Sethe's name resembles that of Osiris' ancient enemy, what she does re-enacts Isis' role and function: like Isis, Sethe laments the dead's passing and lays them to rest. Whereas Kant, even while citing Isis' inscription, remains fixated on her veil and Derrida fears her as a murderess, Morrison performs the rites for which Isis was renowned: celebrating and burying a beloved body.

Beloved's return is the condition for that process to begin. While at the beginning of the novel the white man makes the marks that Amy, Baby Suggs, and Paul D may read but not write, Beloved's presence allows the protagonists to shift position and begin to speak, signifying the transition from reading the marks the other has made to telling the tale of that by which they have been marked. For Sethe, answering Beloved's questions about the past is "an unexpected pleasure" (58); telling her stories becomes "a way to feed her" (58). Beloved is the absent third that is missing from 124, and her insatiable hunger for stories prompts Sethe's and Denver's speech and Paul D's memory. Her presence makes it possible for Sethe to tell the story of being black, a woman, and a mother under slavery; for Denver to reconstruct the story of her birth; and for Paul D to retrieve the feelings he had kept locked in "the tobacco tin lodged in his chest" (113), the place where a real heart used to be. Through their relation to Beloved, the past Sethe and Paul D have tried to "beat back" returns. As Paul D tells Stamp Paid, "She reminds me of something. Something, look like, I'm supposed to remember" (234).

VIII

Beloved enacts the sublime. Appearing in the margins and signifying the presence of the marginal, she also signifies that which is missing or absent and which, like Kant's citation of Isis' inscription, is placed in the margins but nonetheless returns. Just as Kant relegates the sublime to a subordinate position from which it nonetheless escapes, so Beloved betokens the excessiveness of a history that cannot be presented as such. If the novel is about the possibility of addressing the magnitude of a horror that defies representation, Beloved is the figure through which the reader, like the protagonists, may encounter that horror. And if trauma raises in history the same issues that the sublime raises in aesthetics—the experience of an event whose magnitude exceeds representation—Beloved is the figure that attests to that which cannot be figured. Symbolizing the precise opposite of her name, she marks a surplus that exceeds speech but nonetheless impels it.

As both a figure for the border and a borderline figure, Beloved systematically disrupts temporal, spatial, and physical boundaries. Through her Morrison sets up and calls into question a series of oppositions: between life and death, past and present, individual and collective. When she was simply a ghost Beloved haunted 124 and kept its boundaries in constant upheaval; as an incarnate ghost she is quite literally the past embodied and she continues to displace the boundaries of those who reside within 124.[52] Because of Beloved, for example, Paul D first moves into the margins and finally leaves the house; at the same time she draws Sethe and Denver into ever-deepening intimacy. Bringing back to life a past that cannot be kept separate from the present, she conflates what ordinarily would be distinct temporal domains. At once the materialization of Sethe's personal history and a symbol for the institution of slavery, Beloved dramatizes the fragility of the line that divides the realms of past and present; indeed she is a liminal figure who always stands on, and is a figure for, the border.

To tell (or invent) such a "story" involves the presentation of absence, and Beloved is the symbol of absence around which meaning and memory can coalesce. Through her the characters are able to enter into a relationship with loss, for she allows access to a past that is, strictly speaking, irretrievable. At the level of character, Beloved enacts those qualities Morrison finds essential with respect to style: "My language," she told an interviewer, "has to have holes and spaces so the reader can come into it."[53] As the signifier of absence, Beloved allows both characters and reader a point of entry to that which has been absent in our history.

What is lost must be re-found before it can be relinquished. Sethe's relation to Beloved replicates Isis' relation to Osiris: the body cannot be mourned, nor can the story of its loss be told, until its fragments have been found. For Isis, whose words "maketh the dead live" and whose inscription epitomizes Kant's sublime, also performs the work of mourning: she discovers the members of Osiris' body, builds sepulchers to mark the place of their burial, and finds the words in which to lament his loss. Recovering the fragments of a beloved body, or in this case the fragments of a dispersed and ruptured past, shows the connection between the ritual of mourning and the art of storytelling, for each is a way of keeping the dead alive in memory. Burial performs at the level of ritual what storytelling enacts at the level of language; neither seeks to replace or recapture what has been lost but is rather a process of commemorating and symbolizing our attachment to it. Here memory bears witness to an irrecoverable past, and burying the dead "with proper and artistic ceremony" is a matter of burying their remains wherever they are found, resisting the wish to make of the pieces a unified whole or to bring the dead back to life. As Isis finds Osiris' dismembered body, so Beloved's protagonists encounter a repressed and disconnected history.

"Only when the survivor knows he is being heard will he stop to hear—and listen to himself" (71). Laub's account of the role hearing plays in analytic work with Holocaust survivors describes Beloved's function with respect to Denver, Paul D, and Sethe. If, as Amy tells Sethe, pain is "good for you. More it hurts more better it is. Can't nothing heal without pain, you know" (78), Beloved enacts that precept: she brings the protagonists into intimate relation with their pain and one another. Susan Bowers points out that "contemporary research in treatment for post-traumatic stress syndrome indicates that the most crucial part of healing is the unavoidable confrontation with the original trauma and feeling the pain again," and Beloved's return allows that process to begin.[54] For each of the residents of 124, responding to Beloved addresses his or her most intense anguish. Sethe wants to forget having her breast milk stolen and her back beaten to a bloody pulp, murdering her infant daughter to keep her from being enslaved. Paul D wants to forget witnessing the abuse of his fellow slaves at Sweet Home, wearing a bit in his mouth, and working in a chain gang. Denver so desperately wants to forget the rumors she has heard about her younger sister's death that she loses her hearing and leaves school rather than confront suspicious schoolmates. The characters' relationship to Beloved, who symbolizes what in history remains unseen, is the condition for a collective work of mourning to begin.

Beloved both performs the work of mourning and revises Freud's theory of it. As early as *Totem and Taboo* (1913) Freud emphasized that "mourning has a quite specific psychical task to perform: its function is to detach the survivor's memories and hopes from the dead."[55] In his influential essay "Mourning and Melancholia" (1917) he continues to stress that mourning entails the ego's progressive detachment from its "lost objects."[56] As distinct from the "pathological condition" of melancholia, in which the ego establishes "an *identification* . . . with the abandoned object" (249) and which, Freud says, "behaves like an open wound" (253), mourning accomplishes the "detachment of the libido"; once it "is completed the ego becomes free and uninhibited again" (245). For Freud the work of mourning and that of regaining autonomy are one and the same; he defines "normal" mourning as that state in which the ego is able "to sever its attachment to the object that has been abolished" (255). As late as 1926, in *Inhibitions, Symptoms, and Anxiety* Freud continues to insist that successful mourning is a matter of dissolving the ties that bind:

> Mourning occurs under the influence of reality-testing; for the latter
> function demands categorically from the bereaved person that he should
> separate himself from the object, since it no longer exists. Mourning is
> entrusted with the task of carrying out this retreat from the object in
> all those situations in which it was the recipient of a high degree of
> cathexis. That this separation should be painful fits in with what we
> have just said, in view of the high and unsatisfiable cathexis of longing
> which is concentrated on the object by the bereaved person during the

reproduction of the situations in which he must undo the ties that bind him to it.[57]

Published ten years after Freud's essay on mourning and also written in the aftermath of World War I, Virginia Woolf's *To the Lighthouse* (1927) portrays a moment in which Mrs. Ramsay, anxious about her children's late return from an afternoon exploring the edge of the cliffs, is unable to believe that they may come to any serious harm: "after all," she reasons, "holocaust on such a scale was not probable. They could not all be drowned."[58] Woolf's ironic comment (for, unlike her protagonist, she knew full well the likelihood of holocaust) is intensified by Morrison's insistence that catastrophes of such improbable scale do indeed occur and thereby makes explicit a question Freud never entertains: how do we mourn a loss whose magnitude renders it unspeakable? Freud assumes that all losses can be mourned. He does not envision the idea of losses so immense that they may exceed our ability to mourn or represent them. And although he might acknowledge that in mourning we transfer the love previously felt for the dead to the living, his exclusive emphasis upon the process of detachment precludes awareness of what *Beloved* affirms: that mourning consists in sustaining, rather than severing, our continuing love for the dead. The novel not only calls into question Freud's belief that the ego's detachment from its beloved objects is the hallmark of successful mourning but demands a very different account of mourning, one that depends upon affirming and symbolizing our connection to the past.[59]

IX

The sublime attests to this: there is something that cannot be presented. There are also losses that cannot be mourned by a process of separation and detachment such as Freud describes. Just as Isis memorializes Osiris' body by arranging sepulchers to mark the sites of his burial, so *Beloved* functions as a monument that marks the place of what has passed away. Here mourning does not transcend loss but rather imparts a stronger sense of it. If Kant would ban attachment in the name of an economy of disinterestedness and if the sublime continually refers to attachments and emotions that his aesthetic defends against, the act of mourning—here understood as bearing witness to bonds that time cannot destroy—affirms those aspects of the sublime that Kant will not admit.

In *Beloved* mourning becomes possible only when the protagonists are able to symbolize and acknowledge their connection to the past and to one another.[60] Here writing offers a strategy for prolonging attachment, a means of deferring radical separation until the dead have been embraced, if not restored. In the three successive monologues that occur near the end of the novel and present the "unspeakable thoughts, unspoken" (199) of the women of 124, Morrison does not so much speak the unspeakable as push language into border zones that welcome what cannot, but must, be said. At issue in each monologue is the task of articulating, at whatever cost, the extremity and depth of attachment; in each Sethe, Denver, and finally Beloved are able to put their love into language. Each section moves a little farther from narrative, becoming more like music, emphasizing tone and rhythm rather than meaning. In these most poetic sections of the text, mourning becomes synonymous with love's articulation, asserting an intimacy with the dead that proclaims its existence in the here and now, preserving the characters' relatedness to one another in a continuous present in which time's ability to erode connections is denied. Like Isis' songs for her dead brother-lover, loss expresses itself as pure lamentation. Mourning does not "detach the survivors' memories and hopes from the dead," as Freud would have it, but rather underscores the durability of their attachment. In these passages Beloved's return has allowed each character to speak her love and her loss, at first separately and then, at the end, as one. The first is Sethe's, the second is Denver's, the third is Beloved's. A final passage fuses all three.

"Beloved, she my daughter. She mine" (200). In Sethe's monologue, words function as caress and as lament. Sethe begins by explaining that she can speak to Beloved without explanation: "She come back to me of her own free will and I don't have to explain a thing" (200). Beloved already knows everything Sethe thinks and feels: there is no need for narrative. Her presence makes it safe for Sethe to remember. In relation to the daughter who is an intimate part, if not the embodiment of her past, Sethe can relive memories that have had to be hidden: "But you was there and even if you too young to memory it, I can tell it to you" (202). And so she tells Beloved about her longing for her own mother, the rape of her breast milk, the escape from Sweet Home, and finally, about her act of murder. Until her reunion with Beloved, "my mind was homeless . . . I couldn't lay down nowhere in peace, back then. Now I can. I can sleep like the drowned, have mercy. She come back to me, my daughter, and she is mine" (204). A slave owns nothing, including her body; Sethe's use of the possessive pronoun thus proclaims that she is no longer a slave. Knowing what it means to be property, to exist "without the milk that belongs to you" (200), makes Sethe's insistence that Beloved is "mine" all the more poignant. But Sethe does not conceive of her relationship to Beloved as a form of ownership, for if Beloved belongs to Sethe, Sethe also belongs to Beloved: "when I tell you you mine, I also mean I'm yours" (203).

Denver's monologue expresses her fear of Sethe, for she believes that her mother might kill her, as she did Beloved, and her longing for her father. While Sethe remembers being motherless, Denver, also orphaned, cherishes the details about her father she's garnered from her grandmother, Baby Suggs. She describes her daddy as "an angel man," hopes that Beloved has "come to help me wait for my daddy" (208), and plans to protect Beloved from Sethe "till my daddy gets here to help me watch out for Ma'am and anything come in the yard" (207). Most of all, however, this section expresses Denver's love for Beloved, whose blood she swallowed "right along with my mother's milk" (205) and who has been her secret companion since she was little. Like Sethe, Denver affirms the depth and intensity of their connection: "And I do. Love her. I do. She played with me and always came to be with me whenever I needed her. She's mine, Beloved. She's mine" (209).

"I am Beloved and she is mine" (210). This monologue is not narrative—as Barbara Hernstein Smith says, narrative consists of "someone telling someone else that something happened"—for the speaker has no clearly defined, separate identity and cannot be described as "someone."[61] From the first phrase, this section emphasizes the degree to which "she" does not exist apart from her fusion with Sethe: "I am not separate from her there is no place where I stop her face is my own and I want to be there in the place where her face is and to be looking at it too a hot thing" (210). Sethe, however, is both Beloved's real-life mother and the mother of a child at sea on a slave ship, suggesting the extent to which Beloved's subjectivity, bound up with her ancestors and to a diffuse, unrepresentable history, is not one. Her voice speaks for a people, across space and time: it is a composite, both personal and collective, joining the tale of a survivor of the Middle Passage with that of the preconscious "consciousness" of a murdered child.

Beloved's chapter contains no punctuation. Paratactic rather than syn-
tactic, it is both ruptured and connected, employing spaces between
linguistic units rather than grammatical signs to indicate the relations
between words. It is written entirely in the present tense because for
Beloved there is neither past nor future: she exists in a perpetual present
in which "it is always now" (210). And, as Valerie Smith points out,
"only the first person pronoun and the first letter in each paragraph are
capitalized."[62] These pages do not narrate a discrete event or series of
events but rather mark the point at which narration becomes impossible.
The account to which Beloved refers—crouching in the slave ship with
a dead man on top of her; wanting to die, but not dying; watching her
mother "go into the sea" rather than continue to live as a slave; waiting
on a bridge for her mother's face "to come through the water" (213)—
blends the real and the fantastic and insists upon the omnipresence of the
unsayable.

The account chronicles the sensory impressions of a child trapped in
the hold of a slave ship while emphasizing that Beloved is both the survivor
of the Middle Passage and Sethe's real-life daughter. Because crouching
inside the slave ship is also being coiled within her mother's womb,
waiting to die and waiting to be born converge. This section expresses the
child's loss and abandonment when "the woman whose face she wants"
drowns herself: "they do not push the woman with my face through she
goes in they do not push her she goes in the little hill is gone she was going
to smile at me she was going to a hot thing" (212). Beloved's mother has
done to herself what Sethe will eventually do to Beloved: kill herself rather
than be enslaved. Beloved waits "on the bridge because she is under it"
(212) and eventually goes into the water in the hope of finding her mother:
"she knows I want to join she chews and swallows me I am gone now
I am her face my own face has left me I see me swim away a hot thing
I see the bottoms of my feet I am alone I want to be the two of us I want
the join" (213). There is no longer a difference between "I," "me," "she,"
and "her"; the last "paragraph" conflates Beloved's consciousness with
that of the abandoned baby. She comes out of the water to find her way
to the house she had heard the other whisper about and, seeing Sethe's
face, recognizes it as her "own": "Sethe's is the face that left me . . . she
is my face smiling at me doing it at last a hot thing now we can join a hot
thing" (213). Beloved's monologue ends by celebrating her joy in a union
that has been endlessly deferred.

At the level of style the monologues also move toward merger, for each is less differentiated than the one preceding it. In the fourth and final section, for example, the voices become a chorus in which the characters, speaking in union, declare their love for one another. Written without quotation marks or paragraphs, this section looks like a poem: its eight stanzas are composed of single lines and the concluding verses contain no punctuation. Here consolation depends upon an affirmation of attachment and the fusion of individual identities. The monologue begins with Beloved's proclamation that when Sethe "smiles at me . . . it is my own face smiling. I will not lose her again. She is mine" (214). It ends only when the three voices have become indistinguishable:

> Beloved
> You are my sister
> You are my daughter
> You are my face; you are me
> I have found you again; you have come back to me
> You are my Beloved
> You are mine
> You are mine
> You are mine
>
> You forgot to smile
> I loved you
> You hurt me
> You came back to me
> You left me
>
> I waited for you
> You are mine
> You are mine
> You are mine (216–17)

Only when their voices merge can the characters begin to separate from the past and from each other; only when the past's legacy has been acknowledged can the process of letting go of it begin. Thus is the work of mourning accomplished.[63]

But although their merger is necessary, the novel does not end with unequivocal celebration. The union eloquently celebrated in these passages leads toward a symbiosis so intense that Sethe and Beloved become "locked in a love that wore everybody out" (243). Obsessed with Beloved,

Sethe excludes Denver, stops going to work, and starves herself so Beloved will have enough to eat. Denver realizes that Sethe will die unless she does something: "Denver knew it was on her. She would have to leave the yard; step off the edge of the world and go ask somebody for help" (243). Knowing that "nobody was going to help her unless she told it—told all of it" (253), she confides in Janie, the Bodwins' maid. Once again, an act of "telling" allows the possibility of repair. When Janie spreads the word that "Sethe's dead daughter, the one whose throat she cut, had come back to fix her" (255), the community reverses its former antagonism and comes to Sethe's aid. They organize an exorcism and arrive at 124 to free Sethe.

The last part of the novel is structured around a series of reversals, repetitions of earlier scenes that lead to a different outcome. While earlier the community had failed to warn Sethe of the slave captor's approach and thus were indirectly responsible for Beloved's murder, now their generosity prevents Sethe from re-enacting what seems to be the same event. Holding Beloved's hand, Sethe stands at the door to greet the women who assemble outside 124, and when their voices join together to build "the sound that broke the back of words," Sethe trembles "like the baptized in its wash" (261).

In this instance, hearing is a metaphor for rebirth. When Mr. Bodwin drives into the yard to pick up Denver, Sethe, thinking he is Schoolteacher coming for her children, runs at him with an ice pick. This time, the community intervenes. Led by Denver, the first to realize what Sethe intends, the women make "a hill of black people" (262) and wrestle Sethe to the ground. In the process Beloved disappears. She is never seen again.

The community's intervention is not a sufficient exorcism of the past. In the novel's final scene, Paul D returns to 124 and "his coming is the reverse route of his going" (263). Finding Sethe lying on her mother's bed, lamenting the loss of her "best thing" (272), his love brings her back to life. He wants to rub her feet (as Amy did when Sethe gave birth to Denver), to "put his story next to hers" (273). Once again, language symbolizes attachment, for the proximity of one story to another is the most appropriate figure for their intimacy. Perhaps the protagonists can now begin to possess the past, rather than be possessed by it.

X

"I am all that is, that was, and that will be, and no mortal has lifted my veil." Morrison neither raises nor lowers the veil but instead attests to the uncanny border between memory and forgetfulness. The veil, like a bridge, connects the familiar to whatever lies beyond, and the novel makes visible both the struggle to remember and the necessity to forget. Lifting the veil drawn over "proceedings too terrible to relate" also means keeping it in place: at the novel's conclusion the community forgets Beloved "like an unpleasant dream during a troubling sleep" (275). Every trace of her is "disremembered and unaccounted for." All that remains is "weather," and the novel ends by celebrating and lamenting her passing:

> They forgot her like a bad dream. After they made up their tales, shaped and decorated them, those that saw her that day on the porch quickly and deliberately forgot her. It took longer for those who had spoken to her, lived with her, fallen in love with her, to forget, until they realized they couldn't remember or repeat a single thing she said. . . . By and by all trace is gone, and what is forgotten is not only the footprints but the water too and what is down there. The rest is weather. Not the breath of the disremembered and unaccounted for, but wind in the eaves, or spring ice thawing too quickly. Just weather. Certainly no clamor for a kiss. (274–75)

If, having learned to remember, Sethe, Paul D, and Denver can now begin to forget, the reader has been placed in relation to a hitherto unwitnessed history and comes to bear the burden of a "rememory" she has not directly experienced. The story remains in the present tense.

The last two pages state "It was not a story to pass on" twice; in a third version the phrase becomes, "This is not a story to pass on" (274–75). The injunction, which reflects the community's response to Beloved's passing, functions as a chorus that, as Valerie Smith points out, emphasizes "the unspeakability of the subject" and points to "the novel itself, naming the difficulties that attend the project of writing a novel about slavery" (350). The ambiguity of the phrase "to pass on"—meaning both "it was not a story to let die" and "it was not a story to keep alive"—suggests the complexities of transmitting an account that reflects, and indeed comments upon, its own incommunicability. Because "to pass on" means both to transmit and to forget, the novel concludes by "passing on" the very story it proclaims ought not to be transmitted. The phrase's multiple meanings also attest to the untellability of the story that has just been told, for the attempt "to pass on" this story is to occupy the shifting boundary between what can and cannot be said. Morrison's project has been to tell something that resists transmission but must be told, and hearing it links the reader to the untellable. If the community, having confronted the horror of its personal and collective history, has earned the right to forget the past and claim the future, the reader has not. The shift from "It" to "This" and the change in tense from "was" to "is" in the last version of the sentence reflects the shift in responsibility from the community, whose survival depends upon letting go of the past and must now put the story in the past tense, to the reader, who is enjoined not to let the story die. Morrison has refused to pass on "the national amnesia" regarding the subject of slavery in American consciousness. The burden of remembering now depends on us: this is not a story for us to pass on.

Asked about Beloved's past, Paul D says that all she ever said was "something about stealing her clothes and living on a bridge" (235). Beloved tells Paul D she came to 124 because "when I was at the bridge, she told me" (65), and her monologue reveals that she waits "on the bridge because she is under it" (212). The girl who lived on a bridge waiting for a face in the water functions both as a bridge within the novel and as a figure for the novel itself. As the novel's protagonist, Beloved's symbolic function of otherness connects the characters to repressed aspects of the self and to a traumatic past: she is the missing link that fills the gap in 124 and, as Bowers points out, enables "passage to knowledge of the other side that otherwise would be impossible."[64]

But a bridge is also a transitional space between realms that otherwise would remain incommensurable, a place in between where we can go either way, changing direction at any time. Like a bridge, *Beloved* marks the distance between aesthetic and political domains even as it reveals the profound link between them. Like a bridge, it demonstrates the connection between different dimensions even as it attests to what remains unbridgeable, to events "too terrible to relate." Just as reading the scars on Sethe's back signified a brutal political reality at the same time that it changed the meaning of those marks by giving them aesthetic pattern and shape, so *Beloved* demonstrates fiction's capacity to change the meaning of the master's text. Shoshana Felman remarks that "the question for contemporary testimonial narrative is, then, how can it *bridge*, speak over the collapse of bridges, and yet, narrate at the same time the process and event of the collapse" (199), and *Beloved* may be seen as an exemplary response to this challenge. Just as the character Beloved bridges the distance between the past and present, the dead and the living, between stories that can and cannot be told, so the novel creates links between self and other, connecting the reader to buried aspects of the past and unacknowledged chapters of our history as well as to the unpresentable dimension of language that lies within language itself. The novel testifies to its own unspeakability and, if it does not alter the past, it transforms our perception of it, thereby holding out the promise of change in the collective future we create.

If Isis, whose inscription for Kant exemplifies the sublime, is equally important as a goddess of mourning, *Beloved* enacts a work of mourning like that of Isis. Just as Isis buries the fragments of Osiris' body and keeps his memory alive in language, so Morrison bequeaths a "proper and artistic burial" to the "dismembered and unaccounted for," the sixty million and more to whom the novel is dedicated. And if burial's purpose is both to reaffirm our bond with the dead and ritually to mark the place where a beloved body lies, *Beloved* functions as a hitherto absent burial ground, a monument occupying the site of an unmarked grave. Like an inscription on a headstone, the novel commemorates and memorializes the life and death of those who were not, but should have been, loved. At the end of the novel, the narrator suggests that we can only "call," or enter into a relationship with, that which we can also name: "how can they call her if they don't know her name?" (274). By endowing the word "beloved" with multiple significance, Morrison allows access to that which previously was unnamed. As Gwen Bergner points out, "the word 'beloved' names not only the girl baby's return; in the funeral service the word addresses the mourners of the dead," and the novel passes on that name to the reader, who comes to occupy the position of the one who is addressed.[65] The word accrues significance as the novel progresses: what was at first a title becomes a single word on a headstone of a murdered infant, then the name given to the returned ghost of that same child, and finally an injunction.

But the inscription on the headstone that gives *Beloved* its title and initiates its plot also alludes to its epigraph:

I will call them my people,
Which were not my people;
And her beloved;
Which was not beloved.

This quotation from Romans 9:25, which repeats with little difference a passage from the Old Testament book of Hosea, refers to the Apostle Paul's discussion of the Gentiles, who, hitherto ridiculed and despised, have become acceptable. The epigraph prefigures what the novel will perform: reclaiming a lost tribe and calling them by name, it asks us to do what Beloved asks of Paul D: "You have to touch me. On the inside part. And you have to call me my name" (117). In this case, the name is both the text's title and last word, a word that, when divided, functions as an imperative, affirming that what was once reviled must now *be loved*.

At the end of an interview, Morrison describes the qualities she consistently discovers in African-American writing. Comparing the satisfaction and closure classical music gives rise to with the "hunger and disturbance that never ends" produced by jazz, Morrison likens "what black writers do" to black music:

> Jazz always keeps you on the edge. There is no final chord. There may be a long chord, but no final chord. And it agitates you. Spirituals agitate you. No matter what they are saying about how it is all going to be. There is something else there that you want from the music. I want my books to be like that—because I want the feeling of something held in reserve and the sense that there is more—that you can't have it all right now.[66]

Morrison's fidelity to the edge, to writing on and about it, keeps us on edge too. Emphasizing its own refusal of closure, the end of *Beloved* exemplifies the qualities Morrison finds in jazz:

> Take Lena [Horne] or Aretha [Franklin]—they don't give you all, they only give you enough for now. Or the musicians. One always has the feeling, whether it is true or not, they may be absolutely parched, but one has the feeling that there's some more. They have the ability to make you want it, and remember the want. That is a part of what I want to put into my books. They will never fully satisfy—never fully.[67]

Summoning the traces of the dead, of that which, unburied, comes back to haunt, *Beloved* ends by insisting not only that we "remember the want," but also that we must never forget.

Notes

INTRODUCTION

1. Michel Foucault's definition of the subject as "not the speaking consciousness, not the author of the formulation, but a position that may be filled in certain conditions by various individuals" helps us see that individuals are positioned and shaped by the symbolic orders they inhabit. *The Archaeology of Knowledge and the Discourse on Language*, trans. A. M. Sheridan Smith (New York: Pantheon Books, 1972), 115.

2. I do not appeal to the authority of experience for this study's foundation. Because experience is a constructed and historical category, to make substantive claims that rely upon its presumed self-evidence and immediacy is to deny the reality of social mediation. Joan W. Scott quite rightly observes that "when experience is taken as the origin of knowledge . . . questions about the constructed nature of experience, about how subjects are constituted as different in the first place, about how one's vision is structured—about language (or discourse) and history—are left aside. . . . It is not individuals who have experience, but subjects who are constituted through experience" ("The Evidence of Experience," *Critical Inquiry* 17, no. 4 [Summer 1991]: 777, 779). But she also emphasizes that we need the concept of experience and might agree with Diana Fuss's observation that "while experience can never be a reliable guide to the real, this is not to preclude any role at all for experience in the realm of knowledge production" (*Essentially Speaking: Feminism, Nature and Difference* [New York: Routledge, 1989], 118). Teresa de Lauretis suggests that experience should be defined not in terms of transparent immediacy but rather as the "process by which, for all social beings, subjectivity is constructed," and it is this definition, which emphasizes the historical and mediated dimensions of experience, upon which this study relies (*Alice Doesn't: Feminism, Semiotics, Cinema* [Bloomington: Indiana University Press, 1984], 159).

3. In "Toward a Female Sublime" (*Gender and Theory: Dialogues on Feminist Criticism*, ed. Linda Kauffman [New York: Basil Blackwell, 1989], 191–212) Patricia Yaeger defines the female sublime as a particular mode of women's writing. Affirming the woman writer's ability to adopt a mode of writing previously employed by men to establish the preeminence of their identity in society and literature, she proposes a female version of the traditionally male romantic sublime. Adopting Weiskel's notion of a transcendent sublime, Yaeger envisions the female sublime as a mode of empowerment through which the woman writer

can "invent, for women, a vocabulary of ecstasy and empowerment, a new way of reading female experience," and sets out to investigate "the woman writer's strategies for achieving this reinvention" (192). I discuss my considerable differences with Yaeger in connection with *The Awakening* in chapter one but point out here that, by viewing the sublime exclusively as a mode of writing or narrative strategy, Yaeger actually domesticates it. Her sublime, an arena for "intersubjective bliss" and "pleasures" (205), for "revelling" and "ecstasy" (209), becomes a kinder, gentler sublime that isn't sublime at all, for it has become yet another version of the beautiful.

4. Strictly speaking the sublime is not an object but rather the subject's response to whatever it cannot grasp. As Jean-François Lyotard points out, "there are no sublime objects, only sublime feelings" ("The Interest of the Sublime," in *Of the Sublime: Presence in Question*, trans. Jeffery S. Librett [Albany: State University of New York Press, 1993], 126).

5. The following passage from Burke's *Enquiry* demonstrates that race as well as gender offers a powerful metaphor through which to construct the sublime. To substantiate the claim "that the ideas of darkness and blackness are much the same" (and thereby refute Locke's view that "darkness is not naturally an idea of terror"), Burke tells the "very curious story of a boy, who had been born blind, and continued so until he was thirteen or fourteen years old; he was then couched for a cataract, by which operation he received his sight . . . the first time the boy saw a black object it gave him great uneasiness; and . . . some time after, upon accidentally seeing a negro woman, he was struck with great horror at the sight." For Burke, the boy's horrifying vision is proof of the capacity of darkness to produce terror. The doubled figure of race and gender here functions as "natural" evidence of the innate connection between black objects, the feeling of terror, and the power of the sublime (Edmund Burke, *A Philosophical Enquiry into the Origin of Our Ideas of the Sublime and Beautiful*, ed. Adam Phillips [Oxford: Oxford University Press, 1990], 131–33). Subsequent references are to this edition and occur in the text.

6. By ideology I do not mean falsehood or false consciousness but rather, following Althusser, "a system (with its own logic and rigour) of representation (images, myths, ideas, or concepts, depending on the case) endowed with a historical existence and role within a given society," in *For Marx*, trans. Ben Brewster (London: New Left Books, 1977), 231. According to such a view ideology has the function of making socially constructed institutions and values seem "natural," and novels may be said to both reflect and critique it in that they make visible the strategies by which we create social practices and attitudes. For especially germane discussions of ideology see Lennard J. Davis, *Factual Fictions: The Origins of the English Novel* (New York: Columbia University Press, 1983), 212–23; Terry Eagleton, *Criticism and Ideology: A Study in Marxist Literary Theory* (London: Verso, 1978), 11–64; Fredric Jameson, *The Political Unconscious: Narrative as a Socially Symbolic Act* (Ithaca: Cornell University Press, 1981), 17–23, 58–102; and Raymond Williams, *Marxism and Literature* (Oxford: Oxford University Press, 1977), 57–68.

7. The "patriarchal subject" cannot be determined solely through recourse to sex, gender, race, or class. The term does not refer to an essential category but to a position that, consciously or not, respects, conserves, and seeks to perpetuate the effects of patriarchy, in whatever form they may appear.

8. Joseph Addison, *The Spectator*, ed. G. Gregory Smith (New York, Charles Scribner's Sons, 1981), 6:82.

9. Addison, *The Spectator*, 82–83.

10. *"Longinus" on Sublimity*, trans. D. A. Russell (Oxford: Clarendon, 1965), 7. Further references are to Russell's translation and occur in the text.

11. Hélène Cixous, "Sorties," in *The Newly Born Woman*, trans. Betsy Wing (Minneapolis: University of Minnesota Press, 1986), 63–132, and "The Laugh of the Medusa," in *New French Feminisms*, ed. Elaine Marks and Isabelle de Courtivron, trans. Keith Cohen and Paula Cohen (Amherst: University of Massachusetts Press, 1980), 245–64; Julia Kristeva, "From One Identity To An Other," in *Desire in Language: A Semiotic Approach to Literature and Art*, ed. Léon S. Roudiez, trans. Thomas Gora, Alice Jardine, and Léon S. Roudiez (New York: Columbia University Press, 1980), 124–47, and *La révolution du langage poétique* (Paris: Editions du Seuil, 1974).

12. The word "modernism" coincides with both the emergence of the novel and the rise in popularity of theories of the sublime. The term was even coined by a novelist: according to the Oxford English Dictionary its first use occurs in 1737 in a letter from Swift to Pope: "The corruption of English by those Scribblers, who send us over their trash in Prose and Verse, with abominable curtailings and quaint modernisms." If modernism is indeed "a usage, mode of expression, or peculiarity of style or workmanship, characteristic of modern times," then perhaps the novel and the sublime are two of its most representative symptoms. A suggestive remark by Thomas Weiskel (*The Romantic Sublime: Studies in the Structure and Psychology of Transcendence* [Baltimore: Johns Hopkins University Press, 1976]) provides a clue to their affinity: "What created an immediate and growing audience for Longinus was the dilemma or anxiety of modernism. . . . What is new in modernism is an opposition, latent at first, but unavoidable, between authority and authenticity, between imitation, the traditional route to authentic identity, and originality, impossible but necessary. As a state of mind, modernism is an incurable ambivalence about authority" (8).

13. William Wordsworth, "Lines Composed a Few Miles Above Tintern Abbey," in *The Portable Romantic Poets: Blake to Poe*, ed. W. H. Auden and Norman Holmes Pearson (New York: Penguin Books, 1978), 194–95.

14. John Keats, "Letter to Richard Woodhouse, 27 October 1818," in *John Keats*, ed. Elizabeth Cook (Oxford: Oxford University Press, 1990), 418–19.

15. Coleridge's *Miscellaneous Criticism*, ed. T. M. Raysor (London, 1936), 12.

16. Weiskel, *The Romantic Sublime*, 158.

17. I am grateful to Helen Vendler for inviting me to reflect upon the differences between the feminine sublime and the sublime of nineteenth- and twentieth-century male poets. Although this brief discussion of Coleridge, Keats, and

Wordsworth does not perhaps answer her questions, I hope that my reading of Kate Chopin's *The Awakening* makes explicit the differences between Edna Pontellier's final walk into the sea and Giacomo Leopardi's "Thus in this immensity / My meditations drown: / And it is sweet to lose myself in this sea," or John Berryman's "it occurred to me / that one night, instead of warm pajamas / I'd take off all my clothes / and cross the damp cold lawn and down the bluff / into the terrible water and walk forever / under it out toward the island." I also thank her for calling my attention to these two poems. See Giacomo Leopardi, "The Infinite," in *Leopardi: Poems and Prose*, ed. Angel Flores, trans. Edwin Morgan (Bloomington: Indiana University Press, 1966), 61; and John Berryman, "Henry's Understanding," in *Recovery/Delusions, etc.* (New York: Dell, 1973), 53.

18. Luce Irigaray, *Speculum of the Other Woman*, trans. Gillian C. Gill (Ithaca: Cornell University Press, 1985), 230.

19. Judith Butler, *Bodies that Matter: On the Discursive Limits of "Sex"* (New York: Routledge, 1993), ix.

20. Jean-Luc Nancy ("The Sublime Offering," in *Of the Sublime: Presence in Question*, trans. Jeffery S. Librett [Albany: State University of New York Press, 1993]) argues that "as for Kant, he had begun to recognize that what was at stake in art was not the representation of the truth, but—to put it briefly—*the presentation of liberty*. It was this recognition that was engaged in and by the thought of the sublime" (28; emphasis is original—as it is in quotations throughout this book, unless otherwise noted). Jean-François Lyotard ("After the Sublime, the State of Aesthetics," in *The Inhuman: Reflections on Time,* trans. Geoffrey Bennington and Rachel Bowlby [Stanford: Stanford University Press, 1991]) observes that the Kantian sublime involves a sacrifice that is crucial "for the final destination of the mind, which is freedom" (137).

21. The notion that the sublime provokes a crisis in categorization and representation recalls Marjorie Garber's discussion of the "category crisis" introduced in culture by the figure of the transvestite (*Vested Interests: Cross-Dressing and Cultural Anxiety* [New York: Routledge, 1992], 16). Garber argues that "one of the most consistent and effective functions of the transvestite in culture is to indicate the place of what I call 'category crisis,' disrupting and calling attention to cultural, social, or aesthetic dissonances . . . by 'category crisis' I mean a failure of definitional distinctions, a borderline that becomes permeable, that permits of border crossings from one (apparently distinct) category to another: black/white, Jew/Christian, noble/bourgeois, master/servant, master/slave." In chapter two I examine the sublime in relation to transvestism and Burke's writings on the French Revolution. For the moment, it suffices to remark the important connection between the displacement of binaries and the function of the sublime.

22. Jean-François Lyotard, *Lessons on the Analytic of the Sublime*, trans. Elizabeth Rottenberg (Stanford: Stanford University Press, 1994). See also "Representation, Presentation, Unpresentable," in *The Inhuman: Reflections on Time,* trans. Geoffrey Bennington and Rachel Bowlby (Stanford: Stanford University Press, 1991), 124–28.

23. In this regard, see Drucilla Cornell, *Beyond Accommodation: Ethical Feminism, Deconstruction, and the Law* (New York: Routledge, 1991), especially her notion of "an ethical relation to otherness" in which "the subject does not seek to identify or categorize the object, but rather to let the object be in its difference," 148.

24. Bill Readings, "Sublime Politics: The End of the Party Line," *Modern Language Quarterly* (December, 1992): 411, 422–23.

25. Kate Chopin, *The Awakening*, ed. Margaret Culley (New York: Norton, 1976), 8. Subsequent references are to this edition and occur in the text.

CHAPTER 1

1. For a brief discussion of the text's authorship and history see *"Longinus" on Sublimity*, trans. D. A. Russell (Oxford: Clarendon, 1965), x–xii. See also the introduction and notes accompanying Russell's edition of the Greek text *"Longinus" on the Sublime* (Oxford: Clarendon, 1964). Following Neil Hertz, I have also consulted another recent translation, G. M. A. Grube's *Longinus on Great Writing* (New York: Bobbs-Merrill, 1957). Unless otherwise noted all further references to Longinus are to Russell's translation and occur in the text.

2. Sappho's famous ode is preserved only through inclusion in Longinus' treatise. For a discussion of Longinus' and Boileau's treatment of the poem, see Joan DeJean, *Fictions of Sappho: 1546–1937* (Chicago: University of Chicago Press, 1989), 84–87.

3. The reader may wish to read Sappho's ode in the original Greek and then compare Julia Dubnoff's literal translation of it with those provided by Russell and Grube:

φαίνεταί μοι κῆνος ἴϲος θέοιϲιν
ἔμμεν' ὤνηρ, ὄττιϲ ἐνάντιόϲ τοι
ἰϲδάνει καὶ πλάϲιον ἆδυ φωνεί-
ϲαϲ ὑπακούει
καὶ γελαίϲαϲ ἰμέροεν, τό μ' ἦ μὰν
καρδίαν ἐν ϲτήθεϲιν ἐπτόαιϲεν,
ὡς γὰρ ἔϲ ϲ' ἴδω βρόχε' ὤς με φώναι-
ϲ' οὐδ' ἓν ἔτ' εἴκει,
ἀλλ' ἄκαν μὲν γλῶϲϲα †ἔαγε λέπτον
δ' αὔτικα χρῶι πῦρ ὑπαδεδρόμηκεν,
ὀππάτεϲϲι δ' οὐδ' ἓν ὄρημμ', ἐπιρρόμ-
βειϲι δ' ἄκουαι,
†έκαδε μ' ἴδρως ψῦχρος κακχέεται† τρόμος δὲ
παῖϲαν ἄγρει, χλωροτέρα δὲ ποίας
ἔμμι, τεθνάκην δ' ὀλίγω 'πιδεύης
φαίνομ' †αι
ἀλλὰ πᾶν τόλματον ἐπεὶ †καὶ πένητα†

That man to me seems equal to the gods,
the man who sits opposite you
and close by listens
to your sweet voice

and your enticing laughter—
that indeed has stirred up the heart in my breast.

> For whenever I look at you even briefly
> I can no longer say a single thing,
>
> but my tongue is frozen in silence;
> instantly a delicate flame runs beneath my skin;
> with my eyes I see nothing;
> my ears make a whirring noise.
>
> A cold sweat covers me,
> trembling seizes my body,
> and I am greener than grass.
> Lacking but little of death do I seem.
>
> But all must be endured since . . .

I have relied upon the versions of Sappho that appear in Russell and Grube primarily because these are the translations Neil Hertz cites, and it is his particular reading of Sappho's lyric that is the object of this critique.

4. Peter De Bolla interestingly defines sublime discourse as discourse that produces the very excessiveness it purports to describe (*The Discourse of the Sublime: Readings in History, Aesthetics, and the Subject* [New York: Basil Blackwell, 1989], 12): "the discourse of the sublime . . . is a discourse which produces, from within itself, what is habitually termed the category of the sublime and in doing so it becomes a self-transforming discourse. The only way in which it is possible to identify this newly mutated discursive form is via its propensity to produce to excess. . . . Hence the discourse on the sublime, in its function as an analytic discourse or excessive experience, became increasingly preoccupied with the discursive production of the excess."

5. Neil Hertz, *The End of the Line: Essays on Psychoanalysis and the Sublime* (New York: Columbia University Press, 1985), 1–20. Subsequent references are to this edition and occur in the text.

6. Kate Chopin, *The Awakening*, ed. Margaret Culley (New York: Norton, 1976), 15. Subsequent references are to this edition and occur in the text.

7. Grube, *Longinus on Great Writing*, 4.

8. Suzanne Guerlac, *The Impersonal Sublime: Hugo, Baudelaire, Lautréamont* (Stanford: Stanford University Press, 1990), 3. Guerlac emphasizes that the Longinian sublime is not "merely rhetorical" but "occurs as a force of enunciation determined neither by subjective intention nor by mimetic effect" (11). Thus, she argues, "the Longinian emphasis on the act of enunciation, and, in particular, the call for the dissimulation of figurative language, is incompatible with the mimetic structure of metaphor that is at the basis of the analyses of the romantic sublime" (194). Unlike Weiskel, for whom the sublime functions as a transcendent turn, Guerlac finds in the sublime "the site within the metaphysical tradition, and within the tradition of aesthetics, of resistance to mimesis, to metaphorical recuperation or 'resolution' and to aesthetics" (194–95); see 182–93 for Guerlac's discussion of Weiskel's *Romantic Sublime* (which I cite in note 12).

9. Ronald Paulson ("Versions of a Human Sublime," *New Literary History* 16, no. 2 [Winter 1985]: 427) points out that while "studies of the sublime, from Burke

to Monk and Hipple, used to focus on the enumeration of qualities in the sublime object or, more precisely, as they are reflected in the mind of the spectator . . . in the last decade, mediated by Nietzsche and Freud, by Harold Bloom and Thomas Weiskel, the focus has shifted to the agon between subject and object. The former is both/either a participant within a sublime confrontation and/or a spectator without."

10. Longinus' assumption that the sublime entails a transformation of conventional power relations anticipates Burke's famous dictum: "I know of nothing sublime which is not some modification of power" (Edmund Burke, *A Philosophical Enquiry into the Origin of our Ideas of the Sublime and Beautiful*, ed. Adam Phillips [Oxford: Oxford University Press, 1990], 59).

11. See in particular Harold Bloom, *The Anxiety of Influence* (New York: Oxford University Press, 1973). For Bloom the poet achieves sublimity only through overcoming the threat represented by the work of a "strong" precursor poet. In addition to Neil Hertz and Thomas Weiskel, recent proponents of this view include Marc W. Redfield who, in a provocative analysis of Fredric Jameson's notion of a postmodern sublime ("Pynchon's Postmodern Sublime," *PMLA* 104, no. 2 [March 1989]: 152), argues that the sublime moves "from a threatening diffusion of signs toward a more structured conflict, which enables a self to prop itself up, so to speak, on its own anxiety, reading the confirmation of its existence in the image of its threatened destruction." In the same issue of the *PMLA*, R. Jahan Ramazani reaffirms the view that the sublime entails confrontation and/or struggle between opposing forces ("Yeats: Tragic Joy and the Sublime," *PMLA* 104, no. 2 [March 1989]: 164). Drawing upon the accounts of Hertz and Weiskel, he interprets the sublime "as a staged confrontation with death" in which "the anticipation of death gives rise to a counterassertion of life." For Ramazani "death precipitates the emotional turning called the sublime, although theorists of the sublime often refer to death by other names, or by what Kenneth Burke terms 'deflections': nothingness, castration, physical destruction, semiotic collapse, defeat by a precursor, and annihilation of the ego. Death is the recurrent obsession for these theorists, from Longinus to Heidegger and Bloom."

12. Thomas Weiskel, *The Romantic Sublime: Studies in the Structure and Psychology of Transcendence* (Baltimore: Johns Hopkins University Press, 1976), 5; Paul H. Fry, "The Possession of the Sublime," *Studies in Romanticism* 26, no. 2 (Summer 1987): 188.

13. Fry, "Possession of the Sublime," 189–90. See also Fry's discussion of Longinus' treatment of Sappho in "Longinus at Colonus," in *The Reach of Criticism: Method and Perception in Literary Theory* (New Haven: Yale University Press, 1983), 47–86.

14. A discussion regarding Longinus' commentary on Sappho occurs between Suzanne Guerlac and Frances Ferguson in *New Literary History* 16, no. 2 (Winter 1985), the issue entitled "The Sublime and the Beautiful: Reconsiderations." Although their dispute does not directly engage Sappho's portrait of desire or Longinus' reaction to it, it does address a closely related topic: the status of the

subject and the kind of subjectivity at stake in the Longinian sublime. Does the sublime as represented by Longinus threaten or uphold the "unified self-identity of the subject" (275)? Guerlac and Ferguson propose very different answers, but both explore the question by examining Longinus' reading of Sappho.

In the article "Longinus and the Subject of the Sublime," Guerlac argues that theorists who emphasize pure "force of feeling" and who read Longinus from an exclusively phenomenological point of view "obscure a more radical force at work in the Longinian sublime, one which threatens the very notion of the subjectivity, or the unified self-identity of the subject" (275). Guerlac proposes to read *On the Sublime* "in terms of a 'rhetoric' of enunciation, instead of expression" in order to show that in the Longinian sublime "the subject of feeling, or the 'aesthetic' subject, is disrupted as well as the subject of certainty or the theoretical subject" (275). The success of Guerlac's argument depends upon her discussion of Longinus' treatment of Sappho. She argues that what Longinus appreciates in the poem of Sappho "is clearly not a representation of unity, or of a unified body. The body is portrayed as broken, fragmented" (282). Rather, Longinus appreciates "the force of enunciation" through which Sappho is able to portray, and ultimately unify, the fragmented body. In Guerlac's view it is this "force of ennunciation which unifies these fragments, combin[ing] them into a single whole; embodying the text and the body—which now serves as a figure for the unity of composition of the text" (282). Although Guerlac appears to challenge the notion that the sublime implies (or helps construct) a unified subject, she does not question the prevailing view that the Longinian sublime entails the achievement of textual unity or dispute his reading of Sappho's lyric. Like Longinus', Guerlac's reading represses Sappho's emphasis on semiotic and erotic transport and reiterates the view that the sublime text functions as an antidote to division. Guerlac's "force of enunciation" repairs, not underscores, fragmentation and helps to maintain textual unity, if it is not indeed equivalent to it. For if the effect of figurative language is to give the semblance of unity, how can it follow that "there is no stable ground or truth or sincerity in the event of sublimity, which, through a force of enunciation, disrupts the stable identity of the subject" (285)? Unity remains the master trope whether the "force of enunciation" or the subject produces it; Guerlac now ascribes to it the unity and power previously ascribed to the subject.

Guerlac fails to notice precisely what Ferguson remarks in her elegant article, "A Commentary on Suzanne Guerlac's 'Longinus and the Subject of the Sublime'": "the capacity of rhetoric to produce what we might call 'a subjectivity effect'" (292). Ferguson argues that although Guerlac substitutes rhetoric for subjectivity and ascribes to the former the function previously reserved for the latter, nothing has really changed. What difference, Ferguson asks, does it make if the *subject* is divided when *language* is not? "Figurativity thus comes in aid of the notion of unity, in substituting for the shattered bodily unity a figurative wholeness. What is thus disconnected in one register is unified in another" (293). While it would be extremely interesting to know Guerlac's response to Ferguson's remarks, particularly noteworthy in this context is that their debate centers on Longinus' reading of Sappho.

15. See Hertz, *The End of the Line*, 59.

16. For a study that explores the relation between gender, narrative, and a blocking agent or obstacle, see Theresa de Lauretis, "Desire in Narrative," in *Alice Doesn't: Feminism, Semiotics, Cinema* (Bloomington: Indiana University Press, 1984), 103–57. De Lauretis not only argues that narrative structure depends upon a certain sadism but holds that the subject of narrative, or mythical hero, is invariably gendered as male, while the obstacle he encounters is female. According to de Lauretis, "the hero must be male regardless of the gender of the text-image, because the obstacle, whatever its personification, is morphologically female and indeed, simply, the woman" (118–19). By its very nature, then, "representation works to support the male status of the mythical subject" (140).

17. Samuel Holt Monk, *The Sublime: A Study of Critical Theories in Eighteenth-Century England* (1935; rpt., Ann Arbor: University of Michigan Press, 1960), 6. Subsequent references are to this edition and occur in the text.

18. According to Hertz, Weiskel locates in "the pre-Oedipal phases . . . the motivating power of the mathematical sublime, then sees them as rejoining a secondary system that is recognizably Oedipal and more clearly manifested in the dynamical sublime" (*The End of the Line*, 52).

19. Writing seven years after "The Notion of Blockage," Hertz concludes *The End of the Line* with an essay entitled "Afterword: The End of the Line" in which he returns to the previously unexamined question of gender that haunted his discussion of Longinus. Here Hertz inquires: "What comes *after* the end of the line . . . at the end of the line, who pays? and why?" (223). His afterword, however, enacts the very pattern of scapegoating he has already described. A discussion of the relation between gender and scapegoating in George Eliot's *Daniel Deronda* prompts Hertz to ask "how her [the Princess'] gender, her being 'The Mother,' [is] linked to her serving as scapegoat?" (229). His response is that exorcism of the princess allows Daniel to put "a pre-Oedipal mother aside when he enters the symbolic order and takes his place under the sign of his Jewish grandfather" (230). Pursuing the discussion of the pre-Oedipal stage that he had raised all too briefly in connection with Weiskel, Hertz interprets Julia Kristeva's "*L'abjet d'amour*" in a way that parallels his readings of Longinus and Kant. Just as Hertz interprets Kant's mathematical sublime through a Wordsworthian grid of blockage and release, now he reads Kristeva's concept of the non-object or "*abjet*" in terms of the mechanism of scapegoating he finds at work in *Daniel Deronda*. Whereas Kristeva's formulation of the *abjet might* have been understood not only as abjection but as the more "radical flux and dispersion of the subject" that Hertz describes in the essay on "The Notion of Blockage," he interprets it as a triumphant staving off of chaos, an instant in which the infant links itself with the paternal function. The casting out of the *vide*, of "that which could have been a chaos and which now begins to become an *abject*" (232), enables the infant's first sense of selfhood, and the movement Kristeva traces becomes a corollary to that

at work in *Daniel Deronda*: "the casting out of the Princess, her abjection, is intended not to collapse the distance between author and surrogate, but to stabilize it as a chosen separation and thus to ground the multiple gestures of mimesis that make up the novel" (233). The Oedipal moment of casting out differences and achieving an identification with the father, previously described as identical to the structure of the sublime, Hertz now locates at the heart of Kristeva's description of the pre-Oedipal stage. In Hertz's reading of Kristeva, the mother comes to serve the name and law of the father, recreating the same "end of the line scenario" that characterizes Hertz's treatment of Sappho. Once again Hertz evokes the possibility of an excess that cannot "be brought back home to the Father" but does so only the better to return it to him.

20. The phrase "language of the unsayable" derives from the title of the book edited by Sanford Budick and Wolfgang Iser, *Languages of the Unsayable: The Play of Negativity in Literature and Literary Theory* (New York: Columbia University Press, 1989).

21. "Selections from *The World As Will and Idea*," Book III, section 39, in *Philosophies of Art and Beauty: Selected Readings in Aesthetics from Plato to Heidegger*, ed. Albert Hofstadter and Richard Kuhns (New York: The Modern Library, 1964), 464.

22. Immanuel Kant, *Critique of Judgment*, section 29, trans. Werner S. Pluhar (Indianapolis: Hackett, 1987), 130. Subsequent references are to this edition and will appear in the text, along with German terms from the original (*Kritik der Urteilkraft*, ed. Wilhelm Weischedel [Frankfurt: Suhrkamp, 1974]) that I add to show that Kant talks about sacrifice and uses concepts of power and subordination to explain the function of the imagination. For an intriguing discussion of this passage, see Paul de Man, "Phenomenality and Materiality in Kant," in *Hermeneutics: Questions and Prospects*, ed. Gary Shapiro and Alan Sica (Amherst: University of Massachusetts Press, 1984), 132–35.

23. For an insightful discussion of the oceanic sublime, see Steven Z. Levine, "Seascapes of The Sublime: Vernet, Monet, and the Oceanic Feeling," *New Literary History* 16, no. 2 (Winter 1985): 377–400.

24. Gerald L. Bruns, "Disappeared: Heidegger and the Emancipation of Language," in *Languages of the Unsayable: The Play of Negativity in Literature and Literary Theory*, ed. Sanford Budick and Wolfgang Iser (New York: Columbia University Press, 1989), 127–28.

25. Theodore W. Adorno, cited in Bruns, "Disappeared," 144.

26. Edna's "flash of terror" of course recalls Burke's dictum that "terror is in all cases whatsoever either more openly or latently the ruling principle of the sublime" (*Enquiry*, 54). We focus upon Burke's sublime and his notion of terror in the following chapter.

27. Sandra M. Gilbert and Susan Gubar, *Sex Changes,* vol. 2 of *No Man's Land: The Place of the Woman Writer in the Twentieth Century* (New Haven: Yale University Press, 1989), 98. Subsequent references are to this edition and occur in the text.

28. Some of the influential readings of *The Awakening* that do not discuss the ocean's role or "voice" include Margaret Culley, "Edna Pontellier: 'A Solitary Soul,'" in her edition of *The Awakening*, 224–28; Anne Goodwin Jones, "Kate Chopin: The Life Behind the Mask," in *Tomorrow is Another Day: The Woman Writer in the South, 1859–1936* (Baton Rouge: Louisiana State University Press, 1981), 135–82; Susan J. Rosowski, "The Novel of Awakening," *Genre* 12 (Fall 1979): 313–32; George M. Spangler, "Kate Chopin's *The Awakening*: A Partial Dissent," *Novel* 3, no. 3 (Spring 1970): 249–55; Margit Stange, "Personal Property: Exchange Value and the Female Self in *The Awakening*," *Genders*, no. 5 (July 1989): 106–119: Ruth Sullivan and Stewart Smith, "Narrative Stances in Kate Chopin's *The Awakening*," *Studies in American Fiction* 1, no. 1 (1973): 62–75; Lawrence Thornton, "*The Awakening*: A Political Romance," *American Literature* 52, no. 1 (March 1980): 50–66; Paula A. Treichler, "The Construction of Ambiguity in *The Awakening*: A Linguistic Analysis," in *Women And Language in Literature and Society*, ed. Sally McConnell-Ginet, Ruth Borker, Nelly Furman (New York: Praeger, 1980), 239–57; Otis B. Wheeler, "The Five Awakenings of Edna Pontellier," *Southern Review* 11, no. 1 (1975): 118–128; and Cynthia Griffin Wolff, "Thanatos and Eros," in Culley's edition of *The Awakening*, 206–18. For a reading that considers Chopin's treatment of Whitman, see Elizabeth Balken House, "*The Awakening*: Kate Chopin's 'Endlessly Rocking' Cycle," *Ball State University Forum* 20, no. 2 (Spring 1979): 53–58. For an overview of critical responses to *The Awakening* prior to 1977, see Priscilla Allen, "Old Critics and New: The Treatment of Chopin's *The Awakening*," in *The Authority of Experience: Essays in Feminist Criticism*, ed. Arlyn Diamond and Lee R. Edwards (Amherst: University of Massachusetts Press, 1977), 224–38.

29. Dale Bauer, "Kate Chopin's *The Awakening*: Having and Hating the Tradition," in *Feminist Dialogics: A Theory of Failed Community* (Albany: State University of New York Press, 1988), 148. Subsequent references are to this edition and occur in the text.

30. Patricia Yaeger, "'A Language Which Nobody Understood': Emancipatory Strategies in *The Awakening*," *Novel* 20, no. 3 (Spring 1987): 204. Subsequent references will be in the text.

31. Jean-François Lyotard, *The Differend: Phrases in Dispute*, trans. Georges Van Den Abbeele (Minneapolis: University of Minnesota Press, 1988), 13. Subsequent references are to this edition and occur in the text.

32. Ludwig Wittgenstein, *Tractatus Logico-Philosophicus*, trans. D. F. Pears and B. F. McGuinness (London: Routledge and Kegan Paul: 1961), prop. 7, 151.

33. "Answering the Question: What is Postmodernism?" in *The Postmodern Condition*, trans. Regis Durand (Minneapolis: University of Minnesota Press, 1984), 81. See also Lyotard's discussion of aesthetic pleasure and the sublime, "Complexity and the Sublime," in *Postmodernism: ICA Documents*, ed. Lisa Appignanesi (London: Free Association Books, 1989), 19–26. Here Lyotard emphasizes that "with the idea of the sublime, the feeling when faced with a work of art is no longer the feeling of pleasure, or not simply one of pleasure. It is a

contradictory feeling, because it is a feeling of both pleasure and displeasure, together. . . . With the sublime, the question of death enters the aesthetic question" (22).

34. For Lyotard's discussion of the relation between an aesthetics of the sublime and questions of representation, see "The Sublime and the Avant-Garde," in *The Lyotard Reader*, ed. Andrew Benjamin, trans. Lisa Liebmann (Cambridge: Basil Blackwell, 1989), 196–211. Lyotard's most comprehensive discussion of Kant's sublime occurs in *Lessons on the Analytic of the Sublime*, trans. Elizabeth Rottenberg (Stanford: Stanford University Press, 1994). On Lyotard's notions of representation and postmodernity, see Bill Readings, *Introducing Lyotard: Art and Politics* (London: Routledge, 1991), 53–85; and David Carroll, *Paraesthetics: Foucault, Lyotard, Derrida* (New York: Methuen, 1987), 155–84.

35. Walter Benn Michaels, "The Contracted Heart," *New Literary History* 21, no. 3 (Spring 1990): 498. Subsequent references will be in the text.

36. Lyotard, *The Postmodern Condition*, 81.

37. Gilbert and Gubar, *No Man's Land*, 97.

38. Jane P. Tompkins, "The Awakening: An Evaluation," *Feminist Studies* 3, nos. 3–4 (Spring–Summer 1976): 24.

CHAPTER 2

1. Edmund Burke, *A Philosophical Enquiry into the Origin of Our Ideas of the Sublime and Beautiful*, ed. Adam Phillips (Oxford: Oxford University Press, 1990), 36. Subsequent references are to this edition and occur in the text.

2. Edith Wharton, *The House of Mirth* (1905; rpt., New York: Penguin Books, 1985), 26. Subsequent references are to this edition and occur in the text.

3. James T. Boulton points out that with Burke the theory of the sublime undergoes important changes. Whereas in the earlier part of the eighteenth century "the sublime is essentially a style of writing, with Burke it becomes a mode of aesthetic experience found in literature and far beyond it. . . . In the time of Boileau 'sublime' is a term primarily for literary critics; later, sublimity is a subject for psychological study by philosophers interested in the relation between human emotion and sublime objects" (introduction to Burke's *Enquiry* [Notre Dame: University of Notre Dame Press, 1958], xlvii).

4. According to Boulton, Burke's wish to dispel uncertainty and confusion and to show that taste operates by fixed and universal principles "illustrates the eighteenth century inclination to discover immutable laws governing human life and activities. In the Newtonian tradition Burke looks for—and finds—immutable laws governing taste" (ibid., xxviii).

5. W. J. T. Mitchell, *Iconology: Image, Text, Ideology* (Chicago: University of Chicago Press, 1986), 128. I am indebted to Mitchell for emphasizing the transformative and speculative qualities of Burke's sublime. I disagree, however, with his view that the discrepancy between Burke's early and late work may be explained by finding "two theories of the sublime in the *Enquiry*. One is based on imagination, the mechanics of sensation and controlled chiefly by visual and

pictorial metaphors . . . the other, which emerges most clearly in the final section of the *Enquiry*, is resolutely anti-visual, anti-pictorial, and employs the terminology of feeling, sympathy, and customary association or substitution" (139–40). Arguing that two theories of the sublime lie dormant in the *Enquiry* allows Mitchell to distinguish between "the false, speculative French sublime and the true English verbal sublime" (140), and therefore to resolve the difference between Burke's aesthetic and political preferences. However, Mitchell's insistence upon two versions of Burke's sublime flies in the face of those very features he has so brilliantly emphasized as characteristic of it. In so far as the sublime involves the "union of two opposites" and implies "the *transformation* of one into the other in the extremes" (128), it undercuts and blurs the difference between the "true, verbal" and "false, speculative" forms of the sublime Mitchell attempts to discern. If, on the one hand, Mitchell identifies Burke's sublime as the principle of the transformation of opposites, he cannot, on the other, divide the sublime into two opposing aspects, for that would be to ignore what he has taken pains to observe: the ability of the sublime to unite opposites, not produce them.

6. The self-contradictory character of Burke's sublime and its capacity to occupy simultaneously both terms of any opposition is reflected by the reputation Burke acquired after his death, for he has been identified with both sides of the political spectrum. What C. B. MacPherson has called "the Burke problem" is, as Phillips observes, "that his writings have been used to support diametrically opposed political positions" (xiii). He has, for example, been claimed as a champion of conservativism and great defender of the traditional hierarchical society (for his counterrevolutionary writings) and, equally, as a spokesman for the liberal cause (for his case against the British government's policy in the American colonies and against the activities of the East India Company). The question MacPherson attempts to resolve is how "the same man [could] be at once the defender of a hierarchical order and the proponent of a liberal market society?" (*Burke* [Oxford: Oxford University Press, 1980], 4).

7. Donald E. Pease, "Sublime Politics," *Boundary 2* 12, no. 3 (Spring/Fall 1984): 259. Although Pease describes the sublime as "a sheer force" that "unsettles every locus of power" and "spontaneously surpasses every designation intended to locate it" (263), he nonetheless holds that "despite all the *revolutionary* rhetoric invested in the term, the sublime has, in what we could call the politics of historical formation, always served conservative purposes" (275). Pease begins by remarking the sublime's transformative capacities, its "power to make trouble for categorizing procedures," but proceeds to divide it into an implicitly positive "power to bring a new form into being" that faces an explicitly negative "destructive power . . . to disrupt any existent form," as if the sublime's very metamorphic power marks it as negative and threatening. I would argue that the tendency to divide the sublime into positive and negative forms is itself a means of defending against its transformative force. Pease's article responds to Hayden White's "Politics of Historical Interpretation: Discipline and De-Sublimation," in *The Content of the Form: Narrative Discourse and Historical Representation* (Baltimore: Johns Hopkins University Press, 1987), 58–82, in which White examines "the domes-

tication of history effected by the suppression of the historical sublime" (75). White's genealogy emphasizes the repression of a specifically historical sublime and its consequences for the politics of interpretation: he traces the persistent demotion of the sublime in favor of the beautiful in eighteenth and nineteenth century historiography from Burke through Hegel and Marx. According to White, "Burke's *Reflections on the Revolution in France* can be seen as one of the many efforts to exorcise the notion of the sublime from any apprehension of the historical process, so that the 'beauty' of its 'proper' development, which for him was given in the example of the 'English Constitution,' could be adequately comprehended" (68). There is, I think, a very real affinity between White's wish to recover "the historical sublime that bourgeois historiography repressed in the process of its disciplinization" (81) and my own wish to uncover a feminine sublime that traditional theories of the sublime repress. From a feminist point of view the sublime's ability to call into crisis existing categories and power-relations not only underwrites the possibility of critique but aligns the sublime with a politically radical perspective, for it entails a permanent receptivity to interrogating and reconfiguring existing configurations of power.

8. My epigraph, "Hypocrisy, of course, delights in the most sublime speculations," is from Burke's *Reflections on the Revolution in France*, ed. J. G. H. Pocock (Indiana: Hackett, 1987), 55. All further references to the *Reflections* are to this edition and occur in the text.

9. For a discussion of Burke's notions of the beautiful and the sublime in relation to the politics of pleasure see Fredric Jameson, "Pleasure: A Political Issue," in *The Ideologies of Theory* (Minneapolis: University of Minnesota Press, 1988), 2:61–74.

10. In *A Vindication of the Rights of Man*, ed. Eleanor Louise Nicholes (Gainesville: Scholars' Facsimiles & Reprints, 1960), Mary Wollstonecraft responds to Burke's *Reflections* by invoking and criticizing his categories of the beautiful and the sublime. She is particularly critical of his notion of the beautiful, for she believes that it enslaves women by encouraging them to be frivolous and weak. She writes, for example: "if virtue has any other foundation than worldly utility, you have clearly proved that one half of the human species, at least, have not souls; and that Nature, by making women *little, smooth, delicate, fair* creatures, never designed that they should exercise their reason to acquire the virtues that produce opposite, if not contradictory, feelings. . . . If we really wish to render men more virtuous, we must endeavor to banish all enervating modifications of beauty from civil society" (113–15). See also Ronald Paulson, *Representations of Revolution (1789–1820)* (New Haven: Yale University Press, 1983), 81–82; and Steven Blakemore, *Burke and the Fall of Language: The French Revolution as Linguistic Event* (Hanover: University Press of New England, 1988), 51–52.

11. Neal Wood, "The Aesthetic Dimension of Burke's Political Thought," *Journal of British Studies* 4 (1961): 42; Blakemore, *Burke and the Fall of Language*, 60; Sara Suleri, *The Rhetoric of English India* (Chicago: University of Chicago Press, 1992), 36. See also Peter Hughes, "Originality and Allusion in the Writings of

Edmund Burke," *Centrum* 4, no. 1 (Spring 1976): 32–43; and Paulson, *Representations of Revolution*, 57–87.

12. Burke's critique of the excesses of British colonialism in India employs the aesthetic categories of the beautiful and the sublime in much the same way as do his counterrevolutionary writings. Burke's attack on Warren Hastings, for example, became the model for his later attack on the Parisian Jacobins. As Isaac Kramnick points out in *The Rage of Edmund Burke: Portrait of an Ambivalent Conservative* (New York: Basic Books, 1977), 126–42, "Hastings signified more than just the bourgeois principle run wild for Burke; he also represented irresponsible, aggressive, and conquering masculinity. Hastings personified for Burke the consequence of unleashed and unrepressed sexuality" (134). Burke also delighted in dwelling upon the sexual horrors Hastings and his minions inflicted upon aristocratic Indian women, particularly the princesses of Oudi in the years of 1782 and 1783. In these writings, Hastings and the Jacobins enact a perverted version of the sublime while the Indian princesses, like the queen of France, exemplify the beautiful. For discussions of Burke's Indian writings see especially Kramnick's book; and Suleri, *The Rhetoric of English India*, 24–74. For a comprehensive overview of the impeachment proceedings, see P. J. Marshall, *The Impeachment of Warren Hastings* (London: Oxford University Press, 1965). For Burke's India writings see the Bohn Standard Library edition of *The Works of the Right Honorable Edmund Burke* (London, 1877–1884), vols. 4–5; and Burke's "Speech on Mr. Fox's East India Bill" in *The Complete Works of the Right Honorable Edmund Burke*, vol. 2 (Boston: Little, Brown, and Co. 1866). Unless otherwise indicated, all citations from Burke's works are noted merely as *Works* and will refer to the Bohn edition.

13. W. J. T. Mitchell, "Visible Language: Blake's Wond'Rous Art of Writing," in *Romanticism and Contemporary Criticism*, ed. Morris Eaves and Michael Fischer (Ithaca: Cornell University Press, 1986), 50.

14. For another account of Burke's notion of the sublime in relation to the social, see Frances Ferguson, "Legislating the Sublime," in *Studies in Eighteenth-Century British Art and Aesthetics*, ed. Ralph Cohen (Berkeley: University of California Press, 1985), 128–47. Here Ferguson examines the variety of ways in which Burke's "sublime, though repeatedly set apart from the claims of society, nonetheless reinforces them" (133), and discusses the role of the sublime in the *Enquiry* and the *Reflections*.

15. House of Commons, 11 April 1794; in *Speeches of the Right Honorable Edmund Burke* (1816), 4:164–65.

16. *Works*, 5:155.

17. Terry Eagleton, *The Ideology of the Aesthetic* (Oxford: Basil Blackwell, 1990), 54–55.

18. Suleri, *The Rhetoric of English India*, 43.

19. Thomas De Quincey, "A Brief Appraisal of the Greek Literature in Its Foremost Pretensions," in *The Collected Writings of Thomas De Quincey*, ed. David Masson (New York: AMS Press, 1968), 10:300–301.

20. For further discussion of Burke's views of sexual difference and the gendering of his aesthetic categories see Blakemore, *Burke and the Fall of Language*, 49–60; Kramnick, *The Rage of Edmund Burke*, 93–97, 121–25; and Mitchell, *Iconology*, 124–42.

21. *Works*, 3:437.

22. *Works*, 5:256.

23. J. G. A. Pocock, editor's introduction to *Reflections on the Revolution in France*, xxxvii.

24. Burke's professed dislike of speculation did not prevent him from indulging his own taste for it. In 1766 he made a great deal of money in the stock market; in 1768 he purchased an estate near London that cost 20,000 pounds, money that was acquired mainly by speculation in stocks and mortgages.

25. *Works*, 1:4. Burke continued to underscore the dangers of imaginative activity throughout his career. In the "Appeal from the New to the Old Whigs" (1791), he wrote: "There is a boundary to men's passions when they act from Feeling; none when they are under the influence of imagination" (*Works*, 3: 98–99).

26. Christopher Reid, "Language and Practice in Burke's Political Writing," *Literature and History*, no. 6 (Autumn 1977): 204.

27. *Works*, 2:29–30. "An Appeal from the New to the Old Whigs" also contains some striking examples of Burke's hatred of gambling, reminiscent of his diatribe against "a nation of gamesters" in the *Reflections*. In a particularly exemplary passage Burke writes: "Do we not see how lightly people treat these fortunes, when under the influence of the passion of gaming? . . . There is also a time of insecurity, when interests of all sorts become objects of speculation. Then it is, that their very attachment to wealth and importance will induce several persons of opulence to list themselves, and even to take a lead, with the party which they think most likely to prevail, in order to obtain to themselves consideration in some new order or disorder of things. . . . Those who speculate on change, always make a great number among people of rank and fortune, as well as amongst the low and the indigent" (*Works*, 3:107–8).

28. I am greatly indebted to Peter de Bolla's discussions of the diverse relationships between the notion of excess and the theory of the sublime which he develops in his study *The Discourse of the Sublime: History, Aesthetics, and the Subject* (New York: Basil Blackwell, 1989), 4–72, 281–300. My own arguments concerning the interconnections between speculation, financial and discursive excess, and the sublime owe much to de Bolla's view that the function of the discourse on the sublime is not only to describe sublime experience, but also to create "the experiential possibility for sublime sensations" (120).

29. Although Burke insists upon the humiliating violation of the nearly naked queen, there is no evidence of Marie Antoinette fleeing "almost naked" (62). According to Kramnick, "the eyewitness account of that night by Madame de la Tour du Pin, an aristocratic Irish lady-in-aid to the queen, is at variance with Burke's account. The queen's guard seems not to have been killed, and the

incident seemed to most courtiers to have been the product less of Jacobin frenzy than of the incompetence of the guards who it was suggested were part of an internal plot orchestrated by Duc D'Orleans. Madame du Pin also notes that the women in the court had been forewarned of potential danger and had not undressed that evening. She makes no reference to the queen's lack of clothing when fleeing, a fact one might expect to be of some importance for an eyewitness chronicler. It would seem that no one even saw the queen flee by the little passage which linked her bedchamber to the king's." Kramnick, *The Rage of Edmund Burke*, 152. See also *Memoirs of Madame de la Tour du Pin*, ed. Felice Harcourt (London: Harvill Press, 1969), 131–37.

30. Kramnick, *The Rage of Edmund Burke*, 151.

31. On feminine transvestism as a metaphor for political chaos, see Blakemore, *Burke and the Fall of Language*, 56–57; Mitchell, *Iconology*, 143–44; and Paulson, *Representations of Revolution*, 81.

32. In *A Letter to a Noble Lord* (1796), Burke employs a similar metaphor to emphasize that monstrosity is gendered as feminine, but here the revolutionary "furies of hell" of the *Reflections* have been replaced by the revolutionary "harpies of France": "The Revolution harpies of France, sprung from night and Hell, or from that chaotic anarchy, which generates equivocally 'all monstrous, all prodigious things,' cuckoo-like, adulterously lay their eggs, and brood over, and hatch them in the nest of every neighboring state. These obscene harpies, who deck themselves in I know not what divine attributes, but who in reality are foul and ravenous birds of prey (both mothers and daughters), flutter over our heads, and souse down upon our tables, and leave nothing unrent, unrifled, unravaged, or unpolluted with the slime of their filthy offal." Particularly striking is Burke's conviction that female mutation, if not femininity itself, lies at the origin of revolutionary activity. It is also noteworthy that while here Burke uses the confusion of sexual difference as a figure for political and moral anarchy, confusion is, in the *Enquiry*, one of the attributes of the sublime (*Works*, 5:120).

33. For a discussion of female kinship in the novel, see Elaine Showalter, "The Death of the Lady (Novelist): Wharton's *House of Mirth*," *Representations* 9 (Winter 1985): 133–49.

34. The commodification of Lily's beauty and the pervasive power of the marketplace has been the source of much critical speculation. See Elizabeth Ammons, *Edith Wharton's Argument with America* (Athens: University of Georgia Press, 1980), 28–43; Wai-Chee Dimock, "Debasing Exchange: Edith Wharton's *The House of Mirth*," in *Edith Wharton: Modern Critical Views*, ed. Harold Bloom (New York: Chelsea House, 1986), 123–34; Judith Fetterly, "'The Temptation to be a Beautiful Object': Double Standard and Double Bind in *The House of Mirth*," *Studies in American Fiction* 5, no. 2 (Autumn 1977): 200–207; Judith Fryer, *Felicitous Space: The Imaginative Structures of Edith Wharton and Willa Cather* (Chapel Hill: University of North Carolina Press, 1986), 86–94; Barbara Hochman, "Representation and Exchange in *The House of Mirth*," *Novel* 24, no. 2 (Winter 1991): 135–58; Amy Kaplan, *The Social Construction of American Realism* (Chicago: Uni-

versity of Chicago Press, 1988), 88–93; Walter Benn Michaels, *The Gold Standard and the Logic of Naturalism: American Literature at the Turn of the Century* (Berkeley: University of California Press, 1987), 225–34; Robert Shulman, "Divided Selves and the Market Society: Politics and Psychology in *The House of Mirth*," *Contemporary Literature* 11, no. 1 (1985): 10–18; Carol Wershoven, *The Female Intruder in the Novels of Edith Wharton* (London: Associated University Press, 1982), 43–49; Cynthia Griffin Wolff, *A Feast of Words: The Triumph of Edith Wharton* (New York: Oxford University Press, 1977), 115–31.

35. Jean François Lyotard, "The Sublime and the Avant-Garde," in *The Lyotard Reader*, ed. Andrew Benjamin, trans. Lisa Liebmann (Cambridge: Basil Blackwell, 1989), 209. Lyotard also discusses Burke's *Enquiry* in this essay, 204–6.

36. Eagleton, *The Ideology of the Aesthetic*, 212. Anglo-American critics such as Eagleton and Jameson have turned to the sublime in order to preserve and reorient Marxist cultural criticism and analysis: see, for example, Jameson's discussion of a "postmodern or technological sublime" in *Postmodernism, or, The Cultural Logic of Late Capitalism* (Durham: Duke University Press, 1991), 34–54, and "Regarding Postmodernism: A Conversation with Fredric Jameson," in *Universal Abandon? The Politics of Postmodernism*, ed. Andrew Ross (Minneapolis: University of Minnesota Press, 1988). For another account of the sublime as ideology, see Slavoj Zizek, *The Sublime Object of Ideology* (London: Verso, 1989). For Zizek "the sublime is an object in which we can experience this very impossibility, this permanent failure of the representation to reach after the Thing . . . the Sublime is therefore the paradox of an object which, in the very field of representation, provides a view, in a negative way, of the dimension of what is unrepresentable" (203). The ideology of the sublime object thus resides in its capacity to represent lack, understood by Zizek as castration and pure negativity.

37. Here I cite *The Complete Works of the Right Honorable Edmund Burke* (Boston: Little, Brown, and Co., 1866), 10:450.

38. Karl Marx, *Economic and Philosophical Manuscripts*, in *Karl Marx: Early Writings*, trans. Rodney Livingstone and Gregor Benton (New York: Vintage Books, 1975), 358. Here Marx writes: "The *quantity* of money becomes more and more its sole *important* property. Just as it reduces everything to its own form of abstraction, so it reduces itself in the course of its own movement to something *quantitative*. *Lack of moderation* and *intemperance* become its true standard." For Marx, as for Burke, money is a form of monstrous sublimity. Gary Shapiro points out that "Marx's extensive notes on the aesthetics of F. T. Vischer, made just a year or two before the completion of *Herr Vogt*, show him taking an explicit interest in Vischer's account of the sublime. Vischer's discussion of the measureless seems to have helped Marx to formulate the economic categories of *Capital* and other later writings. Capital has a tendency toward a continuous and monstrous development in which every boundary of measure is left behind. Like the Kantian mathematical sublime, capital can expand indefinitely as an objective and threatening presence." Gary Shapiro, "From the Sublime to the Political: Some His-

torical Notes," *New Literary History: A Journal of Theory and Interpretation* 16, no. 2 (1985): 228.

39. Dimock, "Debasing Exchange," 123.

40. On "the tyranny of beauty" see Frances Ferguson's discussion of Burke's *Enquiry* in *Solitude and the Sublime: Romanticism and the Aesthetics of Individuation* (New York: Routledge, 1992), 37–54.

41. The implications of the *tableaux vivants* scene have been much discussed. See Peter Conn, *The Divided Mind: Ideology and Imagination in America* (Cambridge: Cambridge University Press, 1983), 185–86; Fryer, *Felicitous Space*, 75–80; Hochman, "Representation and Exchange in *The House of Mirth*," 151; Kaplan, *The Social Construction of American Realism*, 94–98; Michaels, *The Gold Standard*, 239–44; Bruce Michelson, "Edith Wharton's House Divided," *Studies in American Fiction* 12, no. 2 (Autumn 1984): 212–15; Showalter, "The Death of the Lady (Novelist)," 140; Wershoven, *The Female Intruder in the Novels of Edith Wharton*, 49–50; and Wolff, *A Feast of Words*, 125–26.

42. In "An Appeal from the New to the Old Whigs" Burke describes Reynolds as "the excellent and philosophical artist, a true judge, as well as a perfect follower of nature" (*Works*, 3:114).

43. I take issue with Wai-Chee Dimock, who finds Lily's gestures of resistance "eloquent" and "heroic," but "ultimately futile, ultimately contained, absorbed, and exploited by the very system against which it is directed" ("Debasing Exchange," 134). Although Dimock agrees that in repaying Trenor and burning Selden's letters Lily challenges "the very basis of exchange," she concludes that "as every reader must recognize, defiance of this sort is ultimately unavailing. The exchange system can easily accommodate rebellion like Lily's" (131). For Dimock, the very nobility of Lily's action "lies in its fruitlessness, in its utter lack of material consequence, in its erasure from history. . . . Morality, in *The House of Mirth*, provides no transcendent language, no alternative way of being, but feeds directly into the mechanism of the marketplace. Lily's rebellion, which appeals to and presupposes a transcendent moral order, is doomed for that very reason" (135).

In contrast to Dimock, I argue that resistance is possible only from a position within that which one resists. That there is no outside of the marketplace does not preclude effective resistance, nor imply that everything that occurs within it possesses equal value. That a capitalist society can assimilate actions such as Lily's does not imply the futility of such gestures, but rather underscores their importance and necessity, for acts of resistance can occur only within the context of the power-relations they also contest. To charge, as does Dimock, that acts such as Lily's are "ultimately futile," a challenge "in spirit but not in fact" (131) is, I think, to invalidate and overlook the possibility of individual acts of resistance in favor of an idealized view of the political domain. Such a view would mistakenly envision political or public actions as unassimilable in a way that individual ones are not, and would allow us to believe in a realm that could successfully escape recuperation. As I have argued, Lily Bart creates a kind of value that neither transcends the marketplace nor is determined by it, and the novel's political function resides in its ability to make its readers cognizant of the conditions of the marketplace at the same time that it elaborates an alternative course of action. Far from being "futile," Lily's resistance makes legible the normativizing practices of her society and in so doing confronts the reader with her responsibility for that involvement. Rather than presuppose a "transcendent moral order," as Dimock would have it, Lily's "ethics of risk" resists the ethos of exchange by presenting a radical revision of it, one whose only ground lies in its recognition of the need for perpetual improvisation.

44. Edith Wharton, *A Backward Glance* (New York: D. Appleton-Century, 1934), 207.

45. I contest Walter Benn Michaels's view that Lily Bart exemplifies and embodies market capitalism. Perhaps because Michaels identifies capitalism with "the principle of mutability, the omnipresence and irreducibility of risk" (*The Gold Standard,* 76), he interprets Lily's passion for risk as "an expression of her passion for the market" (230). I argue that successful capitalists do not thrive on taking chances, as Michaels would have it, but rather succeed precisely by minimizing them, and that Lily's passion for chance is not a sign of her commitment to capitalism but evidence of her resistance to it. As Michaels himself observes, "the skillful gambler seeks to minimize risk by exerting a certain control" (230), which is just what Lily, by the end of the novel, no longer attempts—not because she lacks a gambler's skill but because she rejects an economy in which success depends upon eradicating risk. Michaels ignores Lily's development during the course of the novel. I agree that at the beginning Lily's "distaste for the commerce of Wall Street in fact express[es] her complete commitment to the practices of speculation" (228) and that here she does indeed personify the marketplace, yet by the end she affirms a version of speculation that its other practitioners eschew and thereby offers an alternative to it. Successful speculators such as Bertha, Trenor, and Rosedale love profit, not risk; and they, not Lily, are the characters who do indeed embody the marketplace in *The House of Mirth.* In distinct contrast to these figures, Lily resists the market she earlier embodied and does so precisely through her affirmation of risk.

46. Dimock, "Debasing Exchange," 127.

47. Lily's commitment to loss anticipates and enacts Georges Bataille's notion of *dépense* (expenditure), whose goal is not gain or conservation but infinite loss, a loss that offers no possibility of profit ("The Notion of Expenditure," in *Visions of Excess: Selected Writings, 1927–1939,* ed. Allan Stoekl, trans. Allan Stoekl, Carl R. Lovitt, and Donald M. Leslie, Jr. [Minneapolis: University of Minnesota Press, 1985]). Bataille holds that some examples of human comportment toward loss— "luxury, mourning, war, cults, the construction of sumptuary monuments, games, spectacles, arts, perverse sexual activity (i.e., deflected from genital finality)"—are all activities that "have no end beyond themselves" and cannot be accounted for by a logic that insists upon conservation and utility as axiomatic. The burning of Selden and Bertha's correspondence perfectly illustrates Bataille's notion of ex-

penditure: here "the accent is placed on a *loss* that must be as great as possible in order for that activity to take on its true meaning" (118).

48. Jean Paul Sartre, *What is Literature?* trans. Bernard Frechtman and Jeffrey Mehlman (Cambridge, Mass.: Harvard University Press, 1988), 60.

CHAPTER 3

1. Henry James's remark that endings in fiction are never natural and that "we have, as the case stands, to invent and establish them, to arrive at them by a difficult, dire process of selection and comparison, of surrender and sacrifice" suggests that novelistic closure is obtained through the same sorts of sacrificial strategies at play in the Kantian sublime. See the preface "Roderick Hudson," in *The Art of the Novel,* ed. R. P. Blackmur (New York: Scribner's, 1962), 6.

2. A useful definition of patriarchy is that provided by Heidi Hartmann: "relations between men, which have a material base, and which, though hierarchical, establish or create interdependence and solidarity among men that enable them to dominate women." Quoted in Eve Kosofsky Sedgwick, *Between Men: English Literature and Male Homosocial Desire* (New York: Columbia University Press, 1985), 3. Barbara Johnson suggests the following relation between patriarchy, misogyny, and language: "Gynophobia is structured like a language— indeed, more unsettling, language itself is structured like gynophobia. This does not mean—far from it—that women are excluded from language, but that the culpabilization of women is a necessary part of it" ("Response," *Yale Journal of Criticism* 1, no. 2 [Spring 1988]: 177).

3. Steven Knapp, *Personification and the Sublime: Milton to Coleridge* (Cambridge, Mass.: Harvard University Press, 1985), 79.

4. Kant, *Observations on the Feeling of the Beautiful and the Sublime* (1764), trans. John T. Goldthwait (Berkeley: University of California Press, 1960), 78. For an illuminating discussion of the *Observations,* particularly with respect to Kant's sexual politics, see Susan Shell, "Kant's Political Cosmology: Freedom and Desire in the 'Remarks' Concerning *Observations on the Feeling of the Beautiful and the Sublime,*" in *Essays on Kant's Political Philosophy,* ed. Howard Williams (Cardiff: University of Wales Press, 1992), 87–119. I am grateful to James Engell for showing me this essay.

5. Kant's reading and use of the extensive eighteenth-century English literature on aesthetics is detailed in Otto Schlapp, *Kant's Lehre vom Genie und die Entstehung der Kritik der Urteilskraft* (Göttingen, 1901).

6. As Naomi Schor reminds us, Western philosophy "has, since its origins, mapped gender onto the form-matter paradigm, forging a durable link between maleness and form (eidos), femaleness and formless matter" (*Reading in Detail: Aesthetics and the Feminine* [New York: Methuen, 1987], 16).

7. W. J. T. Mitchell, *Iconology: Image, Text, Ideology,* 129.

8. See in particular "Some Psychical Consequences of the Anatomical Distinction between the Sexes" (1925) and "Female Sexuality" (1931) in Sigmund

Freud, *Sexuality and the Psychology of Love*, trans. James Strachey (New York: Collier Books, 1963), 183–211; and "Femininity" (1933) in *New Introductory Lectures on Psychoanalysis*, trans. James Strachey (New York: Norton, 1965).

9. Patricia Parker, *Literary Fat Ladies: Rhetoric, Gender, Property* (London: Methuen, 1987), 179.

10. This may be the point to recall Eve Sedgwick's astute observation that "sex as such not only resembles and conveys but represents power, including—but not only—the power relations of gender" (*Between Man*, 157).

11. On the relation between the rise of the novel as a literary genre and the emergence of the theory of the sublime, see my study "The Rise of the Sublime: Sacrifice and Misogyny in Eighteenth Century Aesthetics," *Yale Journal of Criticism* 5, no. 3 (Fall 1992): 81–99. There I point out that a comparison of publication dates of some of the most popular novels, translations of Longinus' *Peri Hypsous*, and commentaries on the sublime reveals a quite extraordinary overlap: Boileau's translation of Longinus, for example, first appeared in English in 1711 (subsequent editions were published in 1736 and 1752), just eight years before Defoe's *Robinson Crusoe* (1719) and close to the publication of Defoe's *Moll Flanders* (1722) and *Roxana* (1724), and Swift's *Gulliver's Travels* (1726); William Smith's translation, which was to become the standard, first appeared in 1739, remarkably close to the dates of Richardson's *Pamela* (1740–1741) and Fielding's *Joseph Andrews* (1742); John Baille's *Essay on the Sublime* appeared in 1747, two years before Fielding's *Tom Jones*; and Burke's *Enquiry* was published in 1757, close to the date of Sterne's *Tristram Shandy* (1760–1767). In the view of Samuel Holt Monk, whose work *The Sublime: A Study of Critical Theories in Eighteenth-Century England* (1935; rpt., Ann Arbor: University of Michigan Press, 1960) remains the definitive history, Kant's *Critique of Judgment* (1790) stands as the document that coordinates and synthesizes the aesthetic concepts that had been current throughout eighteenth-century England.

12. Monk's study *The Sublime* and Ian Watt's influential *Rise of the Novel: Studies in Defoe, Richardson, and Fielding* (Berkeley: University of California Press, 1957) shed light upon one aspect of the nature of the connection between the sublime and the novel, for Monk's account of the reasons why the sublime became so prominent is surprisingly consistent with Watt's analysis of the novel as a distinctive literary form: both reflect a modern preoccupation with the nature and development of individual identity, and the value and diversity of individual taste. According to Watt, a new emphasis on the primacy of the individual and a correlative privilege of the character's experience as the ultimate arbiter of reality are integral to the novel. This innovation in literary form is accompanied by a parallel development in philosophy, for the very notion of truth is reconceived as a primarily personal and therefore unique, rather than collective and tradition-bound, phenomenon. If the novel "is surely distinguished from other genres and from previous forms of fiction by the amount of attention it habitually accords both the individual acts of its characters and to the detailed presentation of their environment," its technical characteristics also point to the aim that the novelist

of that period shares with the philosopher: "the production of what purports to be an authentic account of the actual experiences of individuals" (Watt, *Rise of the Novel*, 117–18). Similarly, Monk argues that the eminence of the sublime in the eighteenth century was a result of the demand for "a theoretical defense of *individualism* in art" (Monk, *The Sublime*, iii, emphasis added). Longinus came into favor "because he could fill a need; he alone of the ancients could be used to support the idea of 'the liberty of writing'" (26–27). The emerging category of the individual and concern with the varieties of personal experience can be seen as a fundamental reason for the rise of both the novel and the sublime. Just as the former gives priority to the representation of individual identity and experience, so the latter reflects upon the individual's responses to the aesthetic object, and accounts for the subject's experience of pleasure or pain.

13. Watt's classic argument ties the popularity of the novel to the widespread growth of literacy and the expansion of the reading public to include the urban middle classes. But although Watt's argument turns on his attention to the "increasingly important female component" of the reading public, and although he acknowledges that "the majority of eighteenth-century novels were actually written by women," his sole focus is upon woman's role as the consumer and not the producer of fiction. It is surprising that, while two of the most recent and influential studies of the novel challenge Watt, they do not take issue with this point of view. In *The Origins of the English Novel, 1600–1740* (Baltimore: Johns Hopkins University Press, 1987) Michael McKeon argues that "the emerging novel internalizes the emergence of the middle class and the concerns that it exists to mediate" (27), but fails to ask if the concerns of the woman reader, not to mention those of the woman writer, might differ in significant respects from those of the masculine middle class that is his sole focus. And although Nancy Armstrong's brilliant *Desire and Domestic Fiction: A Political History of the Novel* (New York: Oxford University Press, 1987) does make gender a crucial issue by showing that the construction of a new model of female subjectivity was central to the development of novelistic discourse—she argues that "one cannot distinguish the production of a new kind of feminine ideal either from the rise of the novel or from the rise of the new middle classes in England" (8)—Armstrong pays virtually no attention to eighteenth-century women writers; indeed, Austen's *Emma* is the only novel authored by a woman she discusses. Even though Armstrong echoes Woolf's view that, during this period, the fact that women "suddenly began writing and were recognized as women writers strikes me as a central event in the history of the novel" (7), she does not question Watt's assumption that the eighteenth century woman's literary significance is due to her role either as the reader of fiction, or perhaps more important, as the heroine of novels written by men. Neither Armstrong nor McKeon attends to the connection between the emergence of the novel and women's new prominence on the literary scene. In *A Room of One's Own* ([New York: Harcourt Brace Jovanovich, 1957], 65) Virginia Woolf writes, "Thus, towards the end of the eighteenth century a change came about which, if I were rewriting history, I should describe more fully and

think of greater importance than the Crusades or the War of the Roses. The middle-class woman began to write."

14. Although of vastly different social classes and careers, Eliza Haywood (1693?–1756) and Charlotte Smith (1749–1806) are two examples of exceptionally talented women who were able to support themselves entirely by writing. Fanny Burney (1752–1840) and Ann Radcliffe (1764–1823), who originally began to write fiction for pleasure, are also women who came to depend upon the income their novels produced. The more frequent occurrence, however, was for women to supplement their income through novel writing.

15. As B. G. MacCarthy was the first to point out (*Women Writers: Their Contribution to the English Novel, 1621–1744* [Oxford: Basil Blackwell, 1945], 43), "so consistently did women keep step with the advance in novel-writing that to trace their progress is to trace the progress of the novel itself." And as subsequent studies by Patricia Spacks and Jane Spencer attest, the growth of the novel parallels the emergence of a distinctly feminine literary tradition. See Patricia Meyer Spacks, *Imagining a Self: Autobiography and the Novel in Eighteenth-Century England* (Cambridge, Mass.: Harvard University Press, 1976); and Jane Spencer, *The Rise of the Woman Novelist: From Aphra Behn to Jane Austen* (Oxford: Basil Blackwell, 1985).

16. F. G. Black, *The Epistolary Novel in the Late Eighteenth Century: A Descriptive and Bibliographical Study* (Eugene: University of Oregon Press, 1940), 8. Spencer, however, feels that his estimate is "a little high," pointing out that it "relies on always believing the 'By a Lady' claim, which is probably usually true but not an entirely reliable guide" (Spencer, *Rise of the Woman Novelist*, 33 n.7).

17. Spencer, *Rise of the Woman Novelist*, x. Indeed, Spencer's main thesis is that "the gradual acceptance of the woman writer which took place during the eighteenth century considerably weakened this early link between women's writing and feminism. Once writing was no longer considered necessarily unfeminine the woman writer was no longer offering a resistance to male domination" (ibid.).

18. Advertisement in front of E. Boyd's *Female Page* (1737).

19. Susannah Rowson, *Charlotte Temple* (New York: Oxford University Press, 1986), 6. (First American edition under the title *Charlotte: A Tale of Truth*, 1794.)

20. To assert a direct correlation between the emergence of the woman writer and of modern feminism is problematic, for at least until the end of the century, women's fiction by no means challenged patriarchal views of women's role and place. Indeed, as Ruth Perry observes (*Women, Letters, and the Novel* [New York: AMS Press, 1980]): "Novels embellished and perpetuated the myths of romantic love needed to strengthen the new economic imbalances between men and women and necessary to make the lives of the depressed seem fulfilled. . . . They also carried the cultural message that women's lives were to be spent in idleness, daydreams, and romance" (x). And as Spencer points out, the novel played a decisive role in popularizing the ideal of "the pure woman," who "never disturbed her usefulness as male property by any unruly desires of her own" (*Rise*

of the Woman Novelist, 109). Perhaps because women's fiction was perceived as a threat, female novelists compensated by creating characters and plots that underscored feminine docility.

A tradition of feminist thinking was nonetheless beginning to emerge. Perry names Mary Astell as "the first English feminist," citing her Preface to Lady Mary Wortley Montagu's *Turkish Letters* (1724) as a contribution crucial to the development of English feminism. According to Perry, Astell pressed "for women's right to a real education, asking them to set aside their prejudices against a woman's writing and be pleased that a *woman* triumphs, and proud to follow in her train" (*Women, Letters, and the Novel*, 16). And Spencer points out that in the last decade of the century feminism began to play a prominent role in women's fiction. She argues that "amid the ferment of radical ideas at the time of the French Revolution . . . the novel was used by writers on both sides of the political debate to promulgate their ideas, and among the radical novelists feminist ideas were given a central place" (*Rise of the Woman Novelist*, 109). Accordingly, such novels as Elizabeth Inchbald's *Victim of Prejudice* (1799) and Mary Wollstonecraft's *Maria: On the Wrongs of Women* (1798) stand out as "maverick productions of a short-lived revolutionary era" (137). It remains to underscore that these novels are the exception, not the rule.

21. Perry, *Women, Letters, and the Novel*, 22.

22. Spacks, *Imagining a Self*, 60.

23. Eliza Haywood, *The Rash Resolve* (London, 1724), cited in Spencer, *Rise of the Woman Novelist*, 21. Spencer also points out that "the pure woman, for the eighteenth century, was one who never disturbed her usefulness as male property by any unruly desires of her own. It was in the novel that the ideal of pure femininity was most memorably expressed and popularly disseminated" (109–10).

24. Spencer, *Rise of the Woman Novelist*, 186.

25. Spacks, *Imagining a Self*, 57–58.

26. For another view see ibid., 63–71, 87–91. Spacks argues that even while female novelists of the period uphold the established system, they "find images and actions to express profound ambivalence" (63). According to Spacks, "the most successful women writers of the century richly examine what others only imply: the fact that society makes women dwell in a state of internal conflict with necessarily intricate psychic consequences" (89).

27. Greenblatt's theory of "self-fashioning" emphasizes the extent to which the construction of a self depends upon its successful differentiation from a hostile other. See Stephen Greenblatt, *Renaissance Self-Fashioning: From More to Shakespeare* (Chicago: University of Chicago Press, 1980), 3.

28. For critical essays that relate *Frankenstein* to Kantian aesthetics see Marshall Brown, "A Philosophical View of the Gothic Novel," *Studies in Romanticism* 26 (Summer 1987): 275–301; Frances Ferguson, "Legislating the Sublime," in *Studies in Eighteenth-Century British Art and Aesthetics*, ed. Ralph Cohen (Berkeley: University of California Press, 1985), 128–47; and Gayatri Chakravorty Spivak, "Three Women's Texts and a Critique of Imperialism," *Critical Inquiry* 12 (1985): 254–59.

29. Sandra M. Gilbert and Susan Gubar, *The Madwoman in the Attic: The Woman Writer and the Nineteenth-Century Literary Imagination* (New Haven: Yale University Press, 1979), 224.

30. While there is no way to ascertain Shelley's intent with respect to Kant's third *Critique*, her comment upon learning that it was the custom at early dramatizations of *Frankenstein* to place a blank line next to the name of the actor who played the part of the monster, "this nameless mode of naming the un-nameable is rather good," suggests considerable familiarity with Kant's theory of the sublime and a sophisticated and ironic attitude with respect to it (quoted in Gilbert and Gubar, *Madwoman in the Attic*, 241).

31. Jacques Derrida, *The Truth in Painting*, trans. Geoff Bennington and Ian McLeod (Chicago: University of Chicago Press, 1987), 69.

32. Mary Shelley, *Frankenstein or, the Modern Prometheus*, ed. James Rieger (Chicago: University of Chicago Press, 1982), 52. Unless noted otherwise, subsequent citations in the text are to this edition of the 1818 version of the novel.

33. Frances Ferguson, discussing *Frankenstein*'s relationship to nuclear thinking and discourse in "The Nuclear Sublime," *Diacritics* 14, no. 2 (Summer 1984), also points out that the Monster's "skin is too tight." According to Ferguson, "The monster . . . is stretched too thin, as if his skin represented an unsuccessful effort to impose unity on his various disparate parts" (8–9).

34. For discussions of the gender of Frankenstein and his monster, see Gilbert and Gubar, *Madwoman in the Attic*, 213–47; Margaret Homans, *Bearing the Word: Language and Female Experience in Nineteenth-Century Women's Writing* (Chicago: University of Chicago Press, 1986), 100–119; Mary Jacobus, *Reading Woman: Essays in Feminist Criticism* (New York: Columbia University Press, 1986), 99–109; Barbara Johnson, "My Monster/My Self," *Diacritics* 12 (Summer 1982): 1–10; Robert Kiely, *The Romantic Novel in England* (Cambridge, Mass.: Harvard University Press, 1972), 155–73; U. C. Knoepflmacher, "Thoughts on the Aggression of Daughters," and Ellen Moers, "Female Gothic," in *The Endurance of Frankenstein*, ed. George Levine and U. C. Knoepflmacher (Berkeley: University of California Press, 1979), 77–87, 88–119; Anne K. Mellor, "Possessing Nature: The Female in *Frankenstein*," in *Romanticism and Feminism*, ed. Anne K. Mellor (Bloomington: Indiana University Press, 1988), 220–32, and *Mary Shelley: Her Life, Her Fiction, Her Monsters* (New York: Routledge, 1989); Mary Poovey, *The Proper Lady and the Woman Writer* (Chicago: University of Chicago Press, 1984), 114–42; Marc Rubenstein, "'My Accursed Origin': The Search for the Mother in *Frankenstein*," *Studies in Romanticism* 15, no. 2 (Spring 1976): 165–94; William Veeder, *Mary Shelley and Frankenstein: The Fate of Androgeny* (Chicago: University of Chicago Press, 1986); and Paul Youngquist, "*Frankenstein*: The Mother, The Daughter, and the Monster," *Philological Quarterly* 70, no. 3 (Summer 1991): 339–59.

35. Johnson, "My Monster/My Self," 8.

36. As Homans points out, "the demon will much later kill Elizabeth, just as the demon's creation has required both the death of Frankenstein's own mother and the death and violation of Mother Nature. . . . Victor has gone to great

lengths to produce a child without Elizabeth's assistance, and in the dream's language, to circumvent her, to make her unnecessary, is to kill her, and to kill mothers altogether" (*Bearing the Word*, 103).

37. Jacobus, *Reading Woman*, 101.

38. Here I cite the 1831 edition of *Frankenstein* (New York: Collier MacMillan, 1961), 31.

39. Longinus, *On Literary Excellence*, quoted in *Literary Criticism: Plato to Dryden*, ed. Allan H. Gilbert (Detroit: Wayne State University Press, 1962), 174.

40. Martin Heidegger, *The Question Concerning Technology*, trans. W. Lovitt (New York: Harper, 1977), 163–65.

41. Again I cite the 1831 edition: "It was the secrets of heaven and earth that I desired to learn; and whether it was the outward substance of things, or the inner spirit of Nature and the mysterious soul of man that occupied me, still my inquiries were directed to the metaphysical, or, in its highest sense, the physical secrets of the world" (32).

42. Jane Gallop, "The Monster in the Mirror: The Feminist Critic's Psychoanalysis," in *Feminism and Psychoanalysis*, ed. Richard Feldstein and Judith Roof (Ithaca: Cornell University Press, 1989), 15.

43. Jacobus, *Reading Woman*, 85.

44. Gilbert and Gubar, *Madwoman in the Attic*, 240.

45. I quote Dickinson's poem in full. All quotations of Jean Rhys's novel are from *Good Morning, Midnight* (1938; rpt., New York: Perennial Library, 1982) and occur in the text.

46. Mary Lou Emery, "The Politics of Form: Jean Rhys's Social Vision in *Voyage in the Dark* and *The Wide Sargasso Sea*," *Twentieth-Century Literature* 28 (1982): 418–19.

47. Virginia Woolf, "Women and Fiction" (1929) in *Women and Writing* (New York: Harcourt Brace Jovanovich, 1979), 52. Among Rhys's critics, both Judith Kegan Gardiner and Thomas F. Staley note Rhys's implied reference to Woolf. See Judith Kegan Gardiner, "Good Morning, Midnight; Good Night, Modernism," *Boundary 2* 11, nos. 1–2 (Fall/Winter 1982–83): 244–46; and Thomas F. Staley, *Jean Rhys: A Critical Study* (London: MacMillan, 1979), 55–56.

48. Woolf, *A Room of One's Own*, 38–39.

49. Gardiner, "Good Morning, Midnight," 239.

50. Mary Helen Washington cites and expands Alice Walker's notion of the "suspended woman" in "Teaching *Black-Eyed Susans*: An Approach to the Study of Black Women Writers," in *All the Women Are White, All the Blacks Are Men, But Some of Us Are Brave*, ed. Gloria T. Hull, Patricia Bell Scott, and Barbara Smith (Old Westbury: The Feminist Press, 1982), 208–17.

51. Virginia Woolf, *Orlando: A Biography* (1928; rpt., New York: New American Library, 1960), 27.

52. Woolf, *Orlando*, 33.

53. Rhys uses ellipses frequently. Square brackets around ellipses distinguish my deletions from those in the original text.

54. Gardiner, "Good Morning, Midnight," 248–49.

55. Staley, *Jean Rhys*, 97; and Elizabeth Abel, "Women and Schizophrenia: The Fiction of Jean Rhys," *Contemporary Literature* 20, no. 2 (Spring 1979): 167.

56. Elgin W. Mellown, "Character and Themes in the Novels of Jean Rhys," *Contemporary Literature* 13, no. 4 (Autumn 1972): 467.

57. Carole Angier, *Jean Rhys*, Lives of Modern Women Series (London: Penguin Books, 1985), 66.

58. Abel, "Women and Schizophrenia," 167.

59. Arnold E. Davidson, "The Dark is Light Enough: Affirmation from Despair in Jean Rhys's *Good Morning, Midnight*," *Contemporary Literature* 24, no. 3 (Summer 1983): 363.

60. Gardiner, "Good Morning, Midnight," 249.

61. Davidson, "The Dark is Light Enough," 349; and Abel, "Women and Schizophrenia," 167.

62. According to Thomas Weiskel (*The Romantic Sublime: Studies in the Structure and Psychology of Transcendence* [Baltimore: Johns Hopkins University Press, 1976], 94), "the sublime moment recapitulates and thereby reestablishes the Oedipus complex, whose positive resolution is the basis for culture itself."

63. Davidson, "The Dark is Light Enough," 363.

64. Mary Poovey interrogates the idealist assumption that romantic love lies "completely 'outside' ideology" and that, as "an inexplicable, irresistible, and possibly even biological drive," it "flaunts the hierarchy, the priorities, the inequalities of class society" ("*Persuasion* and the Promises of Love," *The Representation of Women in Fiction*, Selected Papers from the English Institute, 1981, no. 7, ed. by Carolyn G. Heilbrun and Margaret R. Higonnet [Baltimore: Johns Hopkins University Press, 1983], 172). She points out that "the fundamental assumption of romantic love—and the reason it is so compatible with bourgeois society—is that the personal can be kept separate from the social, that one's 'self' can even be fulfilled in spite of—and in isolation from—the demands of the marketplace." A materialist-feminist reading of the Rhysian canon underscores precisely this point.

65. Audre Lorde, *Sister Outsider: Essays and Speeches* (Trumansburg: The Crossing Press, 1984), 102.

66. Lorde, *Sister Outsider*, 123.

67. Margaret Atwood, *Surfacing* (New York: Fawcett Crest, 1972), 229. Atwood's injunction might be usefully juxtaposed with Fredric Jameson's criticisms of "left/liberal culture critiques." According to Jameson (*Fables of Aggression: Wyndham Lewis, the Modernist as Fascist* [Berkeley: University of California Press, 1979], 130), such critiques "suggest that cultural change and social renovation can be achieved by changes in thinking, or elevations in the level of consciousness . . . thereby rendering political activity unnecessary." As Atwood would certainly agree, developing the capacity to "refuse to be a victim" is a deeply political concern.

68. Judith Butler, *Gender Trouble: Feminism and the Subversion of Identity* (New York: Routledge, 1990), 123–27; "Imitation and Gender Insubordination" in *Inside/Out: Lesbian Theories, Gay Theories* (New York: Routledge, 1991), 21–27; and the introduction to *Bodies That Matter: On the Discursive Limits of "Sex"* (New York: Routledge, 1993), in which Butler elucidates the notions of performance and performativity not as "primarily theatrical," "not as the act by which a subject brings into being what she/he names, but, rather, as that reiterative power of discourse to produce the phenomena that it regulates and constrains" (12, 2).

CHAPTER 4

1. Toni Morrison, "Unspeakable Things Unspoken: the Afro-American Presence in American Literature," *Michigan Quarterly Review* 28, no. 1 (Winter 1989): 3. Subsequent references are to this edition and occur in the text.

2. The word "spook," a synonym for "ghost," is also used by whites as a derogatory term for Negroes. *Dictionary of American Slang*, ed. Harold Wentworth and Stuart Berg Flexner, 2d ed. (New York: Thomas Y. Crowell, 1975), 510.

3. Toni Morrison, *Playing in the Dark: Whiteness and the Literary Imagination* (Cambridge, Mass.: Harvard University Press, 1992), 5. Subsequent references are to this edition and occur in the text.

4. While in *Playing in the Dark* Morrison explores representations of blackness in the white imagination, in a recent essay bell hooks examines the obverse ("Representing Whiteness in the Black Imagination," in *Cultural Studies*, ed. Lawrence Grossberg, Cary Nelson, and Paula Treichler [New York: Routledge, 1992]). She argues that for blacks whiteness is both synonymous with, and a symbol for, terror (which, as Burke tells us, is "the ruling principle of the sublime"). She also emphasizes that terror and whiteness are central to *Beloved*: "in Morrison's *Beloved* the memory of terror is so deeply inscribed on the body of Sethe and in her consciousness, and the association of terror with whiteness is so intense, that she kills her young so they will never know the terror" (345).

5. In "On the Backs of Blacks," *Time Magazine*, special issue "The New Face of America," Fall 1993, Toni Morrison continues to examine the strategies through which racism and "race-talk" create the appearance of unity. Here she maintains that "although U.S. history is awash in labor battles, political fights and property wars among all religious and ethnic groups, their struggles are persistently framed as struggles between recent arrivals and blacks. In race talk the move into mainstream America always means buying into the notion of American blacks as the real aliens. Whatever the ethnicity or nationality of the immigrant, his nemesis is understood to be African American" (57).

6. Plato, *The Republic*, trans. Allan Bloom (New York: Basic Books, 1968), 74.

7. E. A. Wallis Budge, *Osiris and the Egyptian Resurrection* (New York: G. P. Putnam's Sons, 1911), 1:17.

8. Plutarch, *De Iside et Osiride*, ed. and trans. J. Gwyn Griffiths (Cardiff: University of Wales Press, 1970), 145–46; chapters 15–16 are devoted to Isis' adventures while she searches for Osiris; chapter 9 mentions the inscription on Isis' temple at Saïs (131). For a description of the myth and cult of Isis and Osiris in relation to Plutarch's text, see Griffiths's commentary, 18–75.

9. James Frazer, *The New Golden Bough*, ed. Theodore H. Gaster (New York: New American Library, 1964), 388.

10. For a different interpretation of the Isis-Osiris myth, see Jean-Joseph Goux, "The Phallus: Masculine Identity and the 'Exchange of Women,'" trans. Maria Amuchastegui, Caroline Benforado, Amy Hendrix, and Eleanor Kaufman, *Differences* 4, no. 1 (Spring 1992): 40–75.

11. Robert Graves, *The White Goddess* (New York: Farrar, Straus and Giroux, 1975), 337.

12. Frazer, *New Golden Bough*, 143–44.

13. Graves, *White Goddess*, 232.

14. Ra had grown old and Isis wanted to become mistress of the earth and a mighty goddess, which she could do only by discovering the sun god's secret name. She took some of Ra's saliva, moistened dust and fashioned a snake with it, and laid it in his path. The serpent struck Ra as he passed by and the god suffered terribly from the poison. Ra realized that he was near death, but Isis promised to save him if he would reveal his name to her, and when he consented she immediately uttered the incantation that relieved and healed him. See Budge, *Osiris*, 188.

15. Jacques Derrida's analysis of the notion of the *parergon* in *The Truth in Painting*, trans. Geoff Bennington and Ian McLeod (Chicago: University of Chicago Press, 1987) allowed me to develop this line of thinking. Derrida, however, does not remark the relation Kant establishes between "emotion," *parerga*, and the sublime. And while Derrida argues that "the whole frame of the analytic of the beautiful functions, with respect to that the content or internal structure of which is to be determined, like a *parergon*" (71), my point is that the sublime frames, and thus is parergonal to, Kant's "Analytic of the Beautiful."

16. Kant's comments about pure and mixed colors in the third *Critique* should be read in the context of his 1764 remarks about race in the *Observations on the Feeling of the Beautiful and the Sublime*, trans. John T. Goldthwait (Berkeley: University of California Press, 1960). There he declares that: "The Negroes of Africa have by nature no feeling that arises above the trifling. Mr. Hume challenges anyone to cite a single example in which a Negro has shown talents, and asserts that among the hundreds of thousands of blacks who are transported elsewhere from their countries, although many of them have even been set free, still not a single one was ever found who presented anything great in art or science or any other praiseworthy quality, even though among the whites some continually rise aloft from the lowest rabble, and through superior gifts earn respect in the world. . . . The religion of fetishes so widespread among them is perhaps a sort

of idolatry that sinks as deeply into the trifling as appears to be possible in human nature" (110–11).

17. Derrida, *The Truth in Painting*, 63.

18. Ibid., 39.

19. Marjorie Garber, *Shakespeare's Ghost Writers: Literature as Uncanny Causality* (New York: Methuen, 1987), 129.

20. Jacques Lacan, *The Four Fundamental Concepts of Psycho-Analysis*, ed. Jacques-Alain Miller, trans. Alan Sheridan (New York: W. W. Norton, 1981), 38.

21. Immanuel Kant, "On a Newly Emerged Noble Tone in Philosophy," *Kant*, ed. and trans. Gabriele Rabel (London: Oxford Univ. Press, 1963), 285. Subsequent references are to this edition and occur in the text. Immanuel Kant, "Von einem neuerdings erhobenen vornehmen Ton in der Philosophie," in *Immanuel Kant's Werke*, ed. Ernst Cassirer (Berlin: Bruno Cassirer, 1914), 6:478–96.

22. Jacques Derrida, "Of an Apocalyptic Tone Recently Adopted in Philosophy," trans. John P. Leavey, Jr., *The Oxford Literary Review* 6, no. 2 (1984): 15. Subsequent references to this essay will be in the text.

23. Sarah Kofman, like Derrida, also refers to Isis as "the goddess who murdered Osiris" ("The Economy of Respect: Kant and Respect for Women," *Social Research* 49, no. 2 [Summer 1982]: 400). Her discussion of Isis' appearance in Kant's "On a Noble Tone" not only repeats Derrida's error regarding Isis' actual role with respect to Osiris but, like Kant, she wants "to make of that phantom whatever [she] likes": according to Kofman, Isis is "a phallic castrating mother" (400), the "personification of the law" (402).

24. Garber, *Shakespeare's Ghost Writers*, 130, 172.

25. Barbara Johnson, in a lecture on African-American women's fiction at Harvard University in December 1990, discussed the significance of the missing "three" in the address of the house on Bluestone Road.

26. Toni Morrison, "The Site of Memory," in *Inventing the Truth: The Art and Craft of Memoir*, ed. William Zinsser (Boston: Houghton Mifflin Co., 1987), 106. Subsequent references to this essay are to this edition and occur in the text.

27. Jean-François Lyotard, *Heidegger and 'the jews'*, trans. Andreas Michel and Mark Roberts (Minneapolis: University of Minnesota Press, 1990), 33.

28. Gloria Naylor and Toni Morrison, "A Conversation," *The Southern Review* 21, nos. 3–4 (1985): 585. Theodore Adorno's view that "some art works have the power to break through the social barrier they reach" has strong affinities with Morrison's emphasis upon the responsibility she feels to the people she writes about. In "A Conversation" she says, "the responsibility that I feel for the woman I'm calling Sethe, and for all of these people, these unburied, or at least unceremoniously buried, people made literate in art . . . I feel this enormous responsibility in exactly the way you describe the ferocity you felt when somebody was tampering with a situation that was gonna hurt" (585). And in "Rootedness: The Ancestor as Foundation," in *Black Women Writers (1950–1980): A Critical Evaluation*, ed. Mari Evans (New York: Anchor/Doubleday, 1984), 344, Morrison's

insistence upon the necessary politicality of her work resonates with Adorno's conviction that art can reach and break through social barriers: "If anything I do, in the way of writing novels (or whatever I write) isn't about the village or community or about you, then it is not about anything. I am not interested in indulging myself in some private, closed exercise of my imagination that fulfills only the obligation of my personal dreams—which is to say yes, the work must be political." Theodore W. Adorno might well describe *Beloved* as sublime, for in *Aesthetic Theory*, ed. Gretal Adorno and Rolf Tiedemann, trans. C. Lenhardt (London: Routledge and Kegan Paul, 1984), he defines as sublime "works that transcend their aesthetic shape under the pressure of truth content . . . they polarize spirit and material, only to unite them again" (280).

29. A further connection between *Beloved* and *Their Eyes Were Watching God* is suggested by the similarity of the stories of Sethe's and Nanny's escape from slavery. Both are badly whipped before fleeing, and both barely manage to reach a river. Moreover, Sethe is pregnant with Denver and is about to give birth, while Nanny has just delivered Leafy, Janie's mother, a week earlier. See Zora Neale Hurston, *Their Eyes Were Watching God* (New York: Perennial/Harper and Row, 1990), 16–19.

30. Toni Morrison, *Beloved* (New York: Plume/New American Library, 1987), 5. Subsequent references are to this edition and occur in the text.

31. Toni Morrison, "The Pain of Being Black," interview by Bonnie Angelo, *Time Magazine*, 22 May 1989, 120.

32. Mae G. Henderson, "Toni Morrison's *Beloved*: Re-Membering the Body as Historical Text," in *Comparative American Identities: Race, Sex, and Nationality in the Modern Text*, ed. Hortense J. Spillers (New York: Routledge, 1991), 83.

33. As Valerie Smith points out ("'Circling the Subject': History and Narrative in Toni Morrison's *Beloved*," in *Toni Morrison: Critical Perspectives Past and Present*, ed. Henry Louis Gates and K. A. Appiah [New York: Amistad Press, 1993]), "by setting the novel during Reconstruction Morrison invokes the inescapability of slavery, for the very name of the period calls to mind the havoc and destruction wrought during the antebellum and war years" (345).

34. Shoshana Felman and Dori Laub, *Testimony: Crises of Witnessing in Literature, Psychoanalysis, and History* (New York: Routledge, 1992), 84. Subsequent references are to this edition and occur in the text.

35. Cathy Caruth, editor's introduction to a special issue ("Psychoanalysis, Culture, and Trauma") of *American Imago: Studies in Psychoanalysis and Culture* 48, no. 1 (Spring 1981): 5.

36. The third revised edition of the *Diagnostic and Statistical Manual of Mental Disorders* (Washington, D.C.: American Psychiatric Association, 1987), current until May 1994, defined a traumatic event as one "that is outside the range of usual human experiences" (146). The 1994 edition now defines such an event as one in which "the person experienced, witnessed, or was confronted with an event or events that involved actual or threatened death or serious injury, or a threat to the physical integrity of self or others" (4th ed., 427).

37. Sigmund Freud, *Beyond the Pleasure Principle*, included in *The Standard Edition of the Complete Psychological Works of Sigmund Freud*, ed. James Strachey (London: The Hogarth Press, 1920–1922), 18:29, 13.

38. To cite but a few examples, Lyotard's discussion of the sublime in *Heidegger and 'the jews'*: "There is, however, a sublime feeling . . . this feeling bears witness to the fact that an 'excess' has 'touched' the mind, more than it is able to handle . . . the problematic of the unpresentable as such emerges, a long time ago, with the notion of the sublime" (32, 34); in "Representation, Presentation, Unpresentable": "the task of art remains that of the immanent sublime, that of alluding to an unpresentable which has nothing edifying about it, but which is inscribed in the identity of the transformation of 'realities,'" in *The Inhuman: Reflections on Time*, trans. Geoff Bennington and Rachel Bowlby (Stanford: Stanford University Press, 1991), 128; and in *Peregrinations: Law, Form, Event*: "With the esthetics of the sublime it can be argued that a kind of progress in human history is possible . . . it is indeed not a progress of the beautiful, of the taste of beauty, but of the responsibility to the Ideas of reason as they are negatively presented in the formlessness of such and such a situation which could occur" (New York: Columbia University Press, 1988), 41.

39. Sigmund Freud, *Five Lectures on Psychoanalysis*, included in *The Standard Edition of the Complete Psychological Works of Sigmund Freud*, ed. James Strachey (London: The Hogarth Press, 1910), 11:16.

40. *Diagnostic and Statistical Manual*, 4th ed., 428.

41. Cathy Caruth, "Interview with Robert Jay Lifton," *Psychoanalysis, Culture, and Trauma*, 160.

42. Walter Benjamin, "The Storyteller," *Illuminations*, ed. Hannah Arendt, trans. Harry Zohn (New York: Schocken Books, 1977), 84. Subsequent references are to this edition and occur in the text.

43. The phrase "nobody knows" appears frequently in Morrison's interviews and functions almost as a refrain in *Beloved*, as if to emphasize that the events about which she writes were (and perhaps still are) unwitnessed, unknown, and unseen. In a scene in which Beloved, Sethe and Denver ice-skate together, Morrison repeats the phrase "nobody saw them falling" (174–75) three times, and then changes the phrase to "nobody saw them fall" (175); Sethe recognizes Beloved as her lost daughter when she hears her humming a song Sethe herself had made up, a song "nobody knows . . . but me and my children" (176); and at the end of the novel, Morrison remarks upon the difficulty, or impossibility, of "calling" Beloved: "Everybody knew what she was called, but nobody anywhere knew her name . . . how can they call her if they don't know her name?" (274).

44. Marsha Darling, "In the Realm of Responsibility: A Conversation with Toni Morrison," *The Women's Review of Books* 5, no. 6 (March 1988): 5. Subsequent references to this interview will be in the text.

45. Smith, "Circling the Subject," 347.

46. Toni Morrison mentions that Henry Dumas, whose work she greatly admires, was born in Sweet Home, Arkansas, but does not say whether or not

Sweet Home's name derives from Dumas' birthplace. See "City Limits, Village Values" in *Literature and the Urban Experience: Essays on the City and Literature* (New Brunswick: Rutgers University Press, 1981), 41.

47. Toni Morrison, "Behind the Making of *The Black Book*," *Black World* 23 (February 1974): 89. Subsequent references to this essay will be in the text.

48. Thomas LeClair, "'The Language Must Not Sweat': A Conversation with Toni Morrison," *Toni Morrison: Critical Perspectives Past and Present*, 375.

49. Le Clair, "The Language Must Not Sweat," 375.

50. More than one critic has remarked that *Beloved* retells the myth of Demeter and Persephone. Marilyn Sanders Mobley suggests that Sethe's "pain and mourning over her murdered child recall Demeter's pain in losing Persephone to the underworld." See *Folk Roots and Mythic Wings in Sarah Orne Jewett and Toni Morrison: The Cultural Function of Narrative* (Baton Rouge: Louisiana State Univ. Press, 1991), 174. For Marianne Hirsch, Sethe's story revives "the powerful mythic figure of Demeter . . . like the story of Demeter and Persephone, it is about a temporary, perhaps a cyclical, reunion between the mother and the daughter she lost" (8). "Maternity and Rememory in Toni Morrison's *Beloved*," *Representations of Motherhood*, ed. Donna Bassin, Margaret Honey, and Meryle Mahrer Kaplan (New Haven: Yale University Press, 1994), 97. I thank Marianne Hirsch for graciously allowing me to read her essay in typescript.

Classicists remind us that in many cases the myths of ancient Egypt stand behind those of Greece; some propose that the Demeter-Persephone legend itself is based upon the worship of Isis. J. Gwyn Griffiths, the editor and translator of Plutarch's *De Iside et Osiride*, points out that in the Greek tradition, "Demeter was the counterpoint of Isis." See Griffiths's edition of Plutarch, cited above, p. 43. And according to Joseph Fontenrose, the story of Isis' wanderings and visit to Byblos "is remarkably parallel to the tale of Demeter's wanderings in search of Persephone and visit to Eleusis." See *Python: A Study of Delphic Myth and Its Origins* (Berkeley: University of California Press, 1959), 178.

51. Henderson, "Toni Morrison's *Beloved*," 78.

52. Many of Morrison's critics agree that Beloved symbolizes the presence of the past. Marilyn Sanders Mobley points out that "when Paul D arrives at Sethe's home on 124 Bluestone, Denver seeks to frighten this unwanted guest away by telling him they have a 'lonely and rebuked' ghost on the premises. The obsolete meaning of rebuked—repressed—not only suggests that the ghost represents repressed memory, but that, as with anything that is repressed, it eventually resurfaces or returns in one form or another." See "A Different Remembering: Memory, History, and Meaning in Toni Morrison's *Beloved*," in *Toni Morrison* ed. Harold Bloom (New York: Chelsea House, 1990), 195. For Mae Henderson, "memory is *materialized* in Beloved's reappearance . . . her 'rebirth' represents . . . the uncanny return of the dead to haunt the living, the return of the past to shadow the present," "Toni Morrison's *Beloved*," 72–73. According to Marianne Hirsch, Beloved "is memory itself. She is the story of slavery, the memory of slaves come back to confront the community whose future, until that

point, had been to 'keep the past at bay,'" "Maternity and Rememory," cited above, 105. And Valerie Smith observes that "as a ghost made flesh, she is literally the story of the past embodied. Sethe and Denver and Paul D therefore encounter not only the story of her sorrow and theirs; indeed, they encounter its incarnation," "Circling the Subject," 350.

53. Claudia Tate, "Toni Morrison," *Black Women Writers at Work* (New York: Continuum Publishing, 1983), 125.

54. Susan Bowers, "*Beloved* and the New Apocalypse," *The Journal of Ethnic Studies* 18, no. 1 (Spring 1990): 64.

55. Sigmund Freud, *Totem and Taboo*, included in *The Standard Edition of the Complete Psychological Works of Sigmund Freud*, ed. James Strachey (London: The Hogarth Press, 1913–1914), 13:65.

56. Sigmund Freud, "Mourning and Melancholia," in *The Standard Edition of the Complete Psychological Works of Sigmund Freud*, ed. James Strachey (London: The Hogarth Press, 1914–1916), 14:243. Subsequent references to this essay are to this edition and occur in the text.

57. Sigmund Freud, *Inhibitions, Symptoms, and Anxiety*, included in *The Standard Edition of the Complete Psychological Works of Sigmund Freud*, ed. James Strachey (London: The Hogarth Press, 1925–1926), 20:172.

58. Virginia Woolf, *To the Lighthouse* (New York: Harcourt Brace Jovanovich, 1989), 79.

59. In this regard, see Celeste Marguerite Schenck's provocative essay on women's elegies and the masculine elegiac tradition in "Feminism and Deconstruction: Re-Constructing the Elegy," *Tulsa Studies in Women's Literature* 5 (Spring 1986): 13–26. Here Schenck observes that elegy is "a resolutely patriarchal genre" (13), and argues that because men and women have different styles of mourning, their poetic expressions of loss also differ. Unlike the male elegist, who emphasizes his independence from the poetic master whose death he mourns (and celebrates), the female elegist affirms her refusal to mourn, her unwillingness to render up the dead. Whereas the masculine elegy is "a ritual hymn of poetic conservation during the course of which a new poet presents himself as heir to the tradition" (13), marking "a rite of separation that culminates in ascension to stature" (15), Schenck shows that female elegists construct poems based upon "attachment and recovery, rather than a severing of ties" (19). I would argue that in *Beloved* Morrison transposes the concerns of elegy into a narrative domain. See also Peter M. Sacks, *The English Elegy: Studies in the Genre from Spenser to Yeats* (Baltimore: Johns Hopkins University Press, 1985), 1–37; and Celeste Marguerite Schenck, *Mourning and Panegyric: The Poetics of Pastoral Ceremony* (University Park: Pennsylvania State University Press, 1988), 1–18.

60. For discussions of the role of memory in *Beloved*, see Gayle Greene, "Feminist Fiction and the Uses of Memory," *Signs* 16, no. 2 (Winter 1991): 290–321; and Ashraf H. A. Rushdy, "'Rememory': Primal Scenes and Construction in Toni Morrison's Novels," *Contemporary Literature* 31, no. 3 (1990): 300–323.

61. Barbara Hernstein Smith, "Narrative Versions, Narrative Theories," in *On Narrative*, ed. W. J. T. Mitchell (Chicago: University of Chicago Press, 1980), 228.

62. Smith, "Circling the Subject," 351.

63. In Eric L. Santner's formulation (*Stranded Objects: Mourning, Memory, and Film in Postwar Germany* [Ithaca: Cornell University Press, 1990]), "mourning without solidarity is the beginning of madness" (26). Santner articulates a theory of mourning which is able to find "in the harrowing labor of mourning . . . a source of empowerment" (11) and relates this new "rhetoric of mourning" to the project of postmodern theoretical discourses.

64. Bowers, "*Beloved* and the New Apocalypse," 68.

65. In "Circling the Subject," 351, Smith quotes an unpublished essay by Gwen Bergner.

66. Nellie McKay, "An Interview with Toni Morrison," *Toni Morrison: Critical Perspectives Past and Present*, 411.

67. Ibid.

Index

Compositor: Braun-Brumfield, Inc.
Text: 10.5/13.5 Bembo
Display: Bembo
Printer and Binder: Braun-Brumfield, Inc.